CW01496610

Modern China

Cary Krosinsky

Modern China

Financial Cooperation for Solving Sustainability Challenges

Cary Krosinsky
Yale University
Guilford, CT, USA

ISBN 978-3-030-39203-1   ISBN 978-3-030-39204-8   (eBook)
https://doi.org/10.1007/978-3-030-39204-8

This Palgrave Macmillan imprint is published by the registered company Springer Nature Switzerland AG.
The registered company address is: Gewerbestrasse 11, 6330 Cham, Switzerland

Foreword

It may surprise readers of this book to know that China has become a leader in advancing green finance, not only at home but also in regions around the world.

The past few years has seen China assuming leadership roles, including initiating the Green Finance Study Group within the G20 in 2016, and later helping build an initiative by a coalition of central banks that became known as the Network for Greening the Financial System, or NGFS, with partner central banks of the UK, France, Germany and other nations, formally laying a roadmap for greening finance.

Among the initiatives led by China are the development of green finance taxonomies, introduction of policy incentives for green projects, securitization of green assets that injects liquidity and vibrancy to these markets, as well as the launch of private equities and venture capital funds for the utilization of solar, wind and other alternative energy and related technologies, such as battery storage improvement, thereby significantly reducing the need for government subsidies in these industries.

Technology can and must include the development and rolling out of green finance-oriented digital solutions through mechanisms such as fintech, AI and blockchain, so that green taxonomies can help drive the uptake of green finance in markets, including further application of creative incentives for issuance and better access to green financial products overall.

China has also been aggressively pushing for mandatory disclosures of pollution and other ESG factors by its listed companies, which will make it one of the few large economies with such a rigorous requirement. As China has become one of the top issuers of green bonds in recent years, a disclosure regime will attract more foreign capital, which is essential to the financing of China's green transition.

The support of China's leadership for green finance has been critical. When we (the green finance taskforce launched in 2014) first proposed the idea of developing a green financial system to the central government, it was quickly accepted. China sees support for green finance as economically enhancing, as green-financed industries typically grow faster than the rest of the economy. Greening the Belt and Road Initiative, through efforts such as the Green Investment Principles for the Belt and Road (GIP), also represents a major investment opportunity. The trillions of RMB in green finance issuances are major opportunities for financial institutions both in and outside China as its financial markets and systems open up.

In general, there are five secrets behind China's leadership in green finance:

First, China started its green finance agenda by building a political consensus, not merely holding the technical debate. China backed green finance with a political push from the very top. The highest decision-making bodies in China, including the CPC Central Committee and the State Council, endorsed a 14-action roadmap for developing the green finance system as early as 2015. The political backing by China's president and premier carried enormous weight in setting policies, mobilizing resources and facilitating inter-departmental consensus on green finance.

Second, China's approach to designing the green financial system has been top-down and not purely market-led. The successful development of green finance requires essential ingredients including green taxonomies and definition of green activities, environmental disclosures by corporations and financial institutions, rules and standards for green finance products and incentives to corporations and financial institutions. The effective development of these arrangements, in developing countries like China, requires strong actions from government bodies and regulators which have the convening power.

Third, China emphasized coordination among key ministries, division of labor and an implementation timetable. China recognized at the policy-designing stage that green finance was not merely the responsibility of the central bank or a financial regulator; rather, it requires policy support and resources from many other agencies and regulators, including fiscal support, environmental regulations and industrial policies. That is why seven ministries jointly developed the green finance guidelines in 2016.

Fourth, China defined roles of industrial bodies such as national and local Green Finance Committees. In 2015, the People's Bank of China (or PBoC) launched the Green Finance Committee (GFC) of China Society for Finance and Banking. The GFC, with 240 financial institutions, environment-related companies and research bodies as members, quickly became the main disseminator of green finance knowledge, the organizer of green finance product innovations, a key source of policy recommendations and the coordinator for capacity-building and international collaboration. At the local level, about 20 regional GFCs play similar roles promoting green finance market development.

Fifth, China encourages regional innovations in green finance. Since China's economy has vast regional differences, it is imperative to encourage local players to innovate in their approaches. In June 2017, the State Council approved pilot programs on green finance reform and innovation in five provinces and eight cities. In the last two years, many valuable experiences and innovations were identified. The PBoC organizes annual meetings of these pilot cities, summarizes the best practices and promotes them throughout the country.

This book presents a very good overview of China's green finance development from a Western scholar's perspective. I am also pleased to read that this book calls for more cooperation between China and the rest of the world. A greater understanding of China's on-the-ground perspective and experience helps readers not only appreciate its challenges and progresses made toward improving its environment, but also identify the enormous opportunities as we together create a roadmap for a sustainable world.

(Ma Jun is Chairman of the Green Finance Committee of the China Society for Finance and Banking, Co-Chair of the G20 Green [Sustainable] Finance Study Group, Co-Chair of the Steering Committee of Green Investment Principles for the Belt & Road and Director of the Research Center for Green Finance Development at Tsinghua University.)

Ma Jun

Acknowledgments

A book like this is possible only through successful collaboration, very much an example for how we can all work together to make badly needed progress on issues such as climate change, so we are grateful to have the chance to thank the following for their help in producing this book.

First and foremost, Sustainable Finance Institute Co-founder Huang Zhong was most instrumental in shaping the book's flow and content, providing critical on-the-ground insights from current innovation trends as to why China has emerged as a global economic power and beyond. He is a renaissance man in fact, and it was great to work with him on this text.

Then we must thank the amazing students of Brown University who contributed so much to the nuts and bolts of the book, providing clear insights on China from its long history up to its current workings. Brown University is a special place and I'm honored to even be a small part of it. The grounded, thoughtful students from Brown are a wonderful resource who will be leaders in whatever paths they choose. The world needs their practical, energetic leadership more than ever. Thanks as well to Ella Warshauer, Patrick Reed and Sophie Purdom for their usual top organizational skills and insights as well as Eleni E. Papapanou and Jimena Terrazas Lozano for their able editing assistance. And great thanks as well to Justin Kew, Rongrong Huo and China's wonderful Dr. Ma Jun for their kind contributions.

Also, special thanks to my wife, Valerie Brown, whose insights were extremely valuable and her patience as always is very much appreciated.

Last but not the least, great thanks to the fine team at Palgrave Macmillan, especially the excellent Tula Weis and Lucy Kidwell. The process was smooth and the interactions always positive. And, of course, to you the reader, who we hope will come away with a better sense of China and the imperative before us to get along to solve the world's pressing problems, which in all likelihood we can only achieve together.

Contents

Notes on Contributors

Jackson Barkstrom is an undergraduate at Brown University and co-president of the Brown China Summit. He studies applied mathematics, and he has researched statistical methods to identify gerrymandering as well as the hot hand phenomenon in basketball. In the summer of 2015 he taught English at Qiaoqi Experimental Primary School in Jiangsu Province, China, and in the summer of 2019 he interned as a data scientist at Dominion Energy.

Devyn Collado-Nicol graduated from Brown in 2020 with a degree in Environment and Enterprise—an independently designed degree focused on the nexus of business, society and climate change. He has worked as an ESG analyst in Brown's Investment Office and has helped teach Brown's class on "The Theory and Practice of Sustainable Investing."

Mae Fullerton is a senior at Brown University studying the intersection between decision-making and finance. She has studied Mandarin in China through Harvard in Beijing and led Brown China Summit as co-president, in addition to working at Arabesque, a leading provider of corporate sustainability data. Mae hopes to work to improve US-Sino bilateral relations in the future, which she sees as critical to greening international financial markets.

Nimish Garg is a sophomore at Brown concentrating in Applied Math, Computer Science and Economics. Nimish's interest lies in how we can use financial instruments, particularly derivatives, to mitigate climate change's impact.

Kara Huang is a senior at Brown University, pursuing a degree in economics and the Economics Section Editor for the Brown Journal of Philosophy, Politics & Economics. She spent the past summer as an investment management intern in New York City. Outside of the classroom, she is an intern at the

Rhode Island Office of the General Treasury. After her time at Brown, she will work as an analyst at PGIM Fixed Income, and hopes to bring this experience in sustainable investing to that role. Kara grew up in Asbury Park, New Jersey, and Tokyo, Japan, and recently came back from a semester abroad in Stockholm.

Justin Kew is Sustainability Manager at Carmignac. Justin joined Carmignac in 2019. He started his career in 2007 as an Associate at J.P. Morgan London, before moving to Schroders as Client Portfolio Manager on Quantitative Global Equity. In 2015, he was appointed Sustainable Investment and Product Manager at J.P. Morgan and in 2017 he joined Fidelity International, where he was Senior ESG analyst, responsible for integrating ESG data in the investment analysis and portfolio management process while designing investment process for clients. Justin holds a Master's degree in Electrical & Electronics Engineering from the University of Sheffield and is a CFA Charter holder since 2012.

Cary Krosinsky is a widely respected educator and leading author and advisor on sustainable finance whose ongoing teaching includes popular courses at Brown University, Yale University and NYU.

Jimena Terrazas Lozano graduated from Brown University with her Sc.B. in environmental science. As an international student from Mexico, she is particularly interested in sustainable finance and environmental law in developing countries. She has interned in different countries and with different organizations, including the Secretary of Environment and Natural Resources in Mexico.

Miranda McDermott was born in Buenos Aires, Argentina, and since then has grown up in Buenos Aires, Philadelphia, PA, and Columbia, SC. She is a graduating senior from Brown University studying International Relations. She has been studying Mandarin, and Chinese society, for the past four years and plans on moving to China after graduation.

Eleni E. Papapanou is a sophomore at Brown studying International Relations. She is particularly interested in environmental policy and bridging political and economic interests to promote sustainable development. Outside of class, Eleni loves writing and politics, and is currently working as senior editor for Brown Political Review's US section. Though unsure of what she specifically wants to do later on, she hopes to be involved in something where she can continue writing as well as promote positive, meaningful change.

Annie Phan is a senior studying Economics and Development Studies at Brown and will be completing a five year's Master's in Data Science at the school. Annie comes from Vietnam and is passionate about sustainable finance, international development and social entrepreneurship. Annie has had experience working in market research in the US and Asia.

Alexander Rafatjoo is an East Asian Studies and Economics double major from Brown University. Alex has spent two summers working in investment banking at Bank of America Merrill Lynch in the firm's Global Power & Renewables group where he will return as an analyst. At Brown, he has served as panel director for the university's China Summit and as co-president of the Brown Finance Club. Alex is interested in the intersection between China's dominant position in the renewable energy space and opportunities to facilitate private sector investment in sustainable energy infrastructure.

Sebastian Sheng is currently a Master's student at Brown studying innovation management & entrepreneurship. He worked at Morgan Stanley, PwC, and most recently at Ramirez as a Public Finance Investment Banker spearheading infrastructure & healthcare advisory and financing projects for governments and public institutions across the US. He has been working to apply technological innovations to infrastructure development and management. He is the co-founder of the education consulting start-up Edgy Career, a board member at the social nonprofit Futures & Options in NYC and a graduate with honors from Lehigh University.

Lucia Winton is a student at Brown University studying Economics and Public Policy. Lucia is interested in a range of subjects but hopes to pursue a future in finance, sustainability and policy.

Huang Zhong is an entrepreneur with over 20 years of hands-on experience in China-US high-tech, aerospace, manufacturing, finance, education and entertainment industries and has advanced degrees in hydrogen energy and fuel cell technology. He is the co-founder and Executive Director for Asia at the Sustainable Finance Institute (SFI), having successfully partnered with Peking University HSBC Business School (PHBS) to co-host one of the region's first and largest conferences on sustainable finance. He is frequently consulted by corporations, ministries and departments on renewable energy, built environment, wetlands and clean transportation. He sits on the boards and advises technology firms on EV battery technology, patent law and the Internet of Things and advises regions in China on creating positive social and environment impact.

List of Figures

List of Tables

1

The Cooperation Imperative

Cary Krosinsky

Asia is half of the world's economy (UNCTAD 2019), home to over two-thirds of the world's largest cities, and China is the dominant player in the region.

The *Financial Times* recently declared without hesitation that "The Asian Century is set to begin" (Financial Times 2019). Few doubts remain that this will come to pass, with China only likely to become more influential on the back of its recent economic rise during the last 40 years.[1]

The implications of this economic balance between East and West may not sink in quickly and are too often viewed in a largely competitive light.

It would be easy then for a tremendous opportunity to be lost, as surrounds the possibility for renewed cooperation and the potential power of combined inspiration and innovation that can help solve the world's most significant environmental, social and economic challenges. At stake is nothing less than the survival of the world as we know it. And this has all become only more important given the outbreak of the novel coronavirus.

All economies need to find ways to flourish without doing further damage to our planet and its endangered ecosystems and increasingly carbon-intensive atmosphere. Although global politicians at times avoid these challenges, or actively set policy courses away from what is necessary, within the scientific community the imperative to take action is crystal clear, as is the global mandate before us all, and that is:

---

[1] China is now a clear second in terms of nominal global GDP (World Bank 2018), is close to being on par with the US in terms of purchasing power parity (ibid.), is three times larger in size than Japan, is the second largest country in Asia, and China has been Asia's main trading partner in recent times with a long and interconnected history of this being the case (South China Morning Post 2018).

© The Author(s) 2020
C. Krosinsky, *Modern China*, https://doi.org/10.1007/978-3-030-39204-8_1

If we really care about solving the global climate change challenge before us all, the need to cooperate with China is the new imperative of our times.

Whether cooperation will be challenging or not, in fact it's often the harder things in life that are most worth pursuing.

It's impossible to see a way forward where we successfully solve for climate change, let alone some of the other more pressing societal issues of the day, without China's direct engagement and involvement. The rest of Asia also needs a successful, positive transition across environmental and societal challenges, one that helps usher in a lower-carbon emissions trajectory for the world, and China's success at this would help them later assist the rest of Asia. Such successful transitions only occur at a necessary pace during conditions of economic vibrancy, making cooperation an essential and new modern-day paradigm.

Former Secretary of State John Kerry was one of the strategic architects of the Paris Agreement and led bilateral negotiations that preceded the establishment of this agreement between the US and China (Axios 2019). While the Paris Agreement itself is insufficient for solving climate change (Reuters 2019), it was the first sign that global cooperation on climate was possible, and serves as a good example as to how future collaboration and cooperation can and must occur. Kerry recently made clear (Yale 2019) that he was aware of dozens of developing world countries which, if the West invested in them along with China, could accelerate each of their own low-carbon energy transitions together as another example of potentially useful future cooperation.

Here in the US, global cooperation is a bipartisan imperative and one that should not be political even if it often is in practice. This is increasingly recognized and called for by leading investors, such as Ray Dalio of Bridgewater Associates, who said "There is a lot to respect about the Chinese culture and approach that led to its remarkable accomplishments. We would do well to learn from each other, cooperate and compete to bring each other up rather than to tear each other down. China is a place we need to continue to evolve with and invest in" (Dalio 2019).

Hank Paulson, former US Secretary of the Treasury for Republican President George W. Bush, helped launch the US China Green Fund (Chap. 12) as part of his extended relationship with China. Former California governor Jerry Brown recently helped create the California China Climate Initiative at the University of California, Berkeley, to develop and scale innovations related to climate change, and politicians across parties such as Michael Bloomberg, John Kasich, Joe Biden and former Secretary of State Henry Kissinger also often reflect on the imperative for better relations and more financial cooperation.

Recent Nobel Prize winner and Yale economist William Nordhaus developed the idea of Carbon Country Clubs, the concept being for the US and China to agree on a carbon price, with tariffs imposed on those who don't choose to participate, which would make this an economic imperative as well for countries that choose not to participate (Nordhaus 2015).

None of this will be easy, but it's time to stare reality directly in the eye and get on with what we need to do together to achieve a necessary low-carbon future. This includes strategies that pertain to the future of state-owned enterprises and the fact that public companies in Asia often have governance considerations that would otherwise be unacceptable to Western investors (see Appendix A for a further synopsis on Sustainable Investing and related strategies and terms commonly used).

There is also insufficient data and transparency that might otherwise be useful and required across all of the developing world, those often being wealthy family-dominated economies, but we must get on with finding and implementing solutions. If we don't get on this at once we won't come close to achieving a necessary transition, particularly as pertains to creating measurably fewer greenhouse gas emissions annually on a global basis. "Bending the curve" on annual carbon emissions won't be easy but it will be the only way to ensure future economic success. The entirety of climate science now makes this abundantly clear (see Appendix B for links to brief climate change explainers).

The need to help Asia with its low-carbon transition becomes even clearer when one considers that China uses half of the world's coal, and that coal represents roughly 40% of the global carbon footprint (Stanford Woods Institute for the Environment 2019), and that Asia's carbon emissions are expected to represent something like 50% of the global total as early as 2030 (EIA 2016).

Asia's rising middle class understandably demands lifestyles long enjoyed in the West, and it's not only India and China; the ASEAN region is expected to become increasingly economically relevant, anticipated to become the fourth largest economy combined by 2050 after China, India and the US (US-ASEAN Business Council 2019).

In developing countries, transitions away from coal are particularly challenging. ASEAN countries such as Indonesia have understandable societal demands from their poorer populations, making it particularly difficult financially to convert away from the cheapest energy sources. This dynamic makes a full, global, low-carbon transition even harder to achieve at the necessary pace and scale, and it is therefore of the essence that this receives more focus, specific planning and coordination. Rather than ignoring this, we need to dive in and find the best way to enable this transition together with Asia.

There is increasingly disturbing tangible evidence at hand of where we are heading as a global society. Accelerating incidents of fire and rapidly melting glaciers in Asia that provide essential drinking water to vast populations are only two examples helping to clarify that a low-carbon transition is of the essence to avoid a series of global calamities. Such disasters would be impossible for anyone to avoid, including the medium-term likelihood of billions more climate refugees, further significantly degraded arable land and forests, projected further incidents of human disease outbreaks, depleted ocean fisheries and the loss of critically important biodiversity.

Global economic vibrancy in such a medium-term future is impossible to imagine, and the only way out is to cooperate at global scale as quickly as possible to avoid financial collapse, while creating robust economies which can thrive together. The establishment of successful low-carbon transitions, which require economic vibrancy in order to occur, would create a self-supporting positive dynamic, arguably the only real possibility of a vibrant economic future.

Successful sustainable transitions also provide better immediate realities on the ground for those being affected directly today, whether in cities across Asia suffering from the ill health effects of significant levels of PM2.5, or for the ongoing survival of the oceans now absorbing unsupportable levels of increased heat, or for minimizing the potentially very high financial and human cost of not only billions of climate refugees, but the overall health and well-being of people everywhere.

We can still avoid all of this, but only if we get rapidly on the case.

The essential transition needs to be fully implemented globally across financial and economic systems, specifically in the form of lower carbon transportation, through more efficient industrial processes, buildings and waste streams, and especially through the increased generation of electricity from lower-carbon sources, as well as through sustainable agriculture techniques and related innovations, while also minimizing deforestation (IPCC 2014).

This type of systemic approach turns out to also be the best way forward for regional economic success, especially for countries that choose to lead the way in developing new technologies that enable this transition, and on this front the race is on (Chap. 3), and no country has arguably been as all-in on this transition as China (Chaps. 9 and 19).

There are other present-day economic realities where more cooperation would be helpful, including as regards levels of slavery which continue to be embedded at unacceptable levels within supply chains of large companies producing much of what we globally consume.

Economically suffering US farmers have also been unable to sell easily in Chinese markets during the recent trade war. Such Chinese markets include what is now the world's largest middle class (China Daily 2017) willing to pay more for food they can trust.

Sitting on the outside and complaining about problems or exacerbating tensions isn't nearly as effective as building trusted relationships and working together to find mutually beneficial solutions and better economic conditions.

The race is also on as pertains to the creation of all sorts of new, enabling technologies such as 5G and 6G to follow, through fintech, as well as blockchain, battery storage, new forms of energy (Chap. 3) and even carbon capture and sequestration, and there are also opportunities for more creative methods such as open global innovation and the creation and use of new materials (Krosinsky et al. 2018).

Winners will thrive within sectors, and some sectors will continue to transform at the expense of technologies that are no longer necessary, including ongoing transitions away from coal and oil such as results from research that Carbon Tracker Initiative and others continue to demonstrate, and thus investing in the status quo comes with its own new risks to now be fully considered.

The death of traditional industries such as the newspaper and music industry is likely just a harbinger of what is to follow across automobile and truck manufacturing, within shipping, and as regards the methods of production of consumer goods and the continuing use of plastics.

Investors thinking these transitions won't occur could well be caught out in the near future (for more on sustainable investing, see Appendix A), and as we concluded in our first book, *Sustainable Investing: The Art of Long Term Performance* (Krosinsky et al. 2008), markets need winners and losers, so actually not everyone needs to be on board for the transition to be successful.

Just enough investment, along with global companies applying better strategies around the world, supported by the right policies, can help tip the scale of the global economy in a more urgent, necessary direction.

But perhaps more than anything, we need more people who want this transition to occur, and maybe hardest of all will be changing the ongoing decisions of the average person. People make up roughly two-thirds of the global footprint when one considers choices of transportation, regional energy mixes and the ongoing consumption of food and goods.

The average voter in many countries decides who sets or doesn't set supportive policies which can make or break the speed of the transition. Especially in the US, the collective voice of individual investors and voters in aggregate is a critical determinant in this regard.

The good news is that in China, none of this is an issue.

The Chinese government is on the hook to deliver better results to justify its keeping control, and therefore wants and arguably needs to meet the increasing demands of its middle class, including the air, food and water quality conditions often taken for granted in more developed parts of the world.

Helping China with its successful transition becomes a necessary paradigm for making global progress on climate change and can also become an important case study for the world to learn from. Any alternative scenario makes solving the global climate challenge that much harder and that much less likely to achieve.

Consumption in the West, outsourced over time to China and Asia more generally, is also at least partly responsible for the local environmental degradation which resulted as a side effect, and hence we bear some responsibility for ensuring this gets resolved.

Fortunately, consumer tastes are also starting to change, with companies such as Tesla and Beyond Meat emerging as chic and financially successful, specifically due to their being seen as providing better solutions to transportation needs and the production of food respectively, as specifically connects to this necessary transition. Increasingly, people also want renewable energy, and over time more people are likely to want sustainable electricity as renewables continue to emerge as the least costly option.

The global unicorns of the future may well be companies which help establish better sustainability and financial outcomes at the same time, creating a positive dynamic for investors who increasingly want to be seen as enabling better societal outcomes without missing out on the next big trend, and this is a global opportunity for investors and entrepreneurs, and a key component of this new cooperation paradigm.

> In fact a lack of cooperation may be one of the only ways we won't succeed at achieving the necessary transition, and—this can't be stressed strongly enough—none of this will be possible without economic vibrancy.

India's 2019 economic slowdown and its ongoing low GDP per capita should be especially noted as just one example of the economic imperative behind necessary low-carbon transitions. If India's economy were to thrive, more of its people would insist on positive changes to the often terrible quality of air in its major cities, but for now it cannot, does not and is not able to transition fully and successfully, not until its economy emerges, and certainly many other countries are similarly situated.

We also need governments to create and keep in place the right policies that help support necessary action on lowering carbon emissions. Instead, increasingly nationalist governments are at times being voted into office and are turning away from climate action at the time when it is needed the most. Such voting results have arguably been due to a lack of good jobs and a general sense of feeling threatened by modernity, not only as was experienced in recent UK and US elections, but also manifesting at times in otherwise primarily progressive countries, as has been seen with the *Gilet Jaunes* movement in France, and the ongoing German political dynamic, which threaten to slow their climate responses. This is also important in China, a country which actually does listen to its citizens, and adopts, learns and changes arguably faster than any country in the world (Chap. 8), but China can't act on its own.

> The sustainable transition then needs to be explained more clearly as to how it will specifically benefit the average person and their families everywhere versus the alternative, which will be much worse for everyone.

Global education, then, particularly on the benefits of the necessary transition versus what will be economically worse alternatives, is now another essential goal to achieve including in countries such as China and also throughout the West. This kind of discourse is strangely often missing from many global political and media platforms, with several countries and organizations stuck in older ways of thinking and doing business, resisting change or otherwise not taking on the urgency of issues such as climate change, and as a result not enough people see the need to act rapidly.

China can get this right, and quickly given the chance, but it will need cooperation to do so.

> It is essential to understand that China will only accelerate on the necessary transition if it itself is economically vibrant; otherwise things will not move forward at the pace that is globally required.

Harvard Business School's case studies are rife with examples of companies which innovated well but didn't combine that with a necessary successful business model to achieve scaled implementation of related solutions, such as battery storage company A123 Systems failed to achieve (Vietor 2011).

Similarly, countries won't have the financial well-being to fully transform without economic vibrancy, and the sort of conditions which allow for investing with confidence at necessary scale.

In fact, China, in response to the economic pressures it is facing, exacerbated as they are by the recent trade war, combined with lessening climate action commitments of countries such as the US, has slowed their own recent progress on climate change in some ways (Wall Street Journal 2019). Without an all-in approach across major countries, adequate and necessary action is likely to lag behind what is required.

China as a case study of transition success could help transform Asia's other economies, providing an example others can learn from. It is also our contention that if one has concerns about any of China's behavior, more success at driving positive change will come by welcoming China into a community of cooperative nations, and even better, becoming an ongoing investor who can make reasonable demands for one's capital rather than by isolating China and making it defensive and more likely to generate worse reactions internally.

Trapped by existing debt, China in fact now essentially requires foreign capital to enable its own sustainable transition, creating an important vector for positive change through the parallel establishment of minimum standards such as those that the NY State Common Retirement Fund has committed to developing recently. ESG (environmental, social and governance) covenants on investment can relate to minimum standards as part of increasing methods for performing reliable and thorough due diligence across asset class.

In this way, developed country investors can help China's transition, and once it is successful, other developing countries can then also transition, learning from the China example, allowing them to compete, innovate and thrive as well.

There is almost certainly no other way out of the climate crisis in front of us, and in the chapters, recommendations and case studies to follow we will suggest best ways forward for investors and others interested in solving these challenges of our time.

First of all, it's important to truly understand China, all too often misunderstood from a distance.

It's important to understand China's 5000-plus-year history, and while there is endless detail that can be covered on this, we will give the reader a perspective on how China's thinking and ethos have come to be what it is, and will discuss how there is much that makes a lot more sense once you take a walk in China's shoes.

Something that is generally not recognized is that China has not typically started or participated in world wars, has not done so for a long time and doesn't appear to have particular ambition in this regard, but does understandably demand respect. China has long wanted to protect its borders and its sovereignty and to keep from falling into the type of chaos the country has experienced many times throughout its history. Not long ago it was significantly affected by outside forces (Chap. 6) and the Great Wall is of course an ancient example.

China does, however, have an innate sociology that builds trusted circles and relationships (Guanxi, see Conclusion) and through gaining trust can come the potential for mutual success, potentially at a very high level, and this is what is needed now at scale to solve societal challenges as well.

China is also extremely transformative and entrepreneurial and learns quickly when it makes a mistake. If we care to solve climate change, those of us in the West have to be much less locally minded and myopic and think more holistically on a global basis. We all need to recognize that this something of a left brain/right brain thing, whereby Asia is half the possibility, and arguably more than half of the potential from a transformation potential perspective. This is an entrepreneurial moment, and also a moment to involve as many people and countries as possible to successfully and fully transform global society.

This really does need to be an all-in movement, one that leaves no one stone unturned in the search for economic systems which can thrive in what will otherwise be a climate-challenged future. How do we get there?

Let's see if our book can at least help lead the way toward establishing common goals and pathways forward for us to achieve what we need to do together. The West isolating China and making it an enemy only makes this transition harder and less likely to occur, reducing the opportunity for successful global transformation.

This will also require China to continue to learn and adapt to give the West space to operate comfortably in the country, and at the same time for the West to fully understand China. Such a new reality will only benefit China, a country with ambitions and goals and a government that can impose clear long- term plans, and with a current environmental and societal landscape that needs fixing, which the Chinese people themselves increasingly want to see achieved. Fortunately, no other country gets on with implementing plans once it sets its mind to it in the way that China can.

We now look at the challenges China faces, its history, its ambition and ethos, its desire to innovate and thrive, and perhaps through aiding this necessary transition and helping to lead the global response to climate change, China can gain the respect it arguably deserves.

The time to come together and cooperate for global success is now, and we likely won't get another chance.

References

Axios. 2019. Inside John Kerry's Shadow Diplomacy on Climate Change. https://www. axios.com/john-kerry-vietnam-diplomacy-climate-change-5912b5f6-27aa-474b-b129-56180427f821.html. Accessed 4 Jan 2020.

China Daily. 2017. China Has the World's Largest Middle Class Population. https:// www.chinadaily.com.cn/a/201712/21/WS5a3b15aea31008cf16da292f.html. Accessed 4 Jan 2020.

Dalio, Ray. 2019. Looking Back on the Last 40 Years of Reforms in China. https://www.linkedin.com/pulse/looking-back-last-40-years-reforms-china-ray-dalio/. Accessed 5 Feb 2020.

Financial Times. 2019. The Asian Century Is Set to Begin. https://www.ft.com/content/520cb6f6-2958-11e9-a5ab-ff8ef2b976c7. Accessed 4 Jan 2020.

IPCC. 2014. AR5 Climate Change 2014, Mitigation of Climate Change. https://www.ipcc.ch/report/ar5/wg3/. Accessed 4 Jan 2020

Krosinsky, Cary, Nick Robins, et al. 2008. *Sustainable Investment: The Art of Long Term Performance*. London: Earthscan.

Krosinsky, Cary, Todd Cort, et al. 2018. *Sustainable Innovation and Impact*. Abingdon/New York: Routledge.

Nordhaus, William. 2015. Climate Clubs: Overcoming Free-Riding in International Climate Policy. *American Economic Review*. https://www.aeaweb.org/articles?id=10.1257/aer.15000001

Reuters. 2019. Scientists Urge Stronger Paris Agreement Pledges to Curb Climate Change. https://www.reuters.com/article/us-un-climatechange-targets/scientists-urge-stronger-paris-agreement-pledges-to-curb-climate-change-idUSKBN1XF26I. Accessed 4 Jan 2020.

South China Morning Post. 2018. How Trade Links Between Southeast Asia and China Have Thrived for More Than 1,000 Years. https://www.scmp.com/presented/news/asia/topics/china-and-southeast-asia/article/2158635/how-trade-links-between. Accessed 4 Jan 2020.

Stanford Woods Institute for the Environment. 2019. Global Carbon Emissions Growth Slows, but Hits Record High. https://news.stanford.edu/2019/12/03/global-carbon-emission-increase/. Accessed 4 Jan 2020.

UNCTAD. 2019. World Economic Situations and Prospects. https://unctad.org/en/PublicationsLibrary/wesp2019_en.pdf. Accessed 4 Jan 2010.

US Energy Information Administration. 2016. https://www.eia.gov/todayinenergy/detail.php?id=26252. Accessed 4 Jan 2020.

US-ASEAN Business Council. 2019. Growth Projections. https://www.usasean.org/why-asean/growth. Accessed 4 Jan 2020.

Vietor, Richard. 2011. A123 Systems. Harvard Business School.

Wall Street Journal. 2019. In Tougher Times, China Falls Back on Coal. https://www.wsj.com/articles/in-tougher-times-china-falls-back-on-coal-11577115096?shareToken=st30cc41c3c455426e858c327498b273b8&reflink=share_mobilewebshare. Accessed 4 Jan 2020.

World Bank. 2018. World Development Indicators. https://data.worldbank.org/indicator/NY.GDP.MKTP.CD?year_high_desc=true. Accessed 4 Jan 2010.

Yale College. Secretary John Kerry's Visit to the Exit Seminar of the Energy Studies Multi-Disciplinary Academic Program (MAP) of April 2019.

2

Environmental, Social and Governance Challenges in China Today

Devyn Collado-Nicol

The rise of China as a global economic superpower is one of the defining features of the twenty-first century. From manufacturing to trade, China continues to help reshape the world, and is quickly making itself known as a global economic force. However, China's ascendance from an underdeveloped country to one of the faster-growing economies in the world has not come without significant cost.

China's recent moves on sustainability notwithstanding, its own environmental and societal challenges are increasingly apparent. Legacy issues of air pollution, smog, water and food scarcity, as well as corporate governance concerns and information asymmetry place China at the center of international scrutiny. Domestically, it also faces increasing pressure, as Chinese residents experience many of these problems on a day-to-day basis, while at the same time seeing their country poised to be one of the great economic success stories of the twenty-first century. Arguably, the most important question in front of China is how they will manage to grow in a sustainable manner. Hence, this chapter outlines in more detail the litany of challenges standing in the way of a sustainable economy in China, and how conditions in China compare to other developed countries around the world.

There are many factors that continue to contribute to the issues China faces today. The most prominent factor is that China's rapid economic growth over the last two to three decades has been coupled with a proportionally meteoric increase in coal production and consumption. This is best encapsulated through the Pollution Haven Hypothesis, which posits that the difference in environmental regulation between developed and developing countries privileges a comparative advantage to the latter when it comes to

© The Author(s) 2020
C. Krosinsky, *Modern China*, https://doi.org/10.1007/978-3-030-39204-8_2

pollution-intensive economic activity (Yuan et al. 2019). Carbon-intensive fossil fuel has literally fueled the growth in the industrial, heavy manufacturing and electricity production sectors of the Chinese economy for years.

This has resulted in an increase in emissions of greenhouse gases and other air pollutants proportional to an increase in Chinese manufacturing and economic activity. Since surpassing the US as the largest coal producer in the world in 1992 (IEA Energy Atlas 2019), China has exponentially increased its coal mining operations. For example, between 2005 and 2009, China added 510,600-megawatt coal power plants, roughly equal to the total output of US coal plants at the time, to its production fleet (Pusceddu 2014). This increase in output helped bring the nation's total domestic coal production up to 46% of all global coal production, with consumption following suit at 49% of global coal consumption by 2014 (almost more than the rest of the world combined) (Ayoub 2014). Nevertheless, despite reports that Chinese coal production was slowing in 2015 (Ayoub 2014), Bloomberg News reported that China is set to increase production by 100 million tons in 2019 (Bloomberg News 2019). Needless to say, this much burning of coal is bound to result in a steady decline in air quality, let alone concerns for future climate implications.

If a dramatic increase in coal consumption is emitting tons of air pollutants into China's airspace, then the rapid expansion and urbanization of Chinese cities are putting it all in one place. Since the 1980s, China has seen an extraordinary rate of urbanization across almost all of its major cities, with the percentage of its total population in urban spaces increasing from a mere 19.6% in 1980 (Han 2019a), to over 58% by 2017 (Han 2019b). For comparison, the US had a rate of urbanization of over 70% by 1970, and by 2016, about 82% of people in the US lived in a city. To put China's 58% urbanization rate into context, 82% of the total population in the US amounts to just around 268 million people. On the other hand, 58% of China's total population comes to over 810 million people. Consequently, China is facing increasing momentum toward rapid consumption and degradation of natural resources such as clean air, land, water and food. Urbanization of Chinese cities is not expected to slow, either, with the nation hoping to reach the 70% mark by 2030 (Han 2019b).

With such a variety of factors contributing to the myriad challenges facing modern China today, it is becoming increasingly clear that the country must rethink its approach to growth and ascension to global power. Inasmuch as China begins to facilitate this mass rotation to a zero-carbon, zero-pollution, socially responsible economy, its focus will continue to be on air pollution and emissions, water and food scarcity, and the many governance challenges tied to instances of corruption and information asymmetry. These legacy issues have real implications both at home for China's citizens and abroad for potential investors.

Air Pollution

Intrinsic to the envisaging of the Chinese city is an image of the opaque smog blanketing it—a wall of white air that you can taste in the winter months. On an average day, visibility is noticeably impaired, and, on some days, ambient air pollution limits people's ability to see past 100 meters (Li 2016). Irrespective of the long-term health implications that have arisen, living day-to-day in these conditions has led to China's legacy air pollution becoming experiential for the average person; this reality has become a personal issue for many and their families.

At the center of China's ambient air pollution challenge is an atmospheric cocktail of greenhouse gases, non-greenhouse organic gases and particulate matter. These pollutants stem from a variety of stationary and non-stationary sources, each posing their own human and environmental health hazards. Unsurprisingly, the northeastern corridor extending from Shanghai to the north of Beijing is home to the highest concentration of many of these pollutants. Perhaps more surprising, however, is the approximately 1.6 million premature deaths that are attributable to excessive exposure to unhealthy air on a consistent basis (Rohde and Muller 2015).

The most dangerous and omnipresent pollutant, aside from carbon dioxide, is 2.5 μm (micrometer) fine particulate matter (PM2.5). Defined as any fine airborne particles smaller than 2.5 μm, PM2.5 affected approximately 72 million people in the labor force, and resulted in economic losses totaling over 346 billion RMB (roughly 1.1% of the country's GDP) in 2016 (Xia et al. 2016). Due to its ability to enter the lungs as a non-gas and also the bloodstream, PM2.5 typically poses very severe health hazards for both healthy and especially at-risk populations (e.g. people with asthma, respiratory and pulmonary illness). Despite these risks, about 78% of China's population in 338 cities was subjected to air with excessive levels of PM2.5 in 2016 (more than 35 μm/m^3), and close to 1 million deaths in China could be attributed to PM2.5 exposure (Maji et al. 2018).

One of the biggest challenges with PM2.5, as well as with many of the other pollutants discussed in this chapter, is understanding where and from which sources pollution is coming from. In a study published by Berkeley Earth, two scientists found that much of the pollution occupying Beijing's air actually comes from industrial activity southwest of the city (Rohde and Muller 2015). The study indicates that cities such as Handan and Shijiahuang over 200 miles away from Beijing, and Hangzhou outside of Shanghai, all emit a series of pollutants as a result of coal burning.

Although PM2.5 has severe public health implications throughout China, it is only the garnish dressing up our atmospheric cocktail metaphor—the base, ozone (O_3). Born out of a complex process involving volatile organic compounds (VOCs), nitrous oxides (NOx) and sunlight, ozone exists as a secondary pollutant, and is primarily a result of motor vehicle emissions. Ground-level ozone is one of the primary culprits behind photochemical smog, and contributes to the white haze that makes China's air pollution so seemingly inescapable. While it is important to note that smog is not unique to China, and is quite common in cities across the globe (Los Angeles has a pretty severe smog problem as well), China stands out as one of the countries most affected by this chemical phenomenon. China has been taking aggressive measures to limit car congestion and pollution in its cities. However, with some of the most densely populated cities in the world, China has a large number of motor vehicles on the road every day. With a fleet of registered vehicles larger than the size of the population of the US (Zheng 2017), congestion and pollution from vehicle emissions are consistently hitting new all-time highs. In fact, so many cars have taken to the streets in the last decade alone, that vehicle emissions topped coal burning as the number one contributor to PM2.5 emissions (China Daily 2019) in 2018. Consequently, the Chinese government has tried many different strategies to curb traffic congestion and mitigate further exacerbation of air quality issues. The most notable of these strategies is Beijing's road-rationing odd-even license plate rule during the 2008 Olympics. Widely successful at the time, the city decided to continue enforcing the rule; it entered its tenth consecutive year in 2018 (Chen 2017).

In addition to day-to-day pollution control solutions, China is making an effort to take a more systemic approach to its car congestion and pollution problems. Through a multipronged strategy involving tighter regulations on vehicles, stricter emissions requirements from coal plants, a general push toward natural gas, incentives for purchase of new energy vehicles (NEVs) and improvements in public transport, China has been at war with its air pollution for a good part of 30 years. However, the fight really kicked up in 2013 when the nation won an $18.18 million grant from the Global Environmental Facility to work with the World Bank to revitalize its public transit through intelligent transport systems and transit-oriented design development projects (Kai 2019). Highly focused on its problems surrounding PM2.5, many of the initiatives taken up since then have been focused on reducing the amount of fine particles in the atmosphere. Taking on a similar path toward increasing emissions standards as Europe, China has modeled many of its early emissions regulations off of early European legislation, and the momentum has not slowed. In July 2019, the nation announced that it will put its more stringent "China VI" vehicle emissions standards into action ahead of schedule—citing that all new buses and heavy diesel vehicles in Beijing will abide by these new rules immediately, with all other vehicles required to comply by July 2020 (Xinhuanet 2019). One of the strictest sets of vehicle emissions regulations in the world, China VI parallels the emissions standards put forth in the Euro 6 standards and also incorporates portions of the US Tier 2 standards on tailpipe and evaporative emissions (China: Light-Duty 2019). These aggressive tactics have been paying off as well, with PM2.5 concentrations dropping by nearly 40% in Eastern China over the course of five years from 2013 to 2017 (Burrows 2018).

China's rapid success in combating PM2.5 in its atmosphere is unprecedented. In essence, it accomplished in 5 years what took the US nearly 30 years to do. However, this incredible accomplishment has not come without its own inherent challenges. Even though PM2.5 concentrations have declined drastically, ground-level ozone throughout Eastern China has been steady on the rise. This is mostly due to the incredibly complex atmospheric processes that create surface ozone and photochemical smog. A study completed by Harvard professors of Atmospheric Chemistry and Environmental Engineering found that much of the PM2.5 in the atmosphere had been acting as a sink that absorbed the molecules that catalyze ozone creation (Li et al. 2018). This is the first ever observance of this phenomenon as no other country has ever achieved such a successful, targeted and rapid reduction in PM2.5.

The complex atmospheric chemistry that goes into ozone creation brings us to the sweets and bitters of our atmospheric cocktail—sulfur dioxide (SO_2), nitrogen oxides (NOx), volatile organic compounds (VOCs), and carbon monoxide (CO). The vast majority of sulfur dioxide in the atmosphere comes from power plants and other industrial facilities that burn fossil fuels. Coal tends to be the worst of the fossil fuels when it comes to sulfur content emitted per unit of energy. However, it can also arrive in the atmosphere via ore mining for some metals, and from vehicles or ships that burn fuel with high concentrations of sulfur; freight container vessels are often notorious emitters of sulfur due to their reliance on bunker fuel. Nevertheless, despite its legacy reliance on coal, and its position as one of the largest exporters in the world, a study out of Sichuan University indicates that China is transitioning from an SO_2-dominated air pollution problem, to a NO_x- and O_3-dominated pollution problem—a mark shared by already industrialized nations (Zeng et al. 2019). According to this study, thanks to robust administrative power, sulfur dioxide has been on the decline for roughly 25 years (Zeng et al. 2019), and has helped reduce many of the environmental and health challenges. Incentive strategies such as tying performance and promotion of government officials to the reductions of these emissions have also played a significant role in actualizing this public health benefit of decreased atmospheric sulfur dioxide. Although the study also finds that surface-level ozone has increased in recent years, the authors cite the decrease in atmospheric NO_x as promising. Moreover, with the implementation of the China VI emissions standards, and the increased emphasis on tailpipe emissions in motor vehicles, carbon monoxide emissions are sure to decline.

Climate Change

There's an uneasy poeticism surrounding the ironic fact that carbon, the building block of all life, is also the building block for our entire socioeconomic society. The ubiquity of carbon in our emissions practices is what makes it especially difficult to limit, as our entire lives are built around the extraction, production and consumption of carbon and carbon-based products. In many respects, carbon dioxide is the icing in our aero chemical medley—present in every vein of emissions, though in different quantities, and slowly immersing itself into the broader atmospheric chemical cocktail hovering above and throughout mainland China. However, systemic reliance on carbon for economic growth and industrial activity is not a narrative only told about China; it applies to virtually every nation. Nevertheless, there are core challenges unique to China that make mitigation efforts more challenging than in other nations. Primarily, China is the manufacturing hub of the world. It is common knowledge that most products are made in China, as many foreign companies have outsourced their manufacturing to Chinese-based factories over the years. Second, the need to pursue rapid solutions to its toxic air pollution challenges understandably takes priority over longer-term concerns like greenhouse gases and climate change. Third, China's growing middle class, coupled with its massive population, promises to only exacerbate the issue as more people will be entering the carbon economy through increased consumption of goods and services, all of which have immeasurable amounts of embodied carbon ineradicably tied to its production and life cycle use.

Known quite famously as "the factory of the world," China sits at the heart of most international trade, and, as a result, absorbs a large sum of embodied carbon via its manufacturing and exports. According to a study published by the Brookings Institute, China's share of global manufacturing output in 2018 was 20%, which totaled over $2 trillion in output (West and Lansang 2018). Moreover, studies indicate that the more nascent and rapid growth since 2000 is mostly a result of China's export-led growth strategies (Yao 2011). China is also the largest source of imports for the US, and total trade between the two countries has risen from a mere $5 billion in 1980, to $660 billion in 2018 (China's Economic Rise 2019). China's rise in export-driven growth is mostly a result of foreign companies relocating their manufacturing practices within the mainland—a tactic meant to take advantage of the cheap labor costs within the country.

These interdependencies of international trade are only further complicated in the discussions around China's role in combating climate change. Much like how it is a net exporter of goods, China is also a net exporter of carbon emissions (Carbon Dioxide Emissions 2019). That is, out of the total emissions produced in China, the majority of them (approximately 54%) are a result of manufacturing practices for products destined for export. This poses an interesting challenge for China as it work to improve carbon regulations around its manufacturing sector in that it has to find a way to mitigate future emissions while also keeping manufacturing costs low to avoid losing foreign investment to neighboring countries. Nevertheless, as other regions continue to grow, China has faced a decline in its status as the world's factory as it loses market share to countries in Africa and other developing nations (So 2014). This decline in foreign-oriented manufacturing, coupled with an overall slowing of the Chinese economy, has caused China to move away from its export-led model, and more toward a domestic-focused model centered around private investments, services and innovation. Articulated by President Xi JinPing as the "new normal" (China Daily 2017), China is embracing this transition away from being the factory of the world—a move that can have positive impacts on its role as a net exporter of carbon. Perhaps the most promising aspect of this new economy transition is the "Made in China 2025" plan, which aims to modernize and upgrade the country's manufacturing foundations in ten key areas. Most notably from a climate perspective, China seeks to rapidly advance its electric and new energy vehicles, agricultural technologies, electrical infrastructure, and maritime engineering; it also is looking to improve its rail systems and develop high-speed rail throughout major corridors. These improvements have the potential to revitalize China's energy and technical wherewithal, which could prove crucial to its emissions mitigation strategies.

Of course, for these strategies to be effective, China will have to find a way to power its transition on fuel that is not coal or even oil in the long run. In this vein, China has rapidly become the largest producer, exporter and installer of solar panels, wind turbines, batteries and electric vehicles in the world (Dudley 2019). In 2017, China accounted for roughly 45% of global renewable energy investment and is leading the world with over 150,000 renewable energy-related patents (A New World 2019). China also has grander visions for interconnectedness in the international realm, namely, the Belt and Road initiative which seeks to create a mass infrastructural network to connect Chinese cities with cities in other nations around the globe, as well as the Global Energy Interconnection, which aims to conjoin every continent into one global green electric grid via underwater transmission cables (GEI Initiative 2019).

Despite the impressive climate upside that has emerged from China's transition into an innovation economy, the nations focused on development of its high-tech capabilities and renewable energy technologies has sparked global concern about China's motivations and its role in what is now being called the fourth industrial revolution, which refers to the nascent revolutions in big data, cloud computing and more. These concerns could have interesting ramifications for global efforts to combat climate change via energy transformation as nations are already responding in the mobile technology sector with China and 5G. It is in this nexus of technology, climate, data and international politics that we will need greater cooperation between the US and China, as will be discussed later in this book.

Water Scarcity and Pollution

Perhaps less well known, yet increasingly critical, in the grand scheme of Chinese environmental challenges are those that have to do with its urban and natural water systems. China's water scarcity issues have been at the forefront of the nation's environmental challenges since the beginning of the reform and opening in the 1970s. However, over the last two decades the issue has grown increasingly severe, especially in the northern parts of the country. Characterized by heavily environmental degradation of freshwater resources and by uneven geographical distributions of supply and demand, China is in its 11th hour as it faces critical decisions about water consumption, distribution and pollution mitigation.

At the beginning of the reform and opening in 1978, the unpolluted freshwater basins accounted for 91.8% of freshwater area (Liu and Qiu 2007).

However, over the last 40 years the freshwater landscape has been significantly altered. Rapid industrialization coupled with limited environmental regulation has hastened the degradation of many of China's lakes and reservoirs. By 1987, over 55% of China's overall freshwater area achieved eutrophic status.

Eutrophication, though deadly to the organisms living in the lake ecosystem, does not automatically preclude lake water from being potable (drinkable). Nevertheless, remnants of algal blooms in tap water have been known to cause undesirable taste and odors, and some are even known carcinogens depending on the waste that catalyzed their growth. Additionally, the released toxins can cause illness and can be tricky to filter out through traditional water treatment processes. As a result, special filtration systems must be built in regions where these toxin-emitting algae are known to bloom—a necessity that can easily run up a bill of millions of US dollars for a medium-sized facility (Liu and Qiu 2007).

In addition to the heavy pollution facing China's freshwater resources, the nation must also tackle an additional challenge tied to the spatial distribution of its water resources relative to its population, and the disproportionate amount of water used in industrial and manufacturing practices relative to its per capita consumption. In 2012, access to a renewable water resource was far below the global average (about 25%). In that same year, water usage per unit of GDP was roughly three times the world average (Liu and Yang 2012). Both of these facts, coupled with the abundance of water in the south and the shortage of water in the north, have contributed immensely to the water challenges facing China today, but have also spurred the country to accelerate its water conservation and distribution efforts. The difference in water supply and demand between north and south is particularly stark when put into numbers: 80% of China's water supply is in the south, while 50% of its people are in the north. In response to this, the communist party announced the south-north water transfer project (SNWTP), which encompasses a large infrastructure project meant to transfer 20.9 billion m^3 per year from southern China to various regions in the north by 2030 (Parton 2018). Despite efforts to move this immense amount of water, it is unclear how much power, and therefore water, will be used to move the 20.9 billion m^3. Additionally, between the years of 2013 and 2014, the Ministry of Water Resource announced a decline in groundwater reserves of about 8 billion m^3, and according to China's Statistical Yearbook, in 2017, water usage distribution was as follows: 62% agriculture, 22% power/industry, 14% humans, 2% other, which raises questions about whether the SNWTP will solve China's water distribution challenges in the long term, and if this project will even solve issues of acute water scarcity and access to potable water on a per capita basis.

Distribution, scarcity and eutrophication have all been problems for many countries in their development phases over the years. The US faced various challenges with water quality from industrialization, urbanization and agricultural practices that prompted the slew of water quality legislations in the 1950s and through the 1970s. Other countries managed to maintain a growing population despite challenges similar to what China faces today. Hence, there is a lot China can learn from the nations that have already gone through this process. For example, the country must be thorough not only in its policymaking, but in its enforcement practices as well. As one study published by the Chinese Academy of Sciences in Nanjing and Henan University found, lack of uniformity across regions in enforcement practices will only lead to polluting entities to move into a jurisdiction with the more relaxed enforcement. Moreover, this effect will be only be aggrandized if policy is a result of reactions to environmental shocks rather than a proactive approach that allows polluters time to improve their technology within the pollution constraints (Yuan et al. 2019). The same can be said with respect to air pollution, especially when considering the fluidity that comes with airborne emissions. Of course, given the imposing level of water intensity and air pollution stemming from coal mining and use, as the country begins to wean off of this fossil fuel it may likely see improved water and air quality countrywide.

Governance in China

As is the case with most other economic-oriented development in China, the emergence of governance as a focus issue for the Chinese government began with the reform and opening in 1978. The first shares issued from an organization in China came from state-owned enterprises (SOEs) in the 1980s, and brought with it the establishment of the Shanghai and Shenzhen stock exchanges in 1990 and 1991, respectively. Quickly after, the first shares of an SOE were issued to foreign exchanges in New York and Hong Kong in 1992 and 1993 respectively (Allen and Li 2018). However, it wasn't until the early 2000s that corporate governance guidelines started becoming part of China's legal infrastructure. In 2001, China released its first ever corporate governance code. Issued by the Chinese Securities Regulatory Commission (CSRC), the regulating body of both Shanghai and Shenzhen stock exchanges, the Code of Corporate Governance for Listed Companies encompassed some of the first legal guidelines centered around corporate governance for companies listed on its stock exchanges (Corporate Governance in China 2017). With this new code, the early 2000s began to see important changes with respect to independent directors, quarterly reporting and board governance (Allen and Li 2018).

More and more international investors are becoming interested in Chinese markets. This comes off the tailwinds of the Morgan Stanley Capital International (MSCI) deciding to include 234 Chinese A share companies in its Emerging Markets Index back in June 2018, and increasing its weighting of Chinese companies from 5% to 20% in MSCI indexes (MSCI 2019). Building off this, there has been exciting news that China is looking to end restrictions on foreign investments in the form of securities, futures and life insurance by 2020, a year ahead of schedule (The Straits Times 2019a). And despite tensions with the US government, major US banks have been courting Chinese officials over talks about internationalization of its capital markets (The Straits Times 2019b).

In response to increasing interest in their capital markets, China has begun to more seriously revamp its corporate governance policies. In 2018, the CSRC revised its corporate governance code for the first time since 2002. These revisions come in tandem with its opening up of financial markets, and use Environment, Social and Governance (ESG) criteria to address various corporate governance concerns from foreign investors. However, there are still a few challenges facing both foreign investors and Chinese companies that, if addressed, could smoothen the integration of Chinese capital markets with the rest of the world. The more obvious corporate governance challenges are centered around Variable Interest Entities (VIE), insider trading and corruption.

A good case study for VIEs and Chinese companies is Alibaba, perhaps the most well-known Chinese company to foreign investors. While certainly not the inventor of the VIE structure (RenRen and Baidu both IPO'd in New York using VIEs), Alibaba's IPO was riddled with questions of risk and legality. The largest concern among investors was the concentration of rights between two of Alibaba's executives, Jack Ma and Simon Xie, and the lack of control offered to shareholders relative to direct ownership. Nevertheless, this seems to be changing as Jack Ma announced that Alibaba was transferring ownership to the Alibaba Partnership in an attempt to decrease key-man risk and improve the company's corporate governance (Soo 2018).

Given the number of high-profile cases plaguing both mainland China and Hong Kong markets over the years, foreign investors have grown weary about insider trading and corruption. Perhaps one of the more notable cases is Hanergy, which rose to glory in 2015. Hanergy Thin Film Power Group Ltd., once the star of the Hong Kong exchange, was on a trajectory to achieve a valuation of $40 billion before it saw 47%, or $18.6 billion, erased in less than 24 hours (Ma et al. 2015). This collapse of their stock price came as a shock to many of its shareholders, some of whom are still stranded with the all but worthless asset after Hong Kong began investigating the company and suspended all trading. The sudden and shocking breakdown of the firm's share price was borne out of the then CEO and China's richest man, Li HeJun, using personal loans from companies in what the *Wall Street Journal* describes as "China's informal 'shadow-banking' sector" (Ma et al. 2015), and in many ways highlights the still somewhat murky corporate environments many investors deem characteristic of China.

Another high-profile case is Toronto's former star Sino-Forest—a firm that fell victim to short selling activist investing firm Muddy Waters. Sino-Forest was exposed by Muddy Waters to have been grossly inflating its assets and revenues. This news sent the stock price plummeting by over 60% (McNish 2017). Soon after the Ontario government found Sino-Forest "engaged in deceitful and dishonest conduct … [that] they knew constituted fraud." However, despite these concerns, President Xi JinPing's anti-corruption campaign has doubled the average number of arrests of high-ranking officials to 50 per year (Jennings 2018), including Xiang JunBo, former head of the now defunct China Insurance Regulatory Commission, a sign that China and President JinPing are not taking existing norms around corruption lightly. Studies show that this campaign has statistically decreased the likelihood of fraud throughout China (Zhang 2016). Nevertheless, there remains plenty of work to be done to combat graft in Chinese markets.

Fortunately, in addition to cracking down on corruption and graft, China has been making major strides toward improving their corporate governance regulation. The Asian Corporate Governance Association's annual report published in partnership with Credit Lyonnais Securities Asia (CLSA) indicates that, in addition to substantially improving its ability to enforce corporate governance regulation, the PRC has also improved its corporate governance rules (Hard Decisions 2018). On October 1st, 2018, the CSRC released an amended corporate governance code—updating it from the 2001 version. Most notably, the new code highlights the role of the chairman and the board of directors in managing shareholder protection in general, with a specific emphasis on disclosure; the code calls for a heightened attention to auditing, and the establishment of an auditing committee by all listed companies. Another noteworthy development is the two chapters added to both encourage asset owners and institutional investors to invest responsibly and engage with their portfolio companies, and for companies themselves to voluntarily contribute to the sustainable development of society and the environment. The code also highlights the need for environment, social and governance considerations both by investors and in corporate governance more generally (Hard Decisions 2018).

If we are truly to bridge the gap between Chinese markets and the rest of the world, effort needs to be made on both ends. In a report posted by Harvard Law School's Forum on Corporate Governance and Financial Regulation, Jamie Allen and Li Rui of ACGA argue for better communication between Chinese companies and foreign investors, citing that both sides need to work harder in order to achieve an equal understanding of corporate governance expectations. Most notably, the report cites a quote from a survey respondent that foreign investors should try to understand "the differences in culture, political context, and the path and stage of economic development between China and the rest of the world" (Allen and Li 2018). Common challenges in this regard are centered around difficulties with language and cultural barriers and gaining access to company management. The report argues for foreign shareholders to spend time on the ground in China and study the complex and nuanced relationship-based business environment, if they are not doing so already.

Overall, while there is still plenty of work to be done, major strides are taking place, making for an interesting and dynamic opportunity for foreign investors to hop on early as Chinese markets continue to open up, if they haven't already fully done so by the time this book is published. Likewise, Chinese companies are also on the verge of getting unfettered access to foreign capital markets that used to be off-limits to all but a few exceptions. Notwithstanding these opportunities and positive steps being taken by investors, companies and Chinese regulators, there is still quite a bit of uncertainty about how all this will play out.

This uncertainty requires a new approach to better relations between Chinese companies, regulators and foreign investors, as China is on the move, innovating, always changing, modernizing and adapting, and is fully expected to soon be the world's largest economy.

References

A New World the Geopolitics of the Energy Transformation. 2019. *A New World the Geopolitics of the Energy Transformation*. IREA. http://geopoliticsofrenewables. org/assets/geopolitics/Reports/wp-content/uploads/2019/01/Global_commission_renewable_energy_2019.pdf

Allen, Jamie, and Li Rui. 2018. Awakening Governance: ACGA China Corporate Governance Report 2018. *Awakening Governance: ACGA China Corporate Governance Report 2018*. Harvard Law School Forum. https://corpgov.law.harvard.edu/2018/08/25/awakening-governance-acga-china-corporate-governance-report-2018/

Ayoub, Joseph. 2014. U.S. Energy Information Administration – EIA – Independent Statistics and Analysis. *China Produces and Consumes Almost as Much Coal as the Rest of the World Combined – Today in Energy – U.S. Energy Information Administration (EIA).* U.S. Energy Information Administration, May 14. https://www.eia.gov/todayinenergy/detail.php?id=16271

Bloomberg News. 2019. China's Mammoth Coal Industry Gets Bigger, Crowding Out Imports, April 8. https://www.bloomberg.com/news/articles/2019-04-09/china-s-mammoth-coal-industry-gets-bigger-crowding-out-imports

Burrows, Leah. 2018. China's War on Particulate Air Pollution Is Causing More Severe Ozone Pollution. *Harvard John A. Paulson School of Engineering and Applied Sciences,* December 31. https://www.seas.harvard.edu/news/2018/12/chinas-war-particulate-air-pollution-causing-more-severe-ozone-pollution

Carbon Dioxide Emissions Embodied in International Trade. 2019. *OECD,* April. https://www.oecd.org/sti/ind/carbondioxideemissionsembodiedininternationaltrade.htm

Chen, Pearl. 2017. Beijing's Car Plate Policies. *Global Times,* April 17. http://www.globaltimes.cn/content/1098345.shtml

China Daily. 2017. New Normal in Economic Development, October 5. http://www.chinadaily.com.cn/china/19thcpcnationalcongress/2017-10/05/content_32869258.html

———. 2019. Coal Burning No Longer Major Source of Beijing PM2.5: Study, May 14. http://www.chinadaily.com.cn/a/201805/14/WS5af94c18a3103f6866ee8415.html

China: Light-Duty: Emissions. 2019. *Transport Policy.* https://www.transportpolicy.net/standard/china-light-duty-emissions/. Accessed 30 Dec.

China's Economic Rise: History, Trends, Challenges, and Implications for the United States. 2019. *China's Economic Rise: History, Trends, Challenges, and Implications for the United States.* Congressional Research Service. https://fas.org/sgp/crs/row/RL33534.pdf

Corporate Governance in China. 2017. *Corporate Governance in China.* MSCI. https://www.msci.com/documents/10199/1d443a3d-0437-4af7-aa27-ada3a2655f6d

Dudley, Dominic. 2019. China Is Set to Become the World's Renewable Energy Superpower, According to New Report. *Forbes,* January 11. https://www.forbes.com/sites/dominicdudley/2019/01/11/china-renewable-energy-superpower/#402f4444745a

GEI Initiative – Global Consensus – Global Energy Interconnection Development and Cooperation Organization: GEIDCO. 2019. *Global Energy Interconnection.* https://en.geidco.org/aboutgei/initiative/. Accessed 30 Dec.

Han, Shu. 2019a. China: Urban and Rural Population 2018. *Statista,* November 8. https://www.statista.com/statistics/278566/urban-and-rural-population-of-china/

————. 2019b. China: Urbanization 2018. *Statista,* November 22. https://www.statista.com/statistics/270162/urbanization-in-china/

Hard Decisions: Asia Faces Tough Challenges in CG Reform. 2018. *Hard Decisions: Asia Faces Tough Challenges in CG Reform.* Hong Kong: Asian Corporate Governance Association and CLSA Limited.

IEA Energy Atlas. 2019. *IEA Energy Atlas.* International Energy Agency. http://energyatlas.iea.org/#!/tellmap/2020991907. Accessed 30 Dec.

Jennings, Ralph. 2018. Bad for Business? China's Corruption Isn't Getting Any Better Despite Government Crackdowns. *Forbes.* Forbes Magazine, March 15. https://www.forbes.com/sites/ralphjennings/2018/03/15/corruption-in-china-gets-stuck-half-way-between-the-worlds-best-and-worst/#cd48ee973d10

Kai, Liao. 2019. Reducing Traffic Congestion and Emission in Chinese Cities. *World Bank.* https://www.worldbank.org/en/news/feature/2018/11/16/reducing-traffic-congestion-and-emission-in-chinese-cities. Accessed 20 Sept.

Li, Jane. 2016. Thick Choking Smog Returns to Blanket Beijing, Visibility Falls Below 100 Metres. *South China Morning Post,* November 4. https://www.scmp.com/news/china/society/article/2042983/thick-choking-smog-returns-blanket-beijing-visibility-falls-below

Li, Ke, Daniel J. Jacob, Hong Liao, Lu Shen, Qiang Zhang, and Kelvin H. Bates. 2018. Anthropogenic Drivers of 2013–2017 Trends in Summer Surface Ozone in China. *Proceedings of the National Academy of Sciences* 116 (2): 422–427. https://doi.org/10.1073/pnas.1812168116.

Liu, Wei, and Rongliang Qiu. 2007. Water Eutrophication in China and the Combating Strategies. *Journal of Chemical Technology & Biotechnology* 82 (9): 781–786. https://doi.org/10.1002/jctb.1755.

Liu, Jianguo, and Wu Yang. 2012. Water Sustainability for China and Beyond. *Science* 337 (6095): 649–650. https://doi.org/10.1126/science.1219471.

Ma, Wayne, Brian Spegele, and Jacky Wong. 2015. How Chinese Billionaire Li Hejun's Solar Bet Soured. *Wall Street Journal,* June 21. https://www.wsj.com/articles/how-chinese-billionaire-li-hejuns-solar-bet-soured-1434925566?mod=article_inline

Maji, Kamal Jyoti, Wei-Feng Shiva Ye, Mohit Arora, and S.M. Shiva Nagendra. 2018. PM2.5-Related Health and Economic Loss Assessment for 338 Chinese Cities. *Environment International* 121 (December): 392–403. https://doi.org/10.1016/j.envint.2018.09.024.

McNish, Jacquie. 2017. Sino-Forest Executives Committed Fraud in Overstating Value, Canadian Regulator Says. *Wall Street Journal,* July 14. https://www.wsj.com/articles/sino-forest-accused-of-fraud-by-canada-regulator-1500048098

MSCI. 2019. *MSCI.* https://www.msci.com/documents/10199/238444/China_A_Further_Weight_Increase_PR_Eng.pdf/43f3ee8b-5182-68d4-a758-2968b4206e54

Parton, Charlie. 2018. China's Looming Water Crisis. China's Looming Water Crisis. *China Dialogue*. https://chinadialogue-production.s3.amazonaws.com/uploads/content/file_en/10608/China_s_looming_water_crisis_v.2__1_.pdf

Pusceddu, Riccardo. 2014. China's Growing Coal Use Is World's Growing Problem. *Climate Central*, January 27. https://www.climatecentral.org/blogs/chinas-growing-coal-use-is-worlds-growing-problem-16999

Rohde, Robert A., and Richard A. Muller. 2015. Air Pollution in China: Mapping of Concentrations and Sources. *PLoS One* 10 (8). https://doi.org/10.1371/journal.pone.0135749.

So, Charlotte. 2014. China Losing Status as 'World's Factory'. *South China Morning Post,* February 3. https://www.scmp.com/business/china-business/article/1419428/china-losing-status-worlds-factory

Soo, Zen. 2018. Alibaba's Jack Ma Is Giving Up Ownership of Chinese Entities – Here's What That Means. *South China Morning Post,* October 5. https://www.scmp.com/tech/enterprises/article/2167002/alibabas-jack-ma-giving-ownership-chinese-entities-heres-what-means

The Straits Times. 2019a. China to Hasten Opening Up of Financial Sector, July 3. https://www.straitstimes.com/asia/east-asia/china-to-hasten-opening-up-of-financial-sector

———. 2019b. Trade War Hasn't Stopped Wall Street's $12b China Rush, September 27. https://www.straitstimes.com/business/banking/trade-war-hasnt-stopped-wall-streets-12b-china-rush

West, Darrell M., and Christian Lansang. 2018. Global Manufacturing Scorecard: How the US Compares to 18 Other Nations. *Brookings,* July 10. https://www.brookings.edu/research/global-manufacturing-scorecard-how-the-us-compares-to-18-other-nations/

Xia, Yang, Dabo Guan, Xujia Jiang, Liqun Peng, Heike Schroeder, and Qiang Zhang. 2016. Assessment of Socioeconomic Costs to China's Air Pollution. *Atmospheric Environment* 139 (August): 147–156. https://doi.org/10.1016/j.atmosenv.2016.05.036.

Xinhuanet. 2019. China Focus: China Starts Implementing Tougher Vehicle Emission Standards, July 2. http://www.xinhuanet.com/english/2019-07/02/c_138190039.htm

Yao, Yang. 2011. China's Export-Led Growth Model. *East Asia Forum,* February 27. https://www.eastasiaforum.org/2011/02/27/chinas-export-led-growth-model/

Yuan, Feng, Yehua Dennis Wei, Jinlong Gao, and Wen Chen. 2019. Water Crisis, Environmental Regulations and Location Dynamics of Pollution-Intensive Industries in China: A Study of the Taihu Lake Watershed. *Journal of Cleaner Production* 216 (April): 311–322. https://doi.org/10.1016/j.jclepro.2019.01.177.

Zeng, Yingying C., Yuanfei C. Cao, Xue C. Qiao, Barnabas C. Seyler, and Ya C. Tang. 2019. Air Pollution Reduction in China: Recent Success but Great Challenge for the Future. *Science of the Total Environment* 663 (May): 329–337. https://doi.org/10.1016/j.scitotenv.2019.01.262.

Zhang, Jian. 2016. Public Governance and Corporate Fraud: Evidence from the Recent Anti-Corruption Campaign in China. *Journal of Business Ethics* 148 (2): 375–396. https://doi.org/10.1007/s10551-016-3025-x.

Zheng, Sarah. 2017. China Now Has Over 300 Million Vehicles … That's Almost America's Total Population. *South China Morning Post,* April 19. https://www. scmp.com/news/china/economy/article/2088876/chinas-more-300-million-vehicles-drive-pollution-congestion

3

China and Innovation

Huang Zhong, Lucia Winton, and Cary Krosinsky

It might surprise readers to know that China is innovating at a rapid pace, helping to explain the country's recent advantage in 5G, and is racing to develop other new technologies as well.

China's re-rise as a leading innovating nation manifests across many sectors with private equity and venture capital thriving regardless of recent relative economic slowdowns or trade war dynamics.

What Is Innovation?

It's always important to clarify what innovation actually is and why it's strategically important. Joe Dwyer, a professor at Northwestern's Kellogg School of Management, an investor, technologist, and serial entrepreneur, posits: *"Innovation is the process of creating value by applying novel solutions to meaningful problems."* (Dwyer 2019)

Under this lens, something is "innovative" if it passes three explicit tests:

* *Is it novel?* The notion of novelty is baked right into the word "in*nov*ation." If the idea is not new, it is more optimization than innovation.
* *Does it solve a meaningful problem?* If not, maybe it's art instead of innovation. That is not to say art isn't valuable, but it's generally not designed to directly solve a problem.
* *Does it create value?* If not, maybe it's an invention rather than an innovation. Inventions can lead to value creation, but usually not until someone applies them through innovation.

© The Author(s) 2020
C. Krosinsky, *Modern China*, https://doi.org/10.1007/978-3-030-39204-8_3

29

China's History as an Innovative Nation

Western views on Chinese innovations often fall into two extremes: either "China steals everything" or "China can make everything!" The truth is of course far more complicated—much like it has experienced throughout its thousands of years of history, China's contribution to innovation has also had its ups and downs.

Most people in China know that their ancestors contributed significantly to the world of science and technology, specifically *The Four Great Inventions*—gunpowder, papermaking, printing and the compass.

This history of Chinese innovation, which spans thousands of years, is a source of great pride in Chinese culture; any three-year-old in China can easily recite these four inventions.

These four central discoveries had profound impacts on the development of civilization throughout the world. But there are numerous other inventions and innovations that had great or greater impact in Chinese culture, economy and lifestyle. To name just a few:

- Using shadow clocks and the abacus, the Chinese were able to record space observations, documenting the first recorded solar eclipse in 2137 BC, and make the first recording of any planetary grouping in 500 BC (Cullen 1996).
- Mathematics in China emerged independently by the eleventh century BC. The Chinese developed number sets, including large and negative numbers, decimals, a place value decimal system, a binary system, algebra, geometry and trigonometry (New York Times 2011, p. 1131).
- In a grand architectural and technological feat, the Chinese built the Great Wall of China under the first Chinese Emperor Qin Shi Huang between 220 and 200 BC (Needham 1978).
- Premodern Chinese used escapement mechanisms in water-powered clock-works since the eighth century and developed the endless power-transmitting chain drive in the eleventh century.
- Scientist Shen Kuo made prescient hypotheses surrounding geology, geomorphology and climate change in his Dream Pool Essays of 1088 (Goetzmann and Rouwenhorst 2005, p. 94).
- China invented paper money in the 1200s. Introduced by Marco Polo to Europe in 1260, paper money was an innovation that reshaped the world (Bohlander 1992).

- China first sailed in the ocean in 1405 to as far as East Africa and the Red Sea. The Chinese sailor Zheng He was almost a century earlier than Christopher Columbus set out to discover the world in 1492 (Elvin 1972, pp. 137–172).

The list of China's innovations is as long as its history of civilization; the country contributed to the world's leading innovations until the late 1600s.

China's Lag in Science and Technology Over the Previous 200 Years

Despite its longer history of innovation, civilization and global prowess, China has lagged in science and technology over the last 200 years. Historians have posited a myriad of causes to explain this: political, cultural and economic. While other countries grew and innovated, transitioning to industrialization and mechanization, China instead relied on its huge population and access to land and labor. Mark Elvin, professor emeritus of Chinese history at Australian National University, delineates a high-level equilibrium trap that existed in China (Shepard 2016). This equilibrium trap argued that the Chinese population was large enough, workers cheap enough and agrarian productivity high enough to not require mechanization; thousands of Chinese workers were perfectly able to quickly perform any needed task. Other events such as the Opium Wars and subsequent resentment toward European influence prevented China from undergoing an Industrial Revolution. Replicating Europe's progress on a large scale would be impossible for a lengthy period of time. Political instability under Cixi rule (characterized by frequent oscillation between modernists and conservatives), the Republican Wars (1911–1933), the Sino-Japanese War (1933–1945), the Communist/Nationalist War (1945–1949) as well as the later Cultural Revolution (1966–1976) further isolated China at critical times for technological growth.

Kenneth Pomeranz, a professor of History at the University of Chicago, further postulates that substantial resources that Europe accessed via the New World made a crucial difference between European and Chinese development. While the Western world's high-speed growth in science and technology drove substantial societal advancement, China saw meager growth during the same 200-year period.

It wasn't until Deng Xiaoping, the leader of China from 1978 to 1992 and the "Architect of Modern China," started to open China for economic reform, development and trade in 1979 that China was able to make significant strides toward growth.

From OEM to ODM to OBM to Ecosystem

When China first opened its economy in the early 1980s, it started from a low-margin, low-tech OEM (original equipment manufacturing) model, and slowly but steadily moved up the value chain, upgrading its business model to ODM (original design manufacturing), then onto OBM (original brand manufacturing) and, finally, to building powerful ecosystems (Fig. 3.1).

Many Chinese producers started out as contract or original equipment manufacturers (OEM), producing already designed products or components for the products of other companies—mostly from the US, Europe, Japan and Singapore (Business Commission 2017). The OEM model fit well in China when Western countries were moving up the value chain, transferring labor-intensive and low-margin jobs to China. China used this opportunity and emphasis on OEM to develop its large young population into a strong workforce, forcing state-owned companies to become more market-oriented.

These Chinese manufacturing companies, which vary in size and industry, have been gradually increasing the complexity and earnings potential of their operations over the past 10 or 20 years. As many manufacturers began developing more sophistication, through observation, absorption, imitation, reverse engineering and eventually investments in R&D with intentional innovation, they began transitioning to original design manufacturing (ODM). ODM describes how these manufacturers started handling many aspects of the total manufacturing and design process, often making complete products which Western companies would simply add their brand name to.

This transition from OEM to ODM happened in almost every industry in China: textiles, fashion, computers and mobile phones and, more recently, the financial industry.

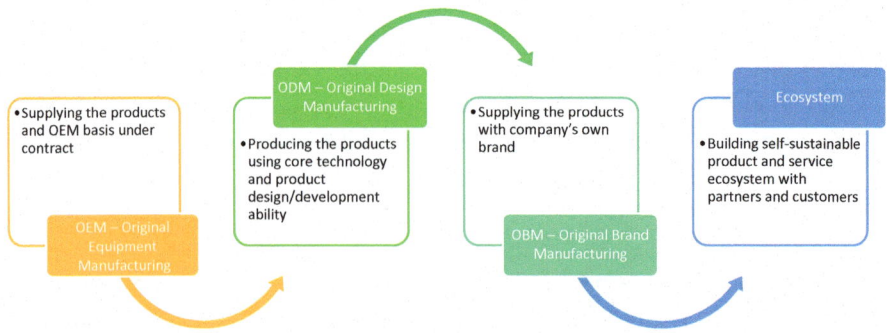

Fig. 3.1 The evolution of the Chinese economy

Well-known companies such as Huawei, ZTE, Xiaomi, Lenovo, BYD, Haier, successfully realized this transformation from OEM to ODM and moved further into OBM, or original brand manufacturing.

Many business observers regard the global financial crisis in 2008 as the turning point for China's transition from relatively profitable ODM to even more lucrative OBM.

When the economic crisis hit global markets, the international demand for Chinese products began decreasing. This sharp decline in demand rattled Chinese manufacturers, who started finding themselves with a lack of contracts to produce their designs and gluts of unsold inventory. Alongside private companies, China's central government also realized the importance of fostering a more successful domestic market. One solution was to start placing their own names on the products they were manufacturing and unloading them in their domestic market.

The transition from ODM to OBM was thus supported through the Chinese domestic market, instead of by global demand. This government push toward building up domestic industries has continued to this day. OBM producers also realize a much higher profit margin than their OEM or ODM counterparts, allowing them to invest more in R&D and branding.

This was the beginning of a movement that would soon permeate through all strata of China's manufacturing empire. Spurred by changes in global markets, China had successfully transitioned from copycat factories once solely bent on getting their handbags to look as much like Gucci as possible into giant high-tech companies shipping tens of millions of phones to markets all around the world.

Long before the recent trade war, prominent companies in China realized that no matter how dominant they were in their industries, there were always competitors who could create better, cheaper products overnight. Consider Kodak, for example. When the digital camera came into the market, Kodak went bankrupt within ten years. What this company lacked was a strong ecosystem of products to protect it in the event of disruptive competition.

Smart companies such as Apple, Google and Microsoft built such an ecosystem by including outside developers and third-party partners to build apps to enhance their core product, the iPhone. Products and services through its core app ecosystem have become Apple's fastest growing segment, driving revenue growth for the company and building partnerships with third-party developers.

Not a single species can survive without the involvements of other species. For a company in the vastly enormous and complex business community, this same logic of survival applies.

Leading Chinese companies such as Huawei, DJI and Tencent are all building their own ecosystems around their core products, Huawei on 5G and related technologies, DJI on drone capacities, Tencent on its most popular WeChat social media app. This transition from OBM to ecosystem is a pivotal step for ongoing success.

Huawei in particular has seen astonishing success in disrupting what was once an exclusive bastion of the developed world, telecommunications and mobile devices. It has done so by building an extraordinary ecosystem of new technology, which includes 5G networks, AI and a brand-new operating system called HarmonyOS. Huawei directly competes with Western companies like Verizon, AT&T, Google's Android service and Apple's iOS software.

Ecosystems, once they reach a healthy balance among key participants, are expansive and harder to destroy.

Transition in Growth

After four decades of rapid growth, China is now entering a new normal of slower growth. China's economy is growing at roughly 6% a year, which, though slower than in the past, remains high by the standards of most middle-income economies. Per capita gross domestic product (GDP) stands at nearly $10,000, about one-fourth of the average for the Organization for Economic Co-Operation and Development (OECD) countries. China has considerable room for future growth.

Despite this slower growth, China's next transformation is well under way, and a "new economy" is emerging. China maintains a strong manufacturing base and is the leading global exporter of manufactured goods, making the country one of the central hubs of the global value chain. Its export products are becoming increasingly more sophisticated, and the share of domestic, value-added exports has been rising steadily in the past decade, as domestic supply chains have deepened. The quality of China's manufacturing exports is improving rapidly, and its manufacturing "fitness," a measure of manufacturing capability, is at par with that of high-income economies. Furthermore, services have taken over manufacturing as the largest share of GDP and are now the largest contributor to GDP growth.

Innovation capabilities are growing rapidly, reducing the gap with leading OECD countries. China's ranking on indexes such as the Global Innovation Index has risen steadily and is now the highest among developing countries. The number of domestic patents filed for inventions has increased to an annual 1.56 million (2018), the highest in the world, although the quality of patents remains tenuous. China's spending on research and development (R&D) has risen significantly, reaching 2.18% of GDP in 2018, compared with the OECD average of 2.4%. Its total spending on R&D is set to pass the US by 2020 (World Bank Group 2019). China is among the global leaders in technologies such as telecommunications, e-commerce, artificial intelligence, fintech, high-speed trains, renewable energy and electric cars.

However, China's productivity growth has been slowing since the global financial crisis and has remained relatively low. Since the crisis, China's growth in total factor productivity (TFP), a broad measure of how productively an economy uses capital and labor, has declined. This decline is especially significant because China's TFP is currently only about half the level of OECD countries (Brookings Institution 2019).

To increase productivity, China will need both higher within-firm productivity growth through innovation and greater gains from the entry and exit of firms and the reallocation of resources to more productive enterprises driven by greater competition (Raiser and Sahib Soh 2019).

China will need to promote new drivers of growth to address its major challenges to productivity. Sustained growth in the long run will depend on continuous productivity improvement.

Innovation as China's Key National Strategy

China's national strategy for economic growth specifically highlights innovation as one of the keys—if not the key—to its continued success in the twenty-first century. In 2006, the Chinese government declared its intention to transform China into "an innovative society" by 2020 and a world leader in science and technology by 2050. This declaration included a commitment to reducing reliance on imported technology to no more than 30% in just a few years, increasing domestic funding for R&D and surpassing foreign rivals in strategic emerging sectors (i.e. biotechnology, energy technology, equipment manufacturing, information technology and advanced materials) (Kirby et al. 2014).

China's Global Innovation Index Ranking on the Rise

China's strategic commitment to innovation has paid off. The Global Innovation Index Report, which provides 80 detailed metrics for 129 economies, ranked China as 14th in the world (Global Innovation Index 2019). Just ten years prior, the same Global Innovation Index ranked China as 43rd for innovation (Global Innovation Index 2010). Since then, China has been consistently rising in ranking as its remarkable pace of innovations has been recognized by global researchers.

Global leaders in technology innovations have sprouted from China in recent years, namely, Baidu, Alibaba and Tencent (also known as BAT). These three tech giants showcase the potential for Chinese innovations to succeed and grow on a huge scale. Baidu, Alibaba and Tencent are now valued at a combined $1 trillion. Alibaba and Tencent alone make up almost $\frac{1}{3}$ of the MSCI China Index and which invest in roughly 50% of China's unicorns, or start-ups valued at over $1 billion (Diamandis 2018). Chinese innovations are making global impacts, disrupting markets, challenging foreign companies to keep pace and reaping financial rewards.

Outside of BAT, innovation in China remains strong. Up-and-coming leaders like news aggregator Toutiao, e-commerce dealer Meituan and ride-sharing provider Didi Chuxing and other giants like Huawei, Xiaomi, DJI, Haier and Midea present further layers of leading innovation pervasive throughout China.

Chinese entrepreneurs are known for their "hustle" and hard work. A new term has been coined to describe their work life: 996, meaning working from 9 a.m. to 9 p.m., 6 days per week. This "hustle," or China Speed (Chap. 8), supported by government policies to spur innovation, helps explain how China's start-ups now claim nearly ¼ of the world's unicorn start-ups (Fannin 2018).

Other indicators that researchers often look at all point to rapid and rampant innovation in China. For example, since 2014, China has built 227 of the world's top supercomputers, while the US has built only 109. For comparison, in just 2008, China produced 12 supercomputers. In education, almost 7 million students obtain a bachelor's degree in China annually; 30% are in engineering compared to 5% in the US. China is now also a leading country in the number of patents, a key indicator of R&D and innovation. In 2016, the US Patent and Trademark Office reported that China was granted 11,000 patents, the equivalent of 8% of US patents, a significant increase from 1066 or 1.2% in 2006 (Atkinson and Foote 2019). Each of these indicators points to accelerating technology growth and levels of innovation.

National Plans and Policies

A central component of China's innovation-driven development plan is the Made in China 2025 initiative. Launched in 2015, the core objective of Made in China 2025 was to advance indigenous innovation in China and to enable the country's role as a manufacturing superpower, revitalizing its historical prowess in technology and innovations. The Made in China 2025 initiative offered a complex architecture of plans and policies to build China into a technological powerhouse and specifically targeted ten sectors: new generation information technology, advanced numerical control machine tools and robotics; aerospace technology, including aircraft engines and airborne equipment; and biopharmaceuticals and high-performance medical equipment (Kania 2018).

In order to transform Chinese cities into leading technology innovators, the government created a policy and regulatory friendly environment for technology and start-ups. China launched 77 initiatives worth $100 billion in tax cuts to stimulate the technology sector. These initiatives include a discounted tax rate for tech firms ranging from 10 to 15 and a range of tax discounts and free land for small or micro businesses. On top of this, the initiative allocated 20% of national security funds to venture capital, launched over 1600 technology business incubators and created 780 government funds for tech entrepreneurs (Jing 2018).

With each of these policies implemented at the national level, innovation in China has not been limited to one region or one sector, but was rather spread across the country in various cities and hubs of innovation. Beijing, one example of a flourishing hub of technology, was ranked the fourth most innovative city in the world, ahead of London, New York and Hong Kong. Beijing has a deep-rooted innovation ecosystem, nurturing most of the unicorns outside of Silicon Valley, and is the third largest destination in the world for venture capital funding (Arcibal 2019). Zhongguancun Science Park, a neighborhood in Beijing, offers a multitude of resources for start-ups, such as shared work spaces and incubators. Zhongguancun Science Park is home to companies like Baidu and Tencent. Innoway, a "start-up village" within Zhongguancun, was developed with $36 million of government funding and offers a glimpse at how government strategy and funding combined with private companies and entrepreneurs spurs effective innovation. In the 200-meter strip of Innoway alone, 300 start-ups reside (Horwitz 2015).

Other cities such as Hangzhou, Shanghai, Shenzhen and Xi'an each sport unique focuses for innovation and development. For instance, Shenzhen, traditionally known for its hardware manufacturing and referred to as the "factory of the world," is now a global center of electronics and communication innovation. The city alone accounted for more than half of China's international patent applications in 2018 and was the birthplace of companies like Huawei, DJI and UBTech Robotics (Yamada 2019).

National strategies like Made in China 2025 along with these widespread hubs of technology have led to world-leading innovations in China. To name a few, China is now home to the world's first qualified robotic doctor (Xiaoyi), the largest floating solar power plant, the first passenger drone (Ehang 248), the first operational drone-delivery program, the largest waste-to-energy plant, the first robot-staffed bank, the first trackless smart train and virtual railway, the first AI-powered teaching assistant, an electric bus fleet and the first landing on the far side of the moon (Coughlin 2019).

Intellectual Property Protection Assisting China's Innovation Transition

China is not only facing pressure from the West to protect intellectual property; domestic companies, especially high-tech companies, are also calling for intellectual property (IP) protection. In response, and in another effort to spur growth in the technology sector, China has made several strides to strengthen judicial protection over IP. Over the past 40 years, China has implemented and continued to improve a modern IP system, primarily through the establishment and growth of a specialized court system for judicial protection of IP. In 2014, China launched three primary IP courts in Beijing, Shanghai and Guangzhou. Shortly afterward, China established IP tribunals in over 18 additional cities (Kaiyun 2019).

The IP caseload of Chinese courts has grown rapidly in recent years. In 2018, China saw a 41% increase in the number of new IP cases received by Chinese courts as well as a 42% increase in the number of cases concluded. China also sports one of the shortest adjudication periods in the world for international IP cases (Huang and Smith 2019). A shift in IP policy represents a positive shift of IP rights in China, critical for incentivizing innovation and providing security to entrepreneurs. Though recent trends in IP protection are positive, issues with IP rights and litigation remain in China. History informs that countries do not enact strong IP rights systems until their ability to innovate domestically replaces a reliance on outside knowledge. The US's own experience in IP protections demonstrates this reality (Derwin 2019).

Chinese NASDAQ: The Science and Technology Innovation Board

Another critical development for Chinese entrepreneurs has been the adoption of a new, regulated listing system, replacing the prolonged regulatory vetting that kept many companies waiting for more than a year before listing their companies on a public stock exchange. In innovating its financial listing system, the Chinese government is making significant strides to loosen its grip on Chinese equity markets, enabling companies to list more easily (Huang 2019). The new exchange, the Science and Technology Innovation Board (Star Market), creates more opportunity for companies to go public.

Beijing adopted this new stock exchange system after tech giants like Alibaba and Baidu chose to list their shares on US exchanges. They were attracted by more tech-friendly regulations in the US, as well as access to abundant capital and the prestige associated with international listings. By introducing the Star Market, China seeks to offer comparable if not greater opportunity for Chinese entrepreneurs to list stocks domestically in China rather than in the US. Within this new exchange are potential opportunities for long-term, value-driven international investors willing to wait for the exchange to gain more maturity and demonstrate success (Huang 2019).

After decades of replicating Western business and economic models, which has led to its transition toward becoming more of an innovative society, Chinese tech companies have also learned the "secret formula" behind Western countries' innovation prowess: talent. Intelligence is the core of any innovation. The Chinese have their own advantages on this front, including large-scale government support, R&D spending that is rapidly catching up with that in the US, a highly skilled workforce trained in engineering and other advanced disciplines and an increasingly competitive education system.

China's Large Pool of STEM Graduates

In 2019, China graduated 8.34 million college graduates, an increase of 140,000 in 2018, the highest ever number of graduates, according to the Ministry of Education. Of this, over half (about 4.7 million) were graduates from STEM (Science, Technology, Engineering and Math) majors (Fig. 3.2).

This new workforce of STEM graduates will be led in the direction of major national programs such as "Made in China 2025," high-tech industries, strategic emerging sectors and advanced manufacturing.

Of course, there remain drawbacks of the Chinese education system. Chinese universities have a track record of successfully teaching students "hard skills," but the inherent test-focused education system has placed little emphasis on the development of anything else. So while graduates from technical or quantitative majors represent great opportunity for the development of technology corporations and industries, the lack of emphasis on "soft" skills and humanities learning is an obvious flaw within the Chinese education system. Yet college graduates born in the age of the internet grew up increasingly

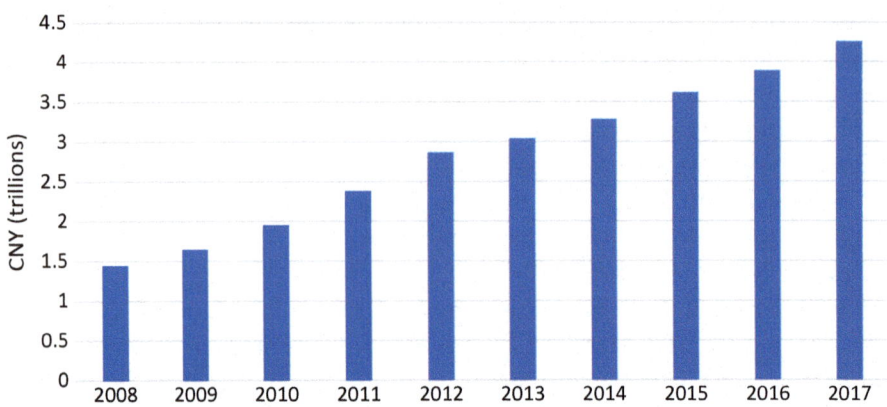

Fig. 3.2 China's annual total spending on education

in wealthy and middle-class families and are developing more innovative mindsets through greater exposure to global perspectives.

China Attracted Global Talent While the US Developed an Anti-Immigration Focus, Inadvertently Benefiting China at the Expense of the US

Before 2012, less than half of Chinese students who graduated or landed a job in the US returned to their home country. Compared with the US, China's technology ecosystem still felt relatively backward at that time, packed with cutthroat copycat companies and thin on venture capital or genuine innovation.

Chinese start-ups were also beginning to attract haigui, a pun on the word for "sea turtle." Haigui refers to folks who return to China after studying or working overseas. The current trade war and recent US anti-immigration policies accelerated this trend of young Chinese citizens gaining education abroad but returning to work in China following graduation, giving China unprecedented advantages attracting foreign educated "haiguis."

As companies like Alibaba, apps like WeChat and ideas such as bike-sharing took off, China's start-up scene began to exert a growing pull on overseas Chinese. Not only was the scene dynamic, but it often offered greater opportunities to aspiring Chinese entrepreneurs who lived abroad. In the US, these students would have to navigate a fraught and increasingly hostile visa process, pitch to investors in their second language and build products for customers from a starkly different cultural background.

Beyond those logistical advantages, China was also steadily narrowing the information and talent gaps that existed for decades. "Now when something happens in the US we get that information almost immediately. It's about the speed of information transfer and that pool of people who have come back," said Li Zhifei, CEO of Chinese start-up Mobvoi and a Ph.D. graduate from John Hopkins University.

US government actions that are driving away highly educated Chinese scientists and engineers threaten America's model as an open economy based on innovation and welcoming talent. China meanwhile happily picks up Western-educated talent and immediately awards them with various practical *treats* from free housing, cash rewards, to the more important *Hukou*—a system of household registration used in mainland China that also has important social benefits, such as education, housing quotas and medical insurance in cities such as Shanghai and Beijing.

Chinese Companies Are Closing the Wage Gap on High-Tech Talent

Ren Zhenfei, CEO of Huawei, said this in early 2019: "One important reason for Huawei's success is investment in R&D and people. We have many foreign scientists working for us. Huawei pays higher salaries than Western companies, so we have many scientists working for us. We have at least 700 mathematicians, over 800 physicists, over 120 chemists. Over 600 basic research experts, and over 60,000 senior engineers and engineers."

According to Chinese media, those in Huawei's higher echelons are extremely well rewarded:

- An entry-level director's annual salary is 1.5 million RMB ($225,000)—Huawei has about 1000 low-level directors.
- Second-level directors get an annual salary of between 5 and 12 million RMB ($745,000–$1.8 million)—Huawei has about 400 directors at this level.
- Top-level directors have an annual salary of 15 million RMB and above ($2.3 million).
- Vice president (VP) annual salaries are 20 million RMB and above ($3 million)—Huawei has dozens of VPs.

On March 1, 2003, China official announced the China Lunar Exploration Project, or the *China Moonshot Project*. On January 3, 2019, China became the first country to land on the far side of the moon.

In 2016, China announced a new initiative to be a world leader in science and technology by 2050, which some deem its *Innovation Moonshot*. The government will do more to implement its innovation-driven development strategy to make the country more "innovative and competitive," Premier Li Keqiang said in his annual speech at the National People's Congress, where he laid out priorities in 2018.

Tech-related initiatives included the fast-tracking of bringing in overseas talent and increasing graduates through its own fast-evolving higher education system. "We have no doubt that by bringing together myriad intellect and pooling everyone's energies, China will break into a sprint of innovation," he said.

China Is Pushing for Innovations to Achieve Sustainable Development Goals

Recent global political events have shaken traditional alliances and structures. Amidst the gloom, how can ambitious global leaders find new opportunities that offer long-term, sustainable growth and value for businesses, but at the same time deliver wider societal benefits?

A recent report "Better World, Better Business" by the Business and Sustainable Development Commission estimates that the global agreement to address some of the most pressing challenges facing the world offers more hope and a huge opportunity valued at $12 trillion by 2030. This analysis comes from an assessment of successfully achieving just some of the 17 United Nations Sustainable Development Goals (SDGs) agreed by the leaders of 193 countries in September 2015.

The report estimates that four of these goals could generate that $12 trillion of new market opportunity within:

- Cities
- Energy and materials
- Food and agriculture
- Health and well-being

Cities

Cities generate over 80% of GDP in China. Many cities struggle with environmental degradation, traffic congestion, inadequate urban infrastructure and a lack of basic services. Maintaining economic growth, while creating sustainable livable cities for all, is the biggest urban challenge facing the country.

As the country is in the middle of a historical transition to urbanization, it focuses on access to housing and basic services, sustainable transport, public spaces, sustainable buildings and policies toward climate change, resource efficiency and disaster risk reduction.

For example, China's high-speed rail (HSR) will soon exceed 18,640 miles (30,000 km), accounting for over two-thirds of the worlds' total length of HSR lines. No nation comes close to rivaling China's HSR construction story. According to a recent report published by the World Bank—which itself financed around 2600 km of Chinese track—other countries would do well to follow Beijing's example.

"China has built the largest high-speed rail network in the world," said Martin Raiser, the World Bank's country director for China. "The impacts go well beyond the railway sector and include changed patterns of urban development, increases in tourism, and promotion of regional economic growth. Large numbers of people are now able to travel more easily and reliably than ever before, and the network has laid the groundwork for potential future reductions in greenhouse gas emissions."

In the meantime, over 300,000 electric buses travel city streets every day. Their widespread adoption in China is enticing other global cities to follow suit. Although these eBuses have higher acquisition prices due to upfront battery costs, their total cost of ownership (TCO) is lower due to their independence from more costly diesel. They also eliminate local particulates, including SO_x, NO_x and CO_2, major issues in most cities today.

In 2018, more electric cars were sold in China than in the rest of the world combined.

The Chinese government spent nearly $60 billion in the last decade to create an industry that builds electric cars, while also reducing the number of licenses available for gasoline-powered cars to increase demand for electric cars, and Beijing plans to spend just as much over the next decade on hydrogen-powered transport.

Starting July 1, 2019, Shanghai entered a new era of compulsory garbage sorting as the country wages war on a growing mountain of garbage to promote green growth and develop a circular economy. With a set of regulations coming into force, individuals, businesses and institutions in the city are ordered to sort garbage into four separate bins—wet garbage (household food), dry garbage (residual waste), recyclable waste and hazardous waste. Anyone who fails to do so could face fines, exemplifying the role the Chinese government plays in green development.

The city is steadily improving its garbage disposal technology and capacity to turn sorted waste into resources. By the end of 2020, the daily disposal capacity of wet trash and dry refuse will increase dramatically with virtually no domestic garbage sent to landfills.

Shanghai, home to about 23 million people, is the first in a nationwide push to raise China's recycling rate, one of the lowest in the region at under 20%. By 2020, China hopes to bring that rate up to 35% in 46 Chinese cities and by 2025 implement a nationwide urban waste sorting system.

Such policy, together with China's unique autocratic political structure and incentives, spurs innovation to make cities more sustainable and livable. The world may soon turn to China for successful urbanization models.

Energy and Materials

The continuing growth in renewable energy around the world is set to boost the power of China while undermining the influence of major oil exporters such as Russia and Middle East states like Saudi Arabia, according to a new report on the geopolitical implications of the changing energy landscape. With a leading position in renewable energy output as well as in related technologies such as electric vehicles, Beijing now finds itself in an influential position which other countries may struggle to counter. "No country has put itself in a better position to become the world's renewable energy superpower than China," says the report issued by the Global Commission on the Geopolitics of Energy Transformation—a group chaired by a former president of Iceland, Olafur Grimsson (Global Commission on the Geopolitics of Energy Transformation 2019).

Geopolitical and socioeconomic consequences of the rapid growth of renewable energy could be profound. Changes are likely to include the emergence of new energy leaders around the world, changing patterns of trade and the development of new alliances. China has taken a leading position in renewable energy and is now the world's largest producer, exporter and installer of solar panels, wind turbines, batteries and electric vehicles. China also has a clear lead in terms of the underlying technology, with well over 150,000 renewable energy patents as of 2016, 29% of the global total. The next closest country is the US, which had a little over 100,000 patents, with Japan and the EU with roughly 75,000 patents each.

While not all patents are useful or valuable, these figures give an indication of how different countries have been focusing on this industry. By contrast, major oil exporters such as Russia, Indonesia and Saudi Arabia had negligible numbers of renewable energy patents.

"The renewables revolution enhances the global leadership of China, reduces the influence of fossil fuel exporters and brings energy independence to countries around the world," said Grimsson, speaking at the launch of the report. "The transformation of energy brings big power shifts."

Food and Agriculture

Driven by self-sufficiency objectives for major grains, China achieved a remarkable expansion of agricultural production. A large country with 1.3 billion people, China feeds 22% of the global population with just 7% of the world's arable land.

However, agriculture is the biggest user of land and water resources, and intensive use of chemical inputs has led to soil degradation, water pollution and damaged bio-diversity. Water resources have reached the limit of sustainable use, particularly in areas where irrigation is intensive or water resources are scarce. The development of intensive livestock has created serious environmental stress, especially on water quality. Climate change is expected to affect agricultural production through rising temperatures, the spread of pests and disease and more frequent severe droughts and floods. Growing competition from other users of land and water may also affect the future of the agriculture sector.

In the twenty-first century, sustainable agriculture in China demands new technology to meet challenges in social, environmental and economic aspects.

Improving the environmental performance of agriculture has become a major objective of agricultural policy in China. In 2015, China announced the Zero-Growth Action Plan for Chemical Fertilizers and Pesticides, which is designed to realize zero growth of the usage of fertilizer and pesticide by 2020. By 2030, the total comprehensive utilization of waste will be realized.

In addition to strengthening environmental regulations, China introduced an incentive mechanism for adopting more environmentally friendly practices and restoring and protecting the environment.

A few successful responses have been developed. Farmers in Sichuan advocated no-tillage crops with the benefits of saving costs and labor, and this is proliferating well now along the Yellow River delta. Slope citrus plantations have been trialed for soil and water conservation in Jiangxi province and a few other regions along the Yangtze River. The merits of this technology include retaining soil fertility and preventing the erosion of soil.

The 13th five-year plan of China includes measures to promote sustainable agriculture in two broad ways. The government will continue to invest in research and development with a view to increasing agricultural productivity, and will also facilitate the creation of more arable land with a number of related partnerships and initiatives taking hold in recent years.

Another important established goal is the restoration of ecology and enhanced ecological functions in China. By 2020, forest coverage rate will reach over 23%, and comprehensive vegetation coverage of grasslands 56%.

Due to the coexistence of challenges and opportunities, sustainable agriculture in China offers a wide platform for innovations to solve current problems and achieve future goals related to economic, environmental and societal progress.

Health and Well-Being

The development of a "Healthy China" is central to the Chinese government's agenda for health and development and has the potential to reap huge benefits for the rest of the world.

In August 2016, China held its National Health Conference, demonstrating the government's tremendous political will in investing in health, followed by the approval of the Healthy China 2030 Planning Outline by China's Central Party Committee and the State Council. This document is the first medium- to long-term strategic plan in the health sector developed at the national level since the founding of China in 1949.

Multisectoral collaboration and innovation also play a key role in a healthy China. With over 20 departments drafting the 2030 plan, a vision has been set for a significantly expanded health industry, which would become a mainstay of the national economy. This would draw on the strength of China's health science and technology innovation, which ranks among the world's best, and would help to considerably improve the quality and level of health service delivered across the country. Through greater technological advances and improvements to the health insurance system, China also hopes to ensure health equity can be achieved by 2030.

Over the last decade, China embarked on the biggest health system reform the world has seen, aiming to extend health services beyond the country's urban centers. At the start of the century, less than one-third of China's population had access to health insurance. Now nearly 100% do. In essence, China has given its huge population a safety net that protects people from being impoverished by the costs of healthcare, making a significant contribution to a fair and prosperous society.

China's investment in health reaps huge dividends for its domestic population, and also for the rest of the world. China's contribution to global health security attracted international attention during the Ebola outbreak in West Africa, supplying well-trained and self-sufficient medical teams when they were needed. More recently China has been supporting the WHO's Emergency Medical Team (EMT) initiative. Shanghai East Hospital was classified in the first batch of EMTs under the WHO Classification List. The Shanghai team is now registered by WHO for emergency deployment when the next regional or global outbreak strikes.

Building on these achievements and its domestic successes, China has a key opportunity to ensure that the huge progress it makes in developing a healthy China at home can deliver great benefits across the world when exported elsewhere.

Implications for Global Investors

With innovation as a nationally mandated strategy and a huge addressable market—there are 772 million internet users in China versus 292 million in the US—opportunities in China for the global investor are plentiful. Private equity firms such as TPG, KKR and Blackrock are all involved in China, hoping to replicate the success found in US innovation hubs such as in Silicon Valley.

Innovation Supported by PE/VC Assisting China's Transition

In 2019, 30% of global VC investing was directed toward Chinese start-ups. This huge amount of venture funding was spurred by expanding exit strategies for Chinese start-ups, evolving exchange markets, state-run initiatives to bolster entrepreneurship and expansive platform strategies developed by leading tech firms like BAT. China is a sensible location for this influx in VC money. In March of 2018, the number of unicorns in China skyrocketed to 164. Combined, these companies were worth a massive $628 billion (Diamandis 2018). Along with these unicorns, 56 Chinese TMT (Technology, Media and Telecommunications) companies went public in 2018 with a combined market capitalization of $222 billion.

These companies, primarily internet giants, are "doing everything," according to the 2019 China Internet Report. This includes new businesses in AI, media, e-commerce, the sharing economy, autonomous cars, fintech, education and gaming ("China Internet Report" 2019). Many of these growing Chinese internet companies are building products that empower the rural population in China. For example, media innovations have allowed 78 million rural users to read the news at least once a month via three primary news apps. Innovation in internet and retail will have equipped 50% of poor villages with e-commerce capacity by 2020. Live streaming technology has enabled more education opportunities for 55 million rural students ("China Internet Report" 2019).

Positive effects of rising innovation and investment spread to the environment as well. With high levels of venture capital investment come increases in green opportunities, which can help China make the necessary transition toward sustainability.

One example of the power of green financing of new innovations is the US China Green Fund (Chap. 12), which finances projects both in the West and in China that yield both financial and environmental returns. Of its $550 million maiden fund, it has poured $420 million in 13 companies in China alone. Some examples of these investments include a marketplace for green home appliances, an energy performance service provider and a real-time parking map designed to mitigate traffic congestion (Liao 2019).

Opportunities to invest in social and environmental innovations are plentiful in China, with a huge population and addressable market, innovation- and environment-focused national strategies, and well-crafted regulatory, policy and financial frameworks. China hosts the world's largest carbon trading exchange, a sizable green bond market (Chap. 19) and initiatives to spur green transport, green industries, green buildings and a green ecosystem. China has crafted aggressive green policies that will lead to aggressive green innovation, and plenty of opportunity for venture and private equity investors to make sustainable investments with competitive financial returns (Joerss et al. 2009).

"Innovation + China Speed + Chinese Market"

Chinese market is potentially ripe for and increasingly friendly to investors, with strategic innovation, China speed and the large Chinese market. It is this combination of unprecedented speed of development (in just two generations, China climbed from an extremely impoverished nation to one of the most affluent in the world) and of the population of 1.4 billion people that gives so much strength to the Chinese marketplace. Global investors can utilize this marketplace to grow their own ideas into successful products.

The Opportunity for Connectivity: China's Belt and Road Initiative

The *Belt and Road Initiative* (BRI) is another Chinese national strategy focused around developing infrastructure and connectivity around China. This initiative focuses on policy coordination, connectivity, unimpeded trade, financial integration and people-to-people bonds with the countries that sign on (Xu and Chen 2019). This project will both build up China's innovation capacity and increase exports of Chinese innovations. With around 152 countries signed onto the initiative, the initiative covers $2/3$ of the world's countries (Cutts 2019). The BRI offers more opportunities for global investment and quick adoption of Chinese innovations in sustainability and beyond.

Win-Win-Win Situation

China's increased focus on and success in building new innovations, opportunities for global investment and a sustainable future represents a potential win-win-win situation. Communities will be able to win the environmental war, governments can win new job opportunities and investors can win heightened returns on sustainable investments. China could arguably be the world's biggest opportunity for successful change, with government strategies focused on both the environment and innovation, and further deployment of sustainable and green finance can be effective tools to leverage technological innovations into practical solutions.

Avoiding Innovation Traps

As outlined throughout this chapter, China offers an abundance of opportunity for the global investor. Innovation is on the rise, sustainable-focused technology is emerging, investment infrastructure is growing and national policies are continuing to push China toward more market-oriented principles. However, while opportunity is potentially plentiful, global investors must also be aware of the drawbacks to investing and working in China, which include underdeveloped IP protections, persistent US-China tensions, political risks and a lack of investment transparency. The greatest opportunity in China comes only when an investor understands the risks and implements plans to mitigate them. Five final key observations then for readers to consider on China and innovation include:

First, innovations in China can be copied quickly. Innovative companies must undergo IP protection, including patenting, trademarking or copyrighting, even if IP law in China is still developing. China has come under intense scrutiny for foreign IP, but also for high levels of domestic IP abuse. While the IP protection landscape is expanding and improving, investors must, nonetheless, look at any investment's IP portfolio with special scrutiny.

Second, Chinese innovation is highly dependent on foreign technology. The risk of US-China decoupling, exacerbated by recent deeper deep divides, would inherently be disruptive to China's innovation ecosystem and connections with foreign partners and suppliers. Understanding China's deep reliance on foreign supply is crucial to properly measuring the risk of investment in China.

Third, political and policy risks continue. Due to China's authoritarian, political system, most Chinese innovations are under the guidance of government planning and only 15% of China's Fortune 500 companies are privately run (Guluzade 2019). Therefore, companies adhering to Chinese government policies may be less risky, but also run contrary to Western views on democracy. Autocratic governance in China inherently involves increased bureaucracy and centralized power, leaving space for human rights infractions and abuse of power. Such abuses have included infractions toward freedom of expression, freedom of religion, women's rights, sexual and gender orientation and more (Human Rights Watch 2019). One example of where successful Chinese business can simultaneously fall short on Western values is TikTok, the popular Chinese-owned social video network. Documents revealed by *The Guardian* in 2019 showed that ByteDance, the technology company that owns TikTok, advances "Chinese foreign policy aims abroad through the app" by censoring news that undermine China such as Hong Kong protests, mentions of Tiananmen Square or references to Tibetan independence (Hern 2019). Investors need to use proper judgment and consult with China experts who have experience dealing with the Chinese government and also understand Western values.

Fourth, if you are an investor in China, you must be active. It is especially important in China to watch your money wisely, keeping track of how and where entrepreneurs and CEOs spend investment dollars. Contrary to norms of Western VC, Chinese companies may invest on something unexpected, potentially even totally unrelated. In some cases, this could yield unprecedented ROIs, but investors have greater risk when left in the dark. Due to this lack of transparency, active investment, paying close attention to a company's expenditures and balance sheet is critical.

Fifth, successful investors must always have an experienced local team, or at a minimum local experts who understand the gaps between China and the investors' worlds—wherever that might be. The value of networking—or in the context of China, *Guanxi* (see Conclusion)—is paramount to the success of investments in China.

References

Arcibal, Cheryl. 2019. Beijing Is More Innovative than New York and London, Report Says. *Inkstone,* May 20. https://www.inkstonenews.com/tech/beijing-ranks-fourth-most-innovative-city-thanks-start-success-says-jll/article/3010901

Atkinson, Robert D., and Caleb Foote. 2019. Is China Catching Up to the United States in Innovation? Information Technology and Innovation Foundation, April. http://ww2.itif.org/2019-china-catching-up-innovation.pdf?_ga=2.247029572.157553926.1554736880-15425082.1554736880

Bohlander, Richard E., ed. 1992. *World Explorers and Discoverers.* New York: MacMillan Publishing Company.

Brookings Institution. 2019. To Sustain Growth, China Can Learn from Previous Transitions to High Income. https://www.brookings.edu/blog/future-development/2019/10/18/to-sustain-growth-china-can-learn-from-previous-transitions-to-high-income/. Accessed 6 Jan 2020.

China Internet Report. 2019. South China Morning Post. https://www.scmp.com/china-internet-report

Coughlin, Daniel. 2019. 28 Incredible 'Made in China' Innovations That Are Changing the World. *msn.com,* April 18. https://www.msn.com/en-us/money/markets/28-incredible-made-in-china-innovations-that-are-changing-the-world/ss-BBRWnlD

Cullen, Christopher. 1996. *Astronomy and Mathematics in Ancient China.* Cambridge: Cambridge University Press.

Cutts, Matthew. 2019. Belt and Road Initiative – Huge Investment Opportunities for Funds. *Arcadis,* April 30. https://www.arcadis.com/en/global/arcadis-blog/matthew-cutts/belt-and-road-initiative-huge-investment-opportunities-for-funds/

Derwin, Jack. 2019. China Has Launched STAR Market, a New Nasdaq-Style Stock Exchange for Tech Companies that Could Fall Apart as Quickly as It Began. *Business Insider,* July 22. https://www.businessinsider.com/what-is-star-market-china-nasdaq-2019-7

Diamandis, Peter H. 2018. Baidu, Alibaba, and Tencent: The Rise of China's Tech Giants. *Singularity Hub,* September 10. https://singularityhub.com/2018/08/17/baidu-alibaba-and-tencent-the-rise-of-chinas-tech-giants/

Dwyer, Joe. 2019. What Is Innovation? *Digital Intent,* September 23. https://digintent.com/what-is-innovation/

Elvin, Mark. 1972. The High-Level Equilibrium Trap: The Causes of the Decline of Invention in the Traditional Chinese Textile Industries. In *Economic Organization in Chinese Society*, ed. W.E. Willmott, 137–172. Stanford, CA: Stanford University Press. isbn:0-8047-0794-4.

Fannin, Rebecca. 2018. Watch for China's Silicon Valley to Dominate in 2018 and Beyond. *Forbes Magazine*, January 1. https://www.forbes.com/sites/rebeccafannin/2018/01/01/watch-for-chinas-silicon-valley-to-dominate-in-2018-and-beyond/#5b2ec9735f1d

Global Commission on the Geopolitics of Energy Transformation. 2019. *A New World: The Geopolitics of Energy Transformation*. IRENA: International Renewable Energy Agency. http://geopoliticsofrenewables.org/report

Global Innovation Index 2010. 2010. Global Innovation Index 2009, Confederation of Indian Industry. https://www.globalinnovationindex.org/userfiles/file/GII-2009-2010-Report.pdf

Global Innovation Index 2019. 2019. Global Innovation Index 2019. https://www.globalinnovationindex.org/gii-2019-report

Goetzmann, William N., and K. Geert Rouwenhorst. 2005. *The Origins of Value: The Financial Innovations that Created Modern Capital Markets*, 94. Oxford: Oxford University Press.

Guluzade, Amir. 2019. Explained, the Role of China's State-Owned Companies. *World Economic Forum*, May 7. https://www.weforum.org/agenda/2019/05/why-chinas-state-owned-companies-still-have-a-key-role-to-play/

Hern, Alex. 2019. Revealed: How TikTok Censors Videos that Do Not Please Beijing. *The Guardian*. Guardian News and Media, September 25. https://www.theguardian.com/technology/2019/sep/25/revealed-how-tiktok-censors-videos-that-do-not-please-beijing

Horwitz, Josh. 2015. Inside Innoway, China's $36 Million Government-Backed Startup Village. *Quartz*, November 27. https://qz.com/534956/inside-innoway-chinas-36-million-government-backed-startup-village/

Huang, Eustance. 2019. Analysts Urge Caution as Stocks on Shanghai's New Nasdaq-Style Tech Board Surge. *CNBC*, July 22. https://www.cnbc.com/2019/07/22/china-markets-analysts-on-shanghais-new-nasdaq-style-star-tech-board.html

Huang, Yukon, and Jeremy Smith. 2019. China's Record on Intellectual Property Rights Is Getting Better and Better. *Foreign Policy*, October 16. https://foreignpolicy.com/2019/10/16/china-intellectual-property-theft-progress/

Human Rights Watch. 2019. World Report 2019: Rights Trends in China. *Human Rights Watch*, January 17. https://www.hrw.org/world-report/2019/country-chapters/china-and-tibet#8b476f

Jing, Meng. 2018. Zhongguancun: Beijing's Innovation Hub Explained. *South China Morning Post*, November 13. https://www.scmp.com/tech/start-ups/article/2172713/zhongguancun-beijings-innovation-hub-centre-chinas-aim-become-tech

Joerss, Martin, Jonathan R. Woetzel, and Haimeng Zhang. 2009. China's Green Opportunity. McKinsey & Company, May. https://www.mckinsey.com/business-functions/sustainability/our-insights/chinas-green-opportunity

Kaiyun, Justice Tao. 2019. China's Commitment to Strengthening IP Judicial Protection and Creating a Bright Future for IP Rights. *WIPO Magazine,* June. https://www.wipo.int/wipo_magazine/en/2019/03/article_0004.html

Kania, Elsa B. 2018. Made in China 2025, Explained. *The Diplomat,* February 1. https://thediplomat.com/2019/02/made-in-china-2025-explained/

Kirby, William, Regina Abrami, and F. Warren McFarlan. 2014. Why China Can't Innovate. *Harvard Business Review,* August 14. https://hbr.org/2014/03/why-china-cant-innovate

Liao, Rita. 2019. This $550M Fund Is Bringing Green Tech from the West to China, Despite Trade Tensions. *TechCrunch,* March 1. https://techcrunch.com/2019/02/28/us-china-green-fund/

Needham, Joseph, Wang Ling, and Lu Gwei-Djen. 1978. *Science and Civilisation in China.* Vol. 4, Part 2, 33. Cambridge: Cambridge University Press.

Raiser, Martin, and Hoon Sahib Soh. 2019. To Sustain Growth, China Can Learn from Previous Transitions to High Income. Brookings Institute, October 18. https://www.brookings.edu/blog/future-development/2019/10/18/to-sustain-growth-china-can-learn-from-previous-transitions-to-high-income/

Shepard, Wade. 2016. The Revolutionary Rise of the Chinese Brand. *Forbes.* Forbes Magazine, May 28. https://www.forbes.com/sites/wadeshepard/2016/05/23/why-chinas-manufacturers-started-building-their-own-brands/#546426cf31b5

The Business Commission. 2017. Report: Better Business, Better World. *Better Business, Better World,* January. http://report.businesscommission.org/report

The New York Times with Introduction by Sam Tanenhaus. 2011. *The New York Times Guide to Essential Knowledge: A Desk Reference for the Curious Mind,* 1131. St. Martin's Press of Macmillan Publishers.

World Bank Group, and the Development Research Center of the State Council, P. R. China. 2019. *Innovative China: New Drivers of Growth.* Washington, DC: World Bank. https://doi.org/10.1596/978-1-4648-1335-1. License: Creative Commons Attribution CC BY 3.0. http://documents.worldbank.org/curated/en/833871568732137448/pdf/Innovative-China-New-Drivers-of-Growth.pdf

Xu, Sitao, and Lydia Chen. 2019. China's Belt and Road Initiative. *Deloitte Insights,* August 16. https://www2.deloitte.com/insights/us/en/economy/asia-pacific/china-belt-and-road-initiative-update.html

Yamada, Shuhei. 2019. Startups Power Shenzhen's Rise as High-Tech Hub. *Nikkei Asian Review,* April 2. https://asia.nikkei.com/Business/China-tech/Startups-power-Shenzhen-s-rise-as-high-tech-hub

4

Implications of the Technology Race

Jackson Barkstrom

What Is the Technology Race; Why Is It Important?

Current tensions between the US and China center around a race for technological supremacy and this technological race raises the stakes for all investors: it increases investment risk and requires further analysis on potential impact and opportunity. Let's call this the "tech race." In this chapter, we underline the basic dynamics and reliances between the US and China, gauge the current and future scope of what is likely to be a constantly unfolding tech race and point out opportunities for investors that might arise in China within the near future.

In short, if the US-China tech race escalates, it could immediately handicap many Chinese businesses and hurt US-China collaboration. Global climate change cooperation could suffer as a result. However, as China and the US race to out-compete each other, the tech race may also provoke flurries of innovation in areas such as information technology, clean energy and biotech. The tech race will prove critical for investors because they can and should have a direct role in improving currently insufficient US-China collaboration as well as utilizing newer tech race-driven innovation.

© The Author(s) 2020
C. Krosinsky, *Modern China*, https://doi.org/10.1007/978-3-030-39204-8_4

Dynamics and Reliances of the US-China Relationship

Fighting While Embracing

The US and China are not only each other's biggest rivals; they are each other's most important trade partners. Their rivalry combined with their trade reliance makes for a complicated relationship. President Xi refers to the US-China relationship as fighting while embracing (chán dòu), and this metaphor is apt because the US and China constantly balance between hostility and cooperation. Trade, for example, teeters between open trade and protectionism.

Rivalry

The stakes of the US-China rivalry rise as China pushes to become a global technological leader. The US wants to maintain its current technological and economic advantages over China, and it shields certain technologies from China and pressures China economically in order to hold onto these advantages.

For both security and economic reasons, the US government fears China getting advanced technology, especially regarding semiconductors or cybersecurity. This rivalry dynamic hurts both countries. The US economy grows more slowly with a lack of adequate trade and collaboration, and China suffers severely under US pressure because China currently depends on the US and global markets for supplies as well as for financing.

Reliance

The US and China depend on each other because each country has different strengths. China has cheap manufacturing, a rapidly developing consumer economy with a high demand for mobile phones and internet-related products and services and a large number of STEM graduates. The US has leading technology, a mature consumer economy and excellent access to global financial markets.

The two countries gain significantly from cross-border trade and investing as well as collaboration opportunities directly because of their different strengths and weaknesses, so much so that they have developed varying degrees of reliance on one another. The US currently relies on China and other countries for most low-cost manufacturing, and China currently relies on the US and other countries for most advanced technology.

Chinese Reliances and Risks: Foreign Technology Supply and Financing

China relies on the global supply of advanced technologies, and this reliance makes China especially vulnerable to US policy. For example, when the US restricted Huawei from using Google's Android operating system on its phones, Huawei suffered losses and had to scramble to build its own operating system to make the phones work again.

Semiconductors, which most know as integrated circuits or computer chips, are China's most pressing supply risk. Semiconductors perform the core processing of phones, computers, smart cars, and so on—you cannot make such devices without them—and these chips are China's Achilles' heel because the US, Taiwan, Korea, Japan and Europe are the only areas in the world capable of designing and manufacturing the most advanced semiconductors, that is, microprocessors (VerWey, July, 2019a). China comprises over half of the global semiconductor demand, but domestic Chinese firms can meet only around 30% of this demand ("China Inside" 2018).

China has plans for future large-scale semiconductor manufacturing, but experts say these efforts will not see success for over ten years due to factors such as lacking human capital (VerWey, August, 2019b). At least for the short term, China will likely rely on global semiconductor supplies to put together most technology. Chinese firms stockpile foreign semiconductors to mitigate this reliance risk, but China remains highly vulnerable to changes in global semiconductor supply (Fig. 4.1).

In addition to China relying on foreign technology such as semiconductors, China relies on a US-dominated global financial system to access capital and conduct international business. A discussion of this reliance is beyond the scope of this chapter, but it is worth noting that the US could potentially use its financial hegemony to put China under great economic pressure (Gewirtz 2019). China may well work to escape this financial reliance.

US Reliances and Risks: Chinese Manufacturing

Many American firms use Chinese manufacturers and would take years to shift manufacturing from China to another country. Apple is a prime example of this reliance: about 50% of its supplier locations are in China, and if Apple moved away from China it would lose significant market share to competitors such as Samsung (Reed 2019). At least in the medium term, many American firms will rely on China to compete globally. It's also important to note that

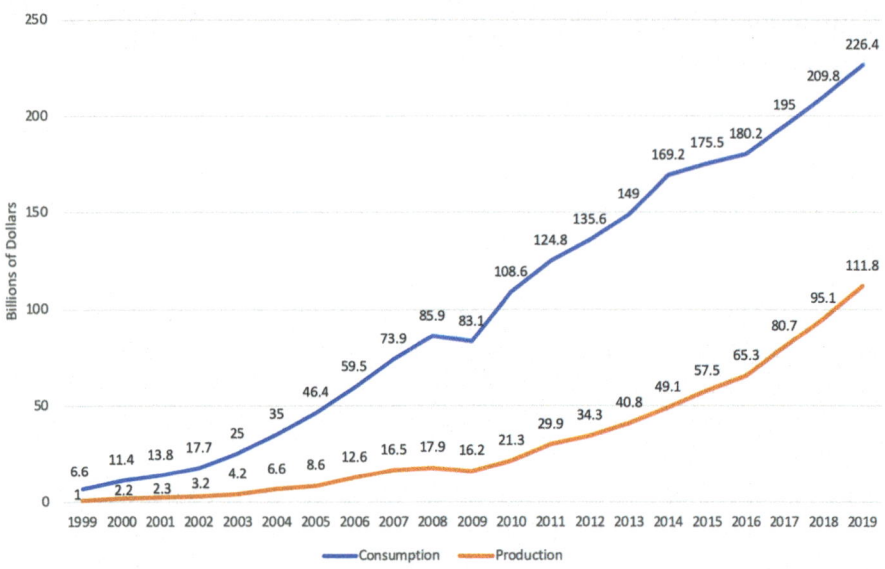

Fig. 4.1 Chinese semiconductor consumption and production by value. (Source: PwC, "China's Impact on the Semiconductor Industry: 2017 Update," November 2017. Data after 2015 is projected)

the China-controlled rare earth element supply is not a major risk to the US. Evidence suggests that a Chinese rare earth element ban would do little more than raise prices of consumer electronics (Hsu 2019). The US can both cut back on rare earth usage and step up rare earth production, whereas China cannot cut back on semiconductor usage or produce the most advanced semiconductors without serious difficulties.

Present and Future Scope of the Technology Race

Rivaling Goals of the US and China

Arguably, the US wants to hold a comprehensive technological and economic advantage over China, while China in response wants to build a self-reliant technological ecosystem near or above the level of the US.

A Rivalry Focused on Technology and Economics

The present conflict between China and the US surrounds technology and economics—headlines focus on tariffs and Huawei contracts, not occupations and annexations—and it's a conflict of which country can develop the best technology and the most powerful economic ecosystem. Niall Fergusson called the US-China relationship the "New Cold War" in a recent editorial in the *New York Times*, but as of now Cold War comparisons seem to be more provocative than meaningful. Although one could argue that the leader of either country might use such a conflict for political gain, the US-China conflict is certainly not a political conflict on the level of what was the US versus USSR Cold War.

Information technology development is central to the tech race because it allows countries to gain reliance advantages. Consider 5G: China is a global leader in 5G development and regulation, and Huawei collaborates on 5G industry standards and makes leading 5G technology at a lower price than any competitor (Thomas 2019).

With its clear competitive advantage, Huawei gets contracts from all over the world in spite of US pressure, and thus many countries rely on Huawei networks. This is a Chinese reliance advantage: countries with Huawei networks rely on Huawei networks to perform and carry their communications. This shouldn't come as too much of a shock: yes, certain countries rely on Huawei networks despite the US's best efforts, but certain Chinese industries also rely on the foreign supply of semiconductors despite China's best efforts. The US currently has many reliance advantages over China that China seeks to eliminate.

Long-Term Chinese Self-Reliance Could Raise the Stakes

China pushes for longer-term technological self-reliance, including the ability to manufacture advanced semiconductors, and these Chinese self-reliance efforts may raise the stakes for the US-China rivalry and for investors. Despite this possibility, some industry experts believe that US-China relations will improve. *Fortune*'s November 2019 Global Tech Forum in Guangzhou, for example, was filled with optimistic perspectives including a Chinese professor who said the entire US-China conflict was rooted in misunderstanding ("Inside the Trade" 2019). The tech race may be a misunderstanding, or it could get worse.

A self-reliant China could decouple from the West and develop its own forms of internet structures, city structures, cybersecurity, and so on, on a level never seen before. This decoupling would increase political risk as well as opportunity. Decoupling in general increases risk for two reasons: First, decoupling leads to less communication between two sides, and less communication increases misunderstanding and risk of conflict. Second, decoupling in some scenarios gives one side an opportunity to dominate the other side without negative consequences. Take this example: if rival countries A and B operate with two completely different R&D pipelines for supercomputers, and A develops an incredibly powerful supercomputer that's years ahead of B, A could potentially sabotage its rival's computer infrastructure with little repercussion (Denning 2019). US-China decoupling, however, also increases opportunity. Investors can combine the best developments from the "China model" and the "US model" and potentially add significant value. As collaboration decreases, the potential value of future collaboration could actually increase.

China may decouple more comprehensively from the West if it achieves more self-reliance. Evidence supporting decoupling includes China's historical emphasis on its uniquely Chinese development models. For example, in 2001, President Xi published an article discussing development economics in China, and in the words of China expert Andrew Batson, "this article could not be a clearer statement of the view that China's model will not and cannot converge with that of Western developed countries" (2019). Additionally, China currently exports its methods of internet censorship and surveillance to other countries (Dave 2018). Evidence opposing decoupling includes plentiful international opportunities for Chinese business, especially in Europe where China already has well-established business networks. We believe China will try to get the best of both worlds and pursue a balanced path between ideological independence and economic opportunity, but this belief assumes a continuation in the current Chinese leadership strategies.

Chinese Innovation Strategy and Sector Outlooks

China's Innovation Strategy of Self-Reliance and Global Leadership

Chinese innovation strategy often aims government intervention at specific sectors, and focuses on (1) developing Chinese self-reliance via initiatives such as semiconductor manufacturing and (2) developing Chinese global leadership via supporting globally important technologies—that is, China's direct and indirect government support of Huawei (Yap 2019)—or via supporting globally underdeveloped technologies such as clean energy or electric vehicles (Naughton 2018, pp. 380–382). Chinese policies focus on both achieving self-reliance and achieving global leadership. China has consistently increased its support for these development policies since they began in 2006 (ibid.).

It's important to note that Chinese innovation policy not only focuses on large and important technological sectors such as semiconductors and artificial intelligence. It also focuses on underdeveloped sectors with no dominant global firms such as electric vehicles, renewable energy and smart cities in order to give Chinese firms a competitive advantage over the rest of the world (ibid.). Leading sustainable technology, for example, could help Chinese firms gain a competitive advantage in sustainability-conscious European markets.

Sector Outlooks

Clean Energy

The Chinese clean energy sector will depend heavily on future Chinese government policy, and future government policy remains unclear (Baxter and Zhe 2019). China heavily supported clean energy from 2016 to 2020 via the 13th Five Year Plan and could still use clean energy for its own pollution problems as well as for business opportunities in Europe. However, a defensive China may also use its abundant coal supply to lessen its reliance on foreign oil, and China has signaled recently that it could increase its coal production and decrease its commitment to sustainability in response to rising global tensions (Wu 2019). The 14th Five Year Plan (2021–2025) will clarify China's position on clean energy.

Biotech

The tech race implications for biotech remain unclear. It remains to be seen if the US will view China's biotech sector as a national security risk and respond with damaging policy (Rapoza 2019), but China is a fertile ground for future biotech innovation, and there is potential for US-China collaboration due to China-specific advantages. For example, China has relatively loose rules for assembling medical datasets and potentially looser rules for experimental therapies ("China's Curing Cancer" 2019). China is also trying to establish medical regulations up to par with peers such as the US, and these regulations would further improve the related investing environment (ibid.). Investors can capitalize on the newest developments in the US and China: an unprecedented Chinese medical dataset, for example, could be shared globally. Solutions to the novel coronavirus outbreak and any further similar outbreaks could also be more rapidly enabled through increased global cooperation.

5G and the Internet of Things (IoT)

Political tensions may continue to rise as the US struggles to come up with an answer to Huawei's dominance. The short-term future of 5G and IoT may well be dominated by Huawei—as mentioned earlier, Huawei's 5G is robust and capable and in addition to 5G, Huawei is building IoT "smart factories" with advanced sensors as well as writing IoT industry standards ("Huawei Founder Predicts" 2019).

For those who don't know, IoT essentially means objects communicating with each other, and an IoT "smart factory" is roughly analogous to a kitchen with appliances that could communicate with each other and make a meal with no human intervention. China has an advantage over the US in terms of IoT development because of its relaxed privacy laws as well as the government's direct role in funding innovation. Under the 2016–2020 Five Year Plan China has invested $74 billion in "smart city" technology ("How China's Smart-City" 2019), where a city monitors citizens in real time and uses the data not only for surveillance but also to improve efficiency in areas such as transportation, energy usage and emergency response.

IoT brings into question a lot of data privacy and monitoring concerns, but as the technology continues to improve it will enable benign efficiency improvements across many different fields.

Supercomputing and Artificial Intelligence (AI)

The US and China may continue to restrict cross-border collaboration and increase funding efforts in the fields of supercomputing and artificial intelligence. Companies and investors will have to deal with proprietary technology in these fields carefully. In terms of supercomputing, a cybersecurity disaster will likely not ensue due to one country being better than the other. The US and China are both making some progress regarding quantum computing, but neither country is likely to develop an ultra-powerful computer that can break encryptions (Naughton 2019). Nonetheless, the US and China may still race to develop powerful computers. In terms of artificial intelligence, the

November 2019 Interim Report from the US Commission on Artificial Intelligence signals that the US is willing to step up funding for AI as well as wall off its AI-related intellectual property from China, and the US and China could be beginning a race for the best AI capabilities. AI completely depends on the data that it's actually using, and for most applications it isn't a magic solution, but American and Chinese governments each have massive stockpiles of data to incentivize AI development.

Manufacturing

The US and China may both protect and develop their own cutting-edge manufacturing capabilities, especially regarding advanced semiconductor manufacturing and 3D printing. In terms of semiconductors, China desperately wants to gain semiconductor self-reliance by catching up to the world's most advanced manufacturers, but it remains years behind global leaders (VerWey, August, 2019b). In terms of 3D printing, China wants to use this along with other manufacturing advances to become a leading supplier of high-tech components and equipment (Naughton 2018, pp. 320–322). The US, however, recently included semiconductor and 3D printing technologies in export restrictions (Alper 2019) and does not want China to surpass its own technological capabilities. We could see another race develop potentially between the two countries.

Conclusion

If the US and China split further from each other, investors who can bridge the gap between countries and choose the best opportunities in either will likely become even more valuable. Thus, as the tech race continues, investors, perhaps especially sustainable investors, working both with and between the US and China can become even more valuable and important as a bridge. Sustainability-minded investors of all stripes can focus on helping advance sectors such as biotech or clean energy that may otherwise fall victim to political conflict, helping enable newly developed technology from both countries to be put to good use.

There are plenty of risks during the current tech race: government policies can change without warning, deals can be blocked and firms can get handcuffed by political worries. However, the tech race should present vigilant investors with worthwhile opportunities.

References

Alper, Alexandra. 2019. U.S. Finalizing Rules to Limit Sensitive Tech Exports to China, Others. *Reuters,* December.

Batson, Andrew. 2019. What Xi Jinping Thinks About Development Economics. *Andrewbatson.com,* December.

Baxter, Tom, and Yao Zhe. 2019. The 14th Five Year Plan: What Ideas Are on the Table? *Chinadialogue.com,* July.

China's Curing Cancer Faster and Cheaper than Anywhere Else. 2019. *Bloomberg,* December.

China's Impact on the Semiconductor Industry: 2017 Update. *PwC,* November.

China Inside: Chinese Semiconductors Will Power Artificial Intelligence. 2018. *Deloitte Insights,* December.

Dave, Paresh. 2018. China Exports Its Restrictive Internet Policies to Dozens of Countries: Report. *Reuters,* November.

Denning, Dorothy. 2019. Is Quantum Computing a Cybersecurity Threat? *American Scientist,* April.

Gewirtz, Julian. 2019. Look Out: Some Chinese Thinkers Are Girding for a 'Financial War.' *Politico,* December.

How China's Smart-City Tech Focuses on Its Own Citizens. 2019. *Financial Times,* June.

Hsu, Jeremy. 2019. Don't Panic About Rare Earth Elements. *Scientific American,* May.

Huawei Founder Predicts Internet of Things Is Next US Battle. 2019. *Financial Times,* July.

Inside the Trade War's Tech Battle that Neither China Nor the U.S. Can Afford to Lose. 2019. *Fortune,* November.

Naughton, Barry. 2018. *The Chinese Economy: Adaptation and Growth.* Cambridge, MA: MIT Press.

Naughton, John. 2019. Will Advances in Quantum Computing Affect Internet Security? *The Guardian,* September.

Rapoza, Kenneth. 2019. Next Up in China Trade War: Biotech Purge?, September.

Reed, J.R. 2019. President Trump Ordered US Firms to Ditch China, but Many Already Have and More Are on the Way. *CNBC,* September.

Thomas, Elise. 2019. Huawei and 5G: What Are the Alternatives? *The Strategist,* March. Australian Strategic Policy Institute.

VerWey, John. 2019a. Chinese Semiconductor Industrial Policy: Past and Present. *United States International Trade Commission Journal of International Commerce and Economics,* July. SSRN.

———. 2019b. Chinese Semiconductor Industrial Policy: Prospects for Future Success. *United States International Trade Commission Journal of International Commerce and Economics,* August. SSRN.

Wu, Yixiu. 2019. Is Coal Power Winning the US-China Trade War? *Chinadialogue.com,* December.

Yap, Chuin-Wei. 2019. State Support Helped Fuel Huawei's Global Rise. *Wall Street Journal,* December.

5

Understanding Chinese History: A Brief Look at China from Its Origins Through the 1700s

Miranda McDermott, Cary Krosinsky, and Huang Zhong

While we are focused primarily on modern-day China, it is important to take at least a small amount of time to understand how the culture of China developed over its long history.

Later chapters focus on aspects of Chinese culture such as China speed, *Guanxi* (or the importance in China of relationship building) as well as the sociology of the average Chinese person, but it's also important to get a sense of China's history to see where the country has been and how this might have influenced its present perspectives. Readers interested in taking a deeper dive into China's history can refer to many other excellent books on China. We recommend a few for your consideration in the Reference section and in Appendix D as we will touch on only a few major themes here to ensure readers have at least a decent starting point perspective (skip to Chap. 8 if this is a familiar territory for you).

Suffice it to say that throughout most of its history, Chinese rulers, including some notable and very effective emperors, imposed conditions of complete and strict control with the alternative being extremely chaotic periods, such as the Warring States Period of roughly 450–210 BC, which led to the Qin dynasty, the first of the Imperial dynasties.

It's interesting to get a sense of China's dynasties, especially when you consider that this dynastic rule lasted for something like 5000 years up through 1912. Put that in perspective, the People's Republic of China just celebrated their 70th anniversary in late 2019, a period less than 2% of the length of China's written history.

Perhaps most useful to know and surprising to some is that China was the world's largest economy back in the 1400s and 1500s, on the back of its

© The Author(s) 2020
C. Krosinsky, *Modern China*, https://doi.org/10.1007/978-3-030-39204-8_5

earlier success as an innovating nation (Chap. 3), making up to 25–30% of global GDP at that time (Business Insider 2017) and so China's recent rise as an economic powerhouse has some precedent. In fact, to most Chinese people, this is just another of such periods that China is returning to its glory.

China of course fell on harder, more turbulent times in the 1800s (Chap. 6) and early 1900s during which chaos and weakness continued up through the establishment of what we now know as the People's Republic of China.

Some other highlights of what readers should know about China's history include:

- The rise of Confucianism (see below)
- Chaotic internal periods and periods of time when China during the course of its long history was at threat from external attack
- The longest-standing, most important emperors and dynasties (see below)
- The Opium Wars (Chap. 6)
- As well as the dramatic turmoil right before the rise of Mao and the Cultural Revolution (Chap. 7)

But China had long periods of stability, largely brought on through Confucian ideology, autocratic strength, discipline and control.

The following significant periods help inform how its history and culture are developed.

Origins of the Chinese Imperial Dynasty

The origins of Chinese history begin with the Bronze Age, dating at least back to 2700 BC. It is commonly recognized that the first emperor, Huang Di, laid the foundation of a stately organized China (the Middle Kingdom) in 2697 BC around the middle and lower reaches of the Yellow River. King Yu, the founder of the Xia dynasty (c. 2070–c. 1600 BC), was the first to yield the principle of hereditary succession, beginning the tradition of a single linear pedigree or "rulership" that would follow for successive dynasties. Xia and its successive dynasties, the Shang and Zhou dynasties, centered geographically in the Central Plain, where their "Chinese" culture that we associate with the China we know today originated (Keay 2011). As historian Patricia Buckley Ebrey mentions, "the term China does not refer to the same geographical entity at all points in history. The historical China was smaller than present-day China and changed in size over time" (Ebrey 2006).

The Birth of Confucianism

The Zhou period was a period "when a hundred schools of thought bloomed" (Ebrey 2006). The emerging thinkers at the time were grouped into three schools: Confucianism, Daoism and Legalism. Confucianism was created by its namesake, Confucius (551–479 BC), who was originally known as Kong Qiu (Keay 2011). As an older man he left his home state of Lu to wander through neighboring states with a small group of students, searching for a ruler who would follow his advice. Confucius believed that the early age of Zhou encapsulated what a perfect society should be like, in which every citizen would devote themselves to fulfill their societal role. Confucius placed significant value on family ties, filial piety, hierarchy and the five cardinal relations: father and son; ruler and ruled; husband and wife; elder and younger brother; and friend and friend. Confucian tradition emphasized studying texts over speculation, meditation and mystical identification with deities— Confucius himself was more concerned with social and political realms rather than the world of gods or spirits. As historian John Keay has explained, "[Confucius] was more of a legitimist than a conservative and he elevated the past into a moral imperative for the present" (Keay 2011). Confucius would die surrounded by only a small circle of disciples. There was no significant Confucius cult until several centuries later, only to serve the rulers at that time.

The Han Dynasty: The First Major Dynasty

The Han dynasty was the first of the five major dynasties that lasted more than two and a half centuries (Han, Tang, Song, Ming and Qing) and is considered by Chinese writers as a golden age in Chinese history. Its predecessor, the Qin dynasty, was founded by Qin Shihuang who is the first emperor that unified the land of China. Qin Shihuang (259–210 BC) unified characters, currencies, weights and measures, which facilitated exchanges amongst people living in a very vast and diverse empire. He also initiated gigantic projects such as the 21,196 km (13,171 mi)-long Great Wall of China and the Terra-Cotta Army. However, such projects put an unbearable burden on civilians. The dynasty was eventually toppled by Liu Bang (r. 202–195 BC) (Huang 1988), who is now known as Emperor Gao. Emperor Gao worked to remove the Qin dynasty's most unpopular features by moving the capital to Chang'an, eliminating some laws, cutting taxes and otherwise lessening the burden on the people. The government's most immediate problem was ruling such a sprawling empire, and they quickly realized that it could not be ruled from the center. Thus, they introduced a provincial composition of ruling that effectively managed the territories on an evolving basis. The following emperor, Emperor Han Wu (r. 141–87 BC), had the greatest impact on Chinese culture and society out of all Han emperors. He proclaimed the first ideological platform for imperial rule: the promotion of Confucianism. He was the first Han emperor to privilege Confucian scholars within the government, making the administration's support of the ideology official. He decreed that officials should be selected on the basis of Confucian virtues and established a national university to train officials in the Confucian classics. This marked the beginning of the Confucian scholar-official system, one of the most distinctive features of imperial China. While expanding the empire through military means Han Wu had to confront and eventually conquered the empire's long-standing enemy—the Xiongnu kingdom in the Ordoos (currently northern Shaanxi). The ethnic group evacuated and the Han dynasty was able to consolidate the land. The expedition also created the now famous Silk Road, leading toward Central Asia.

Cosmopolitan Dynasties and the Return to Glory: The Sui and Tang Dynasties

Yang Jian was the founder of the Sui dynasty, declaring for himself: Sui Wen, the Cultured Emperor (r. 581–604). Sui Wen and his empress were pious Buddhists and drew on Buddhism to legitimize the Sui dynasty. Sui had great ambitions to rebuild the empire comparable to the Han. During this time, the system for civil service recruitment was heavily expanded, with the emperor setting up a Board of Civil Office to centralize all appointments and scrutinize the selection process. The Sui are credited with having promoted the idea and laying down the framework for a genuinely meritocratic civil service (Keay 2011). Another significant achievement of the Sui dynasty was the building of the Grand Canal, which linked the Yellow and Yangtse rivers and would cover a distance of nearly 2500 km. Unfortunately, the cost and magnitude of the project was all too much, and there was serious flooding in the Yellow River in the years 610–611 AD, followed by an increasing demand in resources and manpower for both the army and other public works, which led to the downfall of Sui.

Between 614 AD and 624 AD some 200 mutinies and rebellions reportedly affected practically every province. Li Yuan, the Sui governor of Taiyuan, would become the founder of the Tang dynasty (618–907 AD), which would last three centuries. The Tang government turned away from the military culture and sought officials seeped in Confucian learning. In the Tang system, there were two principal examinations: one tested knowledge of the Confucian classics (*mingjing*) and the other (*jinshi*) required less memorization of the classics but more literary skill (Ebrey 2006). Turkestan, Tibet, Persia, Vietnam, Korea and Japan would fall within the Tang perspective and loom large in imperial policymaking. Still farther afield in India and the Byzantine empire, the political, cultural and productive preeminence of Tang China gained widespread acceptance (Keay 2011).

Tang Gaozu's successor, Tang Taizong (r. 626–649), is widely regarded as the wisest emperor in the history of China for his full consideration of people, especially the peasants. During Han times Emperor Han Wu witnessed his inner Asian empire vanishing into the desert within a matter of decades, but under Tang Taizong, the Tang empire would flourish for well over a century, opening up new perspectives for both the Middle Kingdom and its tribute-bearing satellites, while setting a new benchmark against which subsequent Chinese dynasties, and then republics, would measure their success. It should be noted that, due to the implementation of Confucian doctrine, civilians had definite control over military affairs. Though expansive and downright aggressive, the Chinese empire could be characterized as militaristic during only a few moments in history. Military matters were traditionally treated as a subordinate function of the bureaucracy—under no circumstances should the bureaucracy become a subordinate function of the military. He also created an open atmosphere to bring more frequent economic and cultural contacts between the Tang empire and foreign countries. It was also from that time overseas Chinese began to be called the "Tang People." The Chinatowns around the world these days are in fact in Chinese known as "The Tang People's Town."

Copper money was widely used in the early Chinese empire, but during the chaotic times of the third century AD and the period of fragmentation that followed the fall of the Luoyang capital in 311 AD, it tended to disappear and reappear according to the degree of political stability in the various regions (Elvin 1973). The Tang dynasty in particular experienced a shortage of money. The most important factors for the growing monetary revolution were the growing interdependence of the regional Chinese economies; the actions taken in the field of monetary policy by the central government that would continuously have serious repercussions across the rest of China and provoke numerous countermeasures; the shortage of copper. While bills for the transfer and exchange of cash and commodities had been used since Tang times, it was not until the early eleventh century that true paper money was invented. By the end of the eleventh century paper money had spread into northern China, and in the twelfth century, under the Chin and Southern Song governments, it became established on a regular basis in both the north and the south. By 1161, the Southern Song put about 10 million notes into circulation.

Before the Han dynasty, mercantilism had very little effect on the daily life of the majority of the non-urban population, despite playing an important part in the Chinese economy. Without government permission it was illegal to set up markets other than those officially sanctioned and supervised, thus leading to the creation of a separate system of unofficial markets. These markets were held once every few days and gradually grew up in the countryside to cater to the needs of farmers and the rest of the peasantry. By the latter part of the Tang dynasty such markets were sufficiently numerous. A significant consequence of this was the creation of a national internal customs network that replaced the system of market regulation as the means by which the state controlled and taxed commerce. These economic advances described culminated in an urban revolution, as increased contact with the market made the Chinese peasantry into a class of adaptable, rational, profit-oriented entrepreneurs. Throughout eastern China, cities expanded exponentially into the countryside and spawned many "suburbs." By the thirteenth century, Chinese cities became "the wonder of observers" (Elvin 1973).

The Transition from Tang to Song

The transition between Tang and Song was just as brutal as previous dynastic evolutions. During the final half century of the Tang dynasty, anarchy became rampant as the central government and local officials grew increasingly corrupt. Bandits, gangs and angry mobs took over the countryside, destroying everything in their path as they traveled between provinces. Warlordism in the north and general discord would not be truly resolved until decades later by the imperial army of the new Song dynasty (Fairbank and Goldman 2006).

The Song dynasty (960–1279) oversaw a host of technological developments. From the tenth to the fourteenth century, China was able to advance the threshold of a systematic experimental investigation of nature, eventually creating the world's earliest mechanized industry. In mathematics, a general technique was developed to find the solution of numerical equations containing the unknown. In astronomy, a new level of observational accuracy was achieved. In medicine, they attained more precision in the description of diseases and a number of new remedies were added to the pharmacopoeia.

In metallurgy, coal was beginning to be used for the extraction of iron from iron ore. The invention of block printing technology during the Song dynasty "raised the national level of knowledge to new heights" (Elvin 1973).

Both the securitization of government rule and boom in population growth allowed for serious technological, scientific and economic innovations, as well as enabled China to become one of the most modern countries and economies of the Middle Ages.

This period also saw significant change in the education system and teachings of Confucianism. Printed books gave a great impetus to the education carried on in Buddhist monasteries as well as within families. The government encouraged the establishment of schools by awarding land endowments as well as books, with the goal being that every prefecture would have a school. According to Chaffee (1985), by the early 1100s the state school system had 1.5 million acres of land that could provide a living for some 200,000 students. Becoming classically educated and taking the examinations had become a certification of social status. Confucian training gave these members of the cultural elite a sense of responsibility to keep the world materially and morally in order. Neo-Confucianism emerged from the debates of scholar-officials as their guiding principle. Zhu Xi (1130–1200) synthesized their teachings, providing a broad philosophical view of the universe and the individual. His cosmology asserted dualism between form and material, and behind this dualism existed *Dao*, the Way. According to (Fairbank and Goldman 2006), what Zhu Xi really managed to do was effectively smuggle a "needed element of Buddhist transcendentalism into Confucianism." Through the writing and teaching of this critical sect, Neo-Confucianism became the living faith of China's elite down to the twentieth century. It would become one of the world's most widespread and influential system of ethics (Fairbank and Goldman 2006).

Mongolian and Other Non-Chinese Rulership

The Mongols themselves came from the "Meng" people of north-east Mongolia; however, Chinggis Khan's following included other ethnicities such as Turks and Uighurs (Keay 2011). In 1206, Chinggis Khan was able to unify under his leadership all Mongols in northern China. The Mongols continued into Central Asia and Europe, culminating in Chinggis's final battle against the Song's former enemies, the Tangut Xia. Once the succession to Chinggis had been resolved with his third son, Ögödei, the Mongols resumed their onslaught against China.

With the incorporation of the southern part of the Song empire, four centuries of division came to an end, with all of China, for the first time since the Tang empire, finally being united under one ruler (Keay 2011). The Chinese world order set up by the Han and revived by the Tang as a system of thought and institutions to handle foreign relations collapsed along with the Tang dynasty, and it was under the Mongol and later Manchu conquests that the pattern of dual Sino-nomadic government would reach its peak (Fairbank and Goldman 2006).

Mongol rule in China during the Yuan dynasty (1279–1368) lasted less than a century, and, thus, as Fairbank and Goldman (2006) put it, must be "examined as the seedbed of important phenomena [that would be seen] in the Ming [1368–1644] and Qing [1644–1912] [dynasties]." For example, Yuan was the first dynasty to make Beijing (called Dadu at the time) its capital. The economy grew somewhat due to Yuan dynasty's project of building a second Grand Canal system. This new trade route opportunity combined with the vast size of the empire resulted in such an expansion of foreign trade and foreign relations never before seen in Chinese dynastic history. The Mongols left local communities and Chinese cultural practices and scholarship largely intact, choosing to reshape the region's military institutions and form of government in their own tribal image.

The Ming Dynasty

A significantly higher-than-usual level of rural distress and populist insurgence during the 1340s and a series of warlords in the south reasserting local autonomy in the 1350s greatly contributed to the growing multi-state fragmentation toward the end of the Yuan dynasty. Once the empire was on the brink of collapse, Zhu Yuanzhang, the leader of the rebellious Red Turban Movement, was able to conquer the Yuan capital of Dadu (Beijing). After a century of Mongol rule, China finally returned to Han-Chinese rulership with the founding of the Ming dynasty (1368–1644).

Once crowned emperor, Zhu Yuanzhang, now Ming Taizu, made it his mission to unify China through consolidating the Ming dynasty's grip on power. He decapitated the civil bureaucracy and bolstered agricultural self-sufficiency at the detriment of global trade. His third successor, the Yongler emperor, compounded on this goal of self-sufficiency by restoring and increasing the capacity of the Grand Canal (to ensure internal movement of food and supplies). On the other hand, the emperor opposed the efforts of his father to limit foreign interaction with China by ordering seven voyages to be sent into the "Western" or Indian Ocean. The ships from these voyages reached places such as Qui Nhon in Champa (currently southern Vietnam), Java, Melakka (Malacca, near Singapore), various ports in Sumatra, the south and/or west coasts of Sri Lanka and Koshikodse (currently Calicut). While this event was a sensational achievement given the dynasty's previous disdain for overseas trade, it had little, if any, impact on the expansion of the Ming empire (Keay 2011). The main force behind this project's failure was the Confucian-trained scholar-officials who opposed trade and foreign contact on principle (Fairbank and Goldman 2006).

The stability of the Ming regime and subsequent agricultural reforms finally allowed for significant economic growth during the sixteenth century. This, in turn, increased the empire's newly promoted international trade. Eventually, Chinese trade between European-controlled Peru and Mexico (specifically of silver) grew significantly, and the Portuguese were even allowed to have their own trading base in Macao (Cartwright 2019). This event in particular helped support replacement of paper money with silver as the new continental currency. In the south, ships armed with guns brought Europeans armed with ideas and Christianity, furthering the spread of the religion in the region. The world economy was beginning to slowly integrate China once it developed a more familiar and open profile (Keay 2011).

The Manchu Conquest

The period between the fall of the Ming and the establishment of the Qing dynasty (1644–1912) was short: six weeks. In their rise to power the Manchus took full advantage of their strategic position as a frontier region by being able to learn Chinese ways of life and society while not remaining completely under Chinese rule. They understood that, due to the emphasis on Confucian principles of loyalty within government, the captured government officials (as well as their wives) throughout the provinces would lead their countrymen to suicide rather than join the other side. This allowed for a much smoother conquest and governance over the rest of the former Ming empire.

To guarantee Manchu control over the administration, the Qing made sure that half of the higher-level officials were Manchu (Editors of Encyclopedia Britannica 2019). Finally, the early Manchu rulers took over terminology, forms and ideas of Confucianism and used them for the support and mainte-nance of political authority (Fairbank and Goldman 2006).

During the first century and a half of the dynasty, the Manchus fortunately experienced an unusually long, consistent and strong executive leadership among the first four emperors: Shunzhi emperor (r. 1644–1661), Kangxi (r. 1661–1722), Yongzheng (r. 1722–1736) and Qianlong (r. 1736–1796). Under these emperors, commerce thrived, handicraft industries prospered and China's influence on eighteenth-century European enlightenment grew through its Sino-Jesuit relations (Fairbank and Goldman 2006). It was during the reign of the Qianlong emperor that China attained its maximum territorial expanse: Xinjiang in the west was finally conquered and Myanmar and Annam in the south were forced to recognize Chinese control over their foreign policy and relations. While he was certainly a successful military leader, it must be noted that his success on expanding the frontier was particularly due to the declining strength and disunity of the people in Central Asia. He became particularly infamous for refusing to meet with British trade Ambassador George Macartney, signaling China's refusal to increase its trade with the West.

As the eighteenth century drew to a close, it became clear that, despite Qianlong's and his predecessor's rejections of Western demand for commercial penetration, Britain's persistence and aggressiveness would only continue to grow.

References

Business Insider. 2017. The Rise, Fall, and Comeback of the Chinese Economy Over the Past 800 Years. https://www.businessinsider.com/history-of-chinese-economy-1200-2017-2017-1. Accessed 5 Jan 2020.

Cartwright, Mark. 2019. "Ming Dynasty." Ancient History Encyclopedia. February 6. https://www.ancient.eu/Ming_Dynasty/

Chaffee, John W. 1985. *The Thorny Gates of Learning in Sung China: A Social History of Examinations*. 1st ed. London/New York/Melbourne: Cambridge University Press.

Ebrey, Patricia Buckley. 2006. *China: A Cultural, Social, and Political History*. Boston: Houghton Mifflin.

Elvin, Mark. 1973. *The Pattern of the Chinese Past*. London: Eyre Methuen Ltc.

Fairbank, John King, and Goldman, Merle. 2006. *China: A New History*. Cambridge, MA: Belknap Press, An Imprit of Harvard University Press.

Huang, Ray. 1988. *China: A Macro History*. Armonk: M.E. Sharpe, Inc.

Keay, John. 2011. *China: A History*. New York: Basic Books.

New World Encyclopedia Contributors. "Qianlong Emperor," New World Encyclopedia. //www.newworldencyclopedia.org/p/index.php?title=Qianlong_Emperor&oldid=1020881. Accessed 3 Jan 2020.

The Editors of Encyclopedia Britannica. 2019. "Qing Dynasty." Encyclopedia Britannica. Encyclopedia Britannica, inc., November 26. https://www.britannica.com/topic/Qing-dynasty

6

A Century of Humiliation

Alexander Rafatjoo

In the late eighteenth century, China's historical course began to shift. The country that was once so heavily integrated in global trade was becoming increasingly insular. In *The Wealth of Nations*, published in 1776, Adam Smith remarks, "China has been long one of the richest, that is, one of the most fertile, best cultivated, most industrious, and most populous countries in world. It seems, however, to have been long stationary" (Smith 1979, p. 89). There were notable societal and economic pressures facing China at the turn of the century, and many felt that China's beliefs and institutions were holding the country back. Regarding China's increasing isolation, Smith remarks, "A country which neglects or despises foreign commerce, and which admits the vessels of foreign nations into one or two of its ports only, cannot transact the same quantity of business which it might do with different laws and institutions" (Smith 1979, p. 112). The ensuing period in China's history came to be known as the Century of Humiliation. During this period, China was fragmented politically and socially, lost most of the battles it engaged in and was forced to behave against its own interests in favor of foreign powers.

In the early nineteenth century, as opium became more and more widespread, so did opium addiction. In response, Qing rulers decided to completely halt foreign trade of opium and banned the substance entirely. In the process of doing so, the Qing government held captive many British opium traders and seized their opium. The substance accounted for a significant portion of British trade with China, and British merchants with an oversupply of the product turned to their government for redress. During this period, heightened tensions between British merchants and troops living in China resulted in several bloody outbursts, which only worked to worsen the

© The Author(s) 2020
C. Krosinsky, *Modern China*, https://doi.org/10.1007/978-3-030-39204-8_6

relationship between the two nations. In early 1841, negotiators were sent to address the escalating situation, and the Qing ultimately agreed on a large monetary settlement and the ceding of Hong Kong (then a barren island) to the British as payment for their grievances with the Qing. In addition, the British were to be entitled Canton trade access and a direct line into the Qing court. The outcome of these negotiations infuriated both British and Qing rulers. The Chinese felt they had given too much, while the British felt that the injustices against them were not adequately addressed. The British responded by sending more troops to China. After a series of victories partially due to British technological superiority (Spence 1991, pp. 157–158), the Qing were forced to capitulate. In 1842, the Treaty of Nanjing was signed, ushering in a new era for China.

The treaty had 12 main stipulations that significantly exerted British control over the Qing. This ultimately led to both the US and France creating their own treaties with China and subsequently increasing their influence over the Qing empire. When all was said and done, China owed millions for various reparations; ceded Hong Kong to indefinite British rule; gave foreign nations free trade access to key ports to do business as they saw fit; and allowed for British, American and French extraterritoriality, giving them the right to be exempt from local Chinese laws and instead be tried by their own nation's legal system. Beyond that, however, Britain had inserted a "Favored Nation" clause granting them any rights that additional treaties would award other nations. As a result of these treaties, China had effectively surrendered control of foreign policy, commerce and, to some extent, social and cultural norms. Moreover, these treaties only further increased domestic dissatisfaction with the Chinese government and led to greater political instability.

The ensuing period in China was host to several rebellions, but arguably most notable was the Taiping Rebellion. This rebellion espoused fundamentalist Christian values, and its message was a direct attack on China's Confucian norms. The Taiping Rebellion was one of the longest and bloodiest rebellions in China's history, and China had to rely on help from foreign armies to suppress it. Taking advantage of their vulnerability (Spence 1991, p. 179), the British forced the Chinese to renegotiate their old treaty. As a result, the Treaty of Tianjin was signed in 1858 and imposed even harsher restrictions on China. The British were to be afforded free travel within China and trade boundaries were extended further. In addition, the British mandated that several new port cities open to trade and a British ambassador be given residence in Beijing. Furthermore, internal transport fees were forcibly dropped, and official communications were to be in English.

Following this particularly tumultuous era, however, was a relatively peaceful period of time for China. The Chinese government began sending Chinese students abroad to study at foreign schools and exchange knowledge with the outside world, there was increased technological exchange and adoption and some Chinese soldiers were trained in European military tactics. The underlying sentiment of dissatisfaction with foreign aggression, however, still remained.

In 1894, war broke out between China and Japan over which country would dominate the Korean sphere. Following the successes of the Meiji Restoration, Japan was able to swiftly defeat China, and the Qing sued for peace in April of 1895. The Treaty of Shimonoseki and the loss of the Korean tributary state were humiliating for China, which was accustomed to dominance in East Asia. In addition, China had to pay millions in indemnities, cede land (including Taiwan) to Japan and open more treaty ports to them. The era of relative peace had come to an end, and hope for positive reforms had diminished.

In the last decade of the nineteenth century, foreign powers continued to exert control over China, in effect "carving up" the country for their benefit. In this hostile environment, Chinese nationalism began to develop, and much of this anti-Western sentiment led to the Boxer Uprising in 1900. The rebellion targeted Chinese Christians and the Western missionaries that had converted them; their goal was to "revive the Qing and destroy the foreigners" (Cohen 1997, p. 32). After a series of violent anti-Western attacks broke out, the empress dowager Cixi endorsed the Boxers and declared war against the foreign nations that had oppressed China, "The foreigners have been aggressive towards us, infringed upon our territorial integrity, trampled our people under their feet … Thus it is the brave Boxer followers that have been burning churches and killing Christians" (Ch'ên 1960, pp. 287–308). Two months later, a battalion of approximately 20,000 troops from Britain, France, Japan, Russia and the US went to suppress the Boxer Rebellion, and the Boxer Protocol peace treaty was signed a month later. The treaty required hundreds of millions of dollars in indemnities and further protections for foreigners residing in China. China's attempt to stand up to its foreign oppressors had once again failed.

In 1905, a few years after the Boxer Uprising, the Qing abolished the Confucian imperial examination system. This was one of the many reforms that the Qing court began undertaking to try and maintain their waning authority. The schooling reform meant that a variety of different educational paths became open to students who were looking to pursue successful careers. Furthermore, noting the mounting social pressures against them, the Qing sent emissaries to various countries to study other forms of government and search for ways in which the Qing could reform their weakening government. It was in this atmosphere that the famous reformer Sun Yat-sen began recruiting more aggressively for his anti-Qing society, the Revolutionary Alliance. Sun's republican ideology was heavily influenced by the time he spent studying in Europe, and in this period of educational openness, he was able to recruit more Chinese for the Revolutionary Alliance. The group's members saw the Manchus as unfit rulers and sought to free China from the influences of Japan and the Western countries that had been taking advantage of it. In the ensuing years, many secret societies developed under the umbrella of the Revolutionary Alliance and began to secretly infiltrate the Qing army. Empress dowager Cixi died in 1908, and child emperor Puyi ascended the throne at 2 years and 10 months old surrounded by Manchu advisors and officials.

In October of 1911, a homemade bomb accidentally went off in Wuhan, and it was discovered that the people making these bombs belonged to the anti-Qing forces. Feeling the need to act quickly before their anti-Qing identities were revealed, coalitions of Revolutionary Alliance members who had infiltrated Qing armies mutinied and seized control of local army resources. Similar anti-Qing revolts erupted all over the country, and the Qing ultimately had to comply with the demands of the revolutionary commanders. In November, the Beijing government elected military general Yuan Shikai as the premier of China. This was in an effort to suppress the anti-Qing forces and to move China closer toward a constitutional monarchy as opposed to the republic envisioned by the Revolutionary Alliance. This action continued to feed the Revolutionary Alliance's numbers, and in December of 1911, they took control of Nanjing, the former capital of China. This symbolic victory provided a base and a capital for the anti-Qing forces.

At the end of December 1911, the Revolutionary Alliance had elected Sun Yat-sen as the first Provisional President of the Republic of China; however, the anti-Qing forces recognized that they were weak in comparison to Yuan Shikai's military strength, so they began negotiations. Yuan acted as the intermediary between the Qing and the Revolutionary Alliance during the negotiations, and it was decided that Yuan would take Sun Yat-sen's place as the President of the Republic of China. In the ensuing month, China had both an emperor and a president. Tensions increased when several assassination attempts against the remaining Manchu officials occurred. Ultimately, on February 12, 1912, Puyi—the five-year old "Last Emperor" of China—abdicated the throne, thus marking the end of China's thousands of years of dynastic rule.

References

Ch'ên, Jerome. 1960. The Nature and Characteristics of the Boxer Movement – A Morphological Study. *Bulletin of the School of Oriental and African Studies, University of London* 23 (2): 287–308.

Cohen, Paul A. 1997. *History in Three Keys: The Boxers as Event, Experience, and Myth.* New York: Columbia University.

Smith, Adam, Roy Hutcheson Campbell, Andrew Stewart Skinner, and William Burton Todd. 1979. *An Inquiry into the Nature and Causes of the Wealth of Nations.* Oxford: Clarendon Press.

Spence, Jonathan D. 1991. *The Search for Modern China.* New York: W. W. Norton & Company.

7

1900 to 2001: Chaos, Cultural Revolution and China's Economic Rise

Mae Fullerton

In the two decades from 1895 to the First World War, China's trade began to grow rapidly as it became increasingly integrated into the international economy (Richardson 1999, p. 43). The Treaty of Shimonoseki, which ended the Sino-Japanese War in 1895, had compelled the Chinese government to accept foreign investment. By the turn of the century, Britain, France, Russia, Germany, Japan and other foreign nations had established spheres of control in China (Perdue and Sebring 2016). Foreigners established business enclaves with factories, most of which produced textiles in the cities of Shanghai, Tianjin and Qingdao. As enclaves thrived, their cities molded to support the economic growth. The Bund was built in Shanghai in 1916 to house offices for the Royal Dutch Shell and the Asiatic Petroleum Company and would later become a symbol of Western colonialism. Enclave industrialization spread and quickly caught on with native businessmen who came to play an increasingly large role, such that by the 30s, Chinese firms produced 78% of the value of factory output (Naughton 2018, p. 53).

Between 1911 and 1912, reform-minded officers had organized military revolts that ended in the abdication of the last Qing emperor and established the Republic of China under Sun Yat-sen. The Party struggled at first to establish itself over contending regional warlords but eventually succeeded. Sun Yat-sen's death in 1925 cued Chiang Kai-shek to enter center stage. He broke with the Communists and established the Kuomintang as the Nationalist Party. The Nationalists prioritized industrial development and modern infrastructure such as new transportation and communication links that facilitated the growth of other sectors. The Nationalists began to invest in education and agriculture and drew up plans for an institutional framework for national

© The Author(s) 2020
C. Krosinsky, *Modern China*, https://doi.org/10.1007/978-3-030-39204-8_7

development until fighting broke out between the Red Army and the Nationalist Party in the 30s and escalated into an 18-year-long conflict that would overlap with the Second Sino-Japanese War from 1937 to 1945 (Naughton 2018, pp. 52–53). Mao Zedong emerged as the Communist leader in 1935 during the Communists' "Long March" to a new base in Shaanxi province. Over 20 years of bitter civil war and fighting Japanese aggression had suppressed the economy and divided the country until 1949 when the Communists won and Mao proclaimed the founding of the People's Republic of China. The Nationalists retreated to Taiwan, then a poor agricultural province, and established their own government there. While China's long struggle against foreign aggression had largely come to an end, the resulting Chinese suspicion of Western institutions and worldviews calibrated the population for the closed-door socialist development policies that were implemented soon thereafter.

The Chinese Economy Under Socialist Planning: 1949 to 1978

After its establishment, the Party had two major objectives that would determine the fate of the country for decades to come. The first was to completely reform the economy to model it after the Soviet Union's command economy, and the second was to accelerate economic growth. Despite the lack of a clear roadmap, reform and development were to be pursued simultaneously and at all costs.

Between 1949 and 1956, economic planners transitioned the country into a socialist economic system. This system was characterized by a handful of institutions copied directly from the Soviet Union that were later altered to better fit China's needs. These included expansive state ownership and the substitution of a planning system for markets. The price system was abandoned as the primary mechanism for allocating resources in the economy. Instead, the government directly allocated resources to enterprises. All significant businesses and factories were owned by the state, as well as critical infrastructure enterprises, such as those involved in communication and transportation. The Party decided what a firm's production targets should be and how many resources it should be allocated to achieve those targets. Labor mobility was restricted both at the firm level and on a macro-geographical scale. Firms couldn't change their work forces—hiring or firing people was virtually a nonpractice (Meng 2012, p. 76). Nationwide, labor mobility was restricted by the Hukou system, which was a household registration policy implemented in 1958 to prevent people from flooding into the cities from the countryside (ibid.).

One of the government's first steps was to push public ownership in the countryside via the commune system. Arable land was redistributed such that holdings were equalized among households, effectively removing the power of landlords and wealthy peasants (Kroeber 2016). Within communes existed smaller units known as brigades and work teams. The communes owned the land the farmers worked on, and in return, provided them with food, administrative services and healthcare (Meng 2012, p. 76). In 1953, the state issued mandatory grain procurement, which it collected and sold at artificially low prices in the cities. This need to produce cash crops limited the peasants' ability to produce crops of their choosing. As a result of these policies, rural income growth slowed and per capita production was low (Kroeber 2016, p. 28).

The Chinese Communist Party's development plan, called the Big Push strategy, was also modeled off the Soviet Union. This strategy prioritized national self-reliance by investing in heavy industry. Industries that were in the middle and the top stages of the economy and had multiple linkages to other industries were deemed strategic, such as was the case with oil and steel. A central objective of the new system was to mobilize resources that planners could direct toward their strategic objectives. The government manipulated prices to direct flows of money to favor industrial products over agricultural products. The grain generated by the quotas farmers were forced to meet was collected by government officials and sold in the cities at artificially low prices, while consumer goods produced in factories, such as clothing, were sold at relatively high prices, thus making industry more lucrative, and agriculture less so. This is just one example of how resources were systematically channeled to state-owned enterprises (SOEs), such as all major factories, to make them exorbitantly profitable. It was via this mechanism for "budgetary revenues" that the government generated the majority of its revenue and was able to invest in the Big Push for industrialization (Naughton 2018, pp. 70–72).

In an effort to insulate China's domestic economy while being nurtured by economic decision-makers within the CCP, China had limited openness to the outside world (China's Economic Rise 2019, p. 2). The Party employed a "double air lock" system to insulate the country's domestic economy as part of the Soviet command economy model. An assortment of government-controlled foreign trade companies monopolized the trade of any goods entering or leaving the country and controlled the foreign exchange system with an arbitrary exchange rate and currency that was inconvertible (Steinfeld 2012,

p. 129). This resulted in a price system that artificially benefited the SOEs and made domestic products completely protected from world prices. These insulation mechanisms were put in place as part of a greater "import substitution industrialization" (ISI) strategy for development, by which China would (in theory) promote industrialization by protecting nascent industries, which would be protected from global competition through barriers to industrial imports (China's Sustainable Trade Strategy 2010). Foreign trade was only to provide products that could not be produced domestically, to import cutting-edge technology and, later on, to import much-needed grain. In the 50s, almost half of China's trade was with the Soviet bloc and the majority of the remainder was with Communist countries (Naughton 2018, pp. 67–77). China had turned deeply inward with regard to both trade and diplomacy; by 1971, trade accounted for only 5% of the country's GDP (ibid.). Although the diplomatic ice was broken in 1972 when President Nixon was welcomed in Beijing for his historical meeting with Mao, de facto diplomatic relations were not reestablished with the US until 1979 (BBC 2019).

By the mid to late 50s, however, the pains of rapid societal transformation began to be felt and calls for economic liberalism and a more moderate form of socialism sprang up and eventually penetrated political discussion. Many government planners wanted to think critically about how they had been approaching reform and wanted the ability to discuss it in a more open manner. In response, Mao launched an "Anti-Rightist Campaign" that targeted intellectuals and anyone who spoke out against him, sending many of them to labor camps. Such reactionism re-radicalized the political environment and provided momentum for Mao to introduce a grand plan to further increase the rate of industrial output.

The "Great Leap Forward" (大跃进), launched in 1958, sought to escalate the Big Push development strategy described earlier. Mao's goal was to increase steel production to "catch up" with what he perceived to be the modern world, and, to achieve this, he pushed to increase the rate at which resources were being transferred from agriculture to industry. Communes, which were much larger than any collective, were put in place, among other innovations such as the decentralization of economic decision-making and the rejection of monetary incentives. Most importantly, the effects of two policies in particular combined to become the nail in the coffin for the Chinese population. The government sponsored the diversion of labor away from food production and increased the grain procurement quotas. These policies, in addition to particularly bad weather conditions, led to what is today estimated to be the worst famine in recorded human history (Naughton 2018, pp. 67–77). Other poorly considered policies exacerbated this, such as the Great Sparrow

Campaign (消灭麻雀运动) in which the government publicly declared that "birds are public animals of capitalism" and ordered the mass killing of sparrows because they ate grain seed. Because sparrows eat locusts in addition to seeds, this resulted in massive growth in the locust population, which led to the further destruction of badly needed crop (Phillips 2018). The Great Leap Forward produced economic breakdown and marked the beginning of China's long descendance into international economic isolation.

After a period of crisis management and policy readjustment following the devastating effects of the Great Leap Forward, Mao launched the Cultural Revolution, an ideological and political campaign to purge the Party of bourgeois infiltrators. Although the Cultural Revolution (1967–1969) succeeded in reviving revolutionary spirit, it also caused massive social and political upheaval. Urban members of the upper class, including businesspeople, academics and the educated, were targeted and sent to be reeducated in the countryside by performing hard physical labor (Feng 1985, pp. 45–47). Despite its dramatic social consequences, the Cultural Revolution had little economic significance; production slumped only slightly and quickly bounced back due to effective management (Naughton 2018, pp. 84–85).

Market Transition

Shortly after Mao died in 1976, Deng emerged as the paramount leader of the People's Republic of China. Under Deng, China would witness dramatic economic reform as it transitioned from planned command economy to market liberalization. Contrary to the popular perception that Deng Xiaoping was the sole architect of the Opening Up and Reform (改革开放), Deng was in fact one of many important policymakers during the 80s. Chen Yun, a conservative ideologue who had served on the Central Committee for 47 years and on the Politburo for more than three decades, was elected to the standing committee of the Politburo, the highest policymaking body, in 1978 (Wudunn 1995). He served as a powerful force Deng would have to reconcile with in disputes about how to reform the country; he represented the conservative officials and had further substantial support coming out of the state planning machine. Arthur R. Kroeber, author of *China's Economy* by Oxford Press, and a senior fellow at the Brookings-Tsinghua Center, describes economic reform under Deng as a de facto "balancing act between the adventurous Deng and the look-before-you-leap Chen." Characterized as "two tigers on one mountain top," by a common Chinese saying, Chen Yun was a staunch opponent of Western capitalism and is considered to have served as an important counterbalance to Deng who tended to support radical plans for reform and whose critics accused him of not taking pause to consider the long-term effects. Deng also set the precedent of leaving the management of the economy to his lieutenants, the most important of whom was Zhao Ziyang, who was pivotal to the creation of many reform plans.

Nevertheless, the reforms put in place during the Deng years from 1978 until 1992 when he retired from the Politburo would set China into gear for unprecedented levels of economic growth. The 1978 third plenum of the 11th Central Committee marked a new era in the Chinese economy and launched a host of reforms as part of the Opening Up and Reform (Vogel 2012). It was at this meeting that Deng rose to the forefront as paramount leader and announced the official launch of the "Four Modernizations"—the need to prioritize the modernization of agriculture, industry, national defense, and science and technology. These would come to characterize four key aspects of China's post-Mao development (Four Modernizations 2006).

Deng instituted decentralized economic management as well as rational and flexible long-term planning. In 1980, premier and vice premier of agricultural policy Zhao Ziyang and Wan Li disbanded the communes nationwide and within two years, nearly everyone returned to family farming in which each unit had the right to individually cultivate its own crops. This switch brought about a massive improvement in agricultural livelihood nationwide. Massive swaths of land that had previously been owned and tilled by Mao-era communes were broken up into smaller family-tilled plots, making production soar. Within just five years between 1978 and 1984, rural per capita income more than doubled and grain output was over a third higher than it had been just six years prior (Naughton 2018, pp. 28–29). This positive effect continued throughout the 80s and compounded as higher incomes allowed households to invest in new farming technologies and fertilizers, the demand for which prompted further growth in the industrial sectors that manufactured them (Putterman 1997). Farmers diversified their crops and invested their rising bank savings in the small agricultural businesses that were rapidly sprouting up throughout the countryside.

The increased value in their agricultural output also allowed farmers to seek additional jobs outside the fields to further boost their income. Such trends facilitated the growth of township and village enterprises, otherwise known as TVEs, which peaked in the mid-80s and played an important role in China's economic development in the early years of reform. These were owned or sponsored by local township and village governments or "collectives"; they were the first large-scale solution to harness the surplus of rural laborers and place them into the nascent industrial factories that were created to meet the increasing rural demand for consumer goods (ibid.). Furthermore, TVEs provided a transitional model of semi-private enterprise in an era when the government was still formally discouraging the creation of private business. Despite the fact that TVEs accounted for approximately one-quarter of China's GDP in the mid-90s, they struggled to keep up with the large SOEs and private companies and eventually declined in the latter half of the decade (Kroeber 2016, p. 30).

As part of the Opening Up and Reform, many industrial enterprises were privatized and liberated from the supervision and control of the government. Factory owners were granted newfound freedoms such as the ability to decide their production levels ("Deng Xiaoping" 2019). In essence, China's industrialization resulted from the culmination of both pro-market reform and the implementation of the East Asian developmental strategy (Kroeber 2016, p. 13). Under Deng, China also opened itself to foreign investment and strengthened its trade relations with the West. The "Open Door Policy" welcomed foreign investment into the country and fueled the growth of a nascent market economy and private sector. In 1989, Shenzhen and Shanghai opened their stock markets and by the early 90s the IMF had already ranked China's economy as being the third largest in the world (Deng Xiaoping 2019).

Hong Kong

In 1984 Deng signed a Joint Declaration with Margaret Thatcher on the conditions under which Hong Kong would revert to Chinese rule in 1997. They negotiated the "One Country, Two Systems" policy under which Hong Kong would become part of the Communist-led country but would retain its capitalist economic system and partially democratic political system for 50 years after the handover. Hong Kong is today considered to be a Special Administrative Region of China. It had been under British rule since the last Opium War and had prospered as a highly unregulated capitalist society. While the mainland had been opposed to trade and fluctuated in and out of existential instability, Hong Kong had become a major throughway for trade such that it came to be referred to as the "Pearl of the Orient." For companies situated in Hong Kong, their proximity to the mainland lowered the transaction cost of doing business in the PRC. When China opened its trading system in the 80s, many of the industrial manufacturing jobs left Hong Kong and the region transitioned to specialize in manufacturing-related services

(Tao and Wong 2002). Despite Hong Kongers' angst over the uncertainty of their future as 2047, the end of the 50-year period nears, the Special Administrative Region today closely resembles an independent country for all intents and purposes. It has its own currency, its own passports and its own judicial system.

The 1990s and WTO Accession

When people flooded Tiananmen Square in the spring of 1989, urban residents had enjoyed few of the rewards that rural Chinese had experienced as a result of the agriculture-focused reforms of the 80s. While the reforms of the 80s could be described as tentative and gradual, the reforms of the 90s pushed for a rapid, radical transformation of the entire system. The first stock market, the Shanghai Stock Exchange, opened in 1990 and after Deng made his "Southern Tour" in 1992 to visit and endorse the special economic zones, he reiterated the need for accelerated reform and to prioritize experimentation over ideology. Edward Steinfeld, a professor of China studies at Brown University, describes the change in his book *Playing Our Game; Why China's Rise Doesn't Threaten the West*:

> No longer would reform be a treatment to save socialism, something to be meted out parsimoniously only to the extent that socialist fundamentals remained untrammeled. Instead, reform—radical systemic transformation— would become an end unto itself, a core source of legitimacy for the entire political-economic system. To the extent that socialist intuitions stood in the way, they would have to be dismantled. Reform had once been intended to save socialism for the nation. Now, reform would have to save the nation *from* socialism.

Deng declared development as "the only hard truth" and the Third Plenum of the Fourteenth Party Congress in 1993 set this attitude into gear by providing the blueprint for the reforms that Zhu Rongji would carry out for the next six years. The Party called for a variety of institutions that were necessary for a dramatic switch from market socialism to a "socialist market economy." This entailed the establishment of a standardized federal tax system that broadened the tax base, new management methods and structures for standard monetary policy, a new banking system, a formalized social security system and a new foreign trade system. Privatization spread throughout the SOE, township and village enterprise and collective sectors. The country opened itself to direct foreign investment and devalued its currency (Brent 2019). In 1996, the RMB was allowed to be convertible on the current account, enabling the free flow of money for imports and exports (Yu Le and Simon Rabinovitch 2008).

New company laws forced extensive reform of the state-owned enterprises (SOEs) in a way that countered many of their classically socialist governance structures. Tens of thousands of firms were relinquished from state ownership. In order to join the club of advanced countries, China's SOEs had to cede vulnerability to a myriad of Western investment bankers such as J.P. Morgan and employ the help of experts from Goldman Sachs to navigate the regulatory nuances of IPOs and operating in the global marketplace once listed (Steinfeld 2012, pp. 178–185). While these SOEs are indeed still state-owned, they are now subject to the listing requirements, corporate governance standards, transparency and information disclosure rules of the international stock exchanges. For example, the Party maintained its control of China National Offshore Oil Corporation (CNOOC) by creating the holding company CNOOC Group that owns 64% of the listed subsidiary CNOOC Ltd., as is consistent with the well-known "two-thirds" rule of listing semi-public state-owned enterprises (Steinfeld 2012, pp. 175–216). By the late 90s, newly established price stability and increased competition forced firms to face a new level of market pressure, which drove further corporate restructuring (Naughton 2018). Premier Zhu Rongji announced China's bid to join the World Trade Organization and the national constitution was updated to recognize private ownership and emphasize the need for the rule of law.

China's accession to the WTO on December 11, 2001, symbolized to the world its opening to foreign trade. It was required to grant broader and fairer access to its economy in exchange for more open access for its light manufactured exports to other countries. It made protocol commitments that substantially exceeded those made by any other member of the World Trade Organization, including those that had joined since 1995 (Lardy 2001). China had to commit to giving foreign companies more equal footing with their domestic competitors and to improving the protection of intellectual property rights. It could no longer restrict trade to a finite number of state-owned foreign trade companies and it had to significantly lower tariffs. WTO membership dismantled barriers and made it easier for domestic firms to trade internationally, fueling a massive surge in exports after 2004 ("What Happened When China Joined the WTO? | World101" 2019). Due to these concessions, consumers around the world were able to buy their goods more cheaply and foreign corporations profited from increased access to the largest market in the world.

The outcomes of the reforms described above were astounding. Between the eve of the Opening Up and Reform in 1977 and the year 2000, China's share of total world trade sextupled. By 1995, China had become one of the top ten trading countries in the world. Its foreign direct investment soared (Lardy 2001). Trade in goods between the US and China increased more than 30 times, from less than $8 billion in 1986 to over $578 billion in 2016 ("What Happened When China Joined the WTO? | World101" 2019).

As the world's largest exporter with an economy now 30 times larger than it was in 1979 and over 800 million people lifted out of poverty, China has propelled itself into a new era (ibid.).

References

BBC. 2019. China Profile—Timeline. *BBC.* https://www.bbc.com/news/world-asia-pacific-13017882

Brent, S. 2019. How China Rode the Foreign Technology Wave. *The American Interest.* https://www.the-american-interest.com/2019/10/22/how-china-rode-the-foreign-technology-wave/

China's Economic Rise: History, Trends, Challenges, and Implications for the United States. 2019. *Congressional Research Service.* https://fas.org/sgp/crs/row/RL33534.pdf

China's Sustainable Trade Strategy: An Overview. 2010. *International Institute for Sustainable Development.* https://www.iisd.org/pdf/2010/china_sustainable_trade_strategy.pdf

Deng Xiaoping. 2019. In *Encyclopedia Britannica,* written by the Editors of Encyclopedia Britannica. Encyclopedia Britannica, Inc.

Feng, Sing-Nan. 1985. The Cultural Revolution: A Tragic Legacy. *Change* 17 (2): 41–47. www.jstor.org/stable/40164492

Four Modernizations. 2006. In *A Dictionary of World History,* ed. Edmund Wright. Oxford University Press. https://www.oxfordreference.com/view/10.1093/acref/9780192807007.001.0001/acref-9780192807007-e-1333

Kroeber, R. 2016. *China's Economy: What Everyone Needs to Know.* Oxford: The Oxford University Press.

Lardy, Nicholas. 2001. Issues in China's WTO Accession. *Brookings.* https://www.brookings.edu/testimonies/issues-in-chinas-wto-accession/

Meng, Xin. 2012. Labor Market Outcomes and Reforms in China. *The Journal of Economic Perspectives* 26 (4): 75–101. www.jstor.org/stable/23290281

Naughton, Barry. 2018. *The Chinese Economy: Adaptation and Growth.* Cambridge: The MIT Press.

Perdue, P., and E. Sebring. 2016. The Boxer Uprising I: The Gathering Storm in North China (1860–1900). *MIT Visualizing Cultures.* https://visualizingcultures.mit.edu/boxer_uprising/bx_essay01.html

Phillips, Jack. 2018. China's Worst Environmental Disaster Was a Campaign to Wipe Out the Common Sparrow. *The Epoch Times.* https://www.theepochtimes.com/chinas-worst-environmental-disaster-was-a-campaign-to-wipe-out-the-common-sparrow_2231451.html

Putterman, Louis. 1997. On the Past and Future of China's Township and Village-Owned Enterprises. *World Development* 25 (10): 1639. https://doi.org/10.1016/S0305-750X(97)00060-0.

Richardson, Phillip. 1999. *Economic Change in China, c. 1800–1950*, 43. Cambridge: Cambridge University Press.

Steinfeld, Edward. 2012. *Playing Our Game: Why China's Economic Rise Doesn't Threaten the West*. Oxford: Oxford University Press.

Tao, Z., and R. Wong. 2002. Hong Kong: From an Industrialized City to a Centre of Manufacturing-Related Services. *Urban Studies* 39 (12): 2345–2358. https://doi.org/10.1080/0042098022000033917.

Vogel, Ezra. 2012. *Deng Xiaoping and the Transformation of China*, 231–246. Cambridge: Harvard University Press.

What Happened When China Joined the WTO? | World101. 2019. *Council on Foreign Relations.* https://world101.cfr.org/global-era-issues/trade/what-happened-when-china-joined-wto. Accessed 20 Dec 2019.

Wudunn, Sheryl. 1995. Chen Yun, a Chinese Communist Patriarch Who Helped Slow Reforms, Is Dead at 89. *The New York Times,* April 11.

Yu Le, and Simon Rabinovitch. 2008. TIMELINE: China Milestones Since 1978. *Reuters,* December 8. https://www.reuters.com/article/us-china-reforms-chronology-sb/timeline-china-milestones-since-1978-idUKTRE4B711V20081208

8

China Speed: Modern China's Work Ethic and Sociology

Huang Zhong and Cary Krosinsky

The breakneck speed of China's economic growth over the past four decades has impressed the world, what we like to call "China Speed," which continues to impact the country and increasingly the rest of the world.

China Speed by the Numbers

From 1978 to 2018, China's nominal GDP soared 245 times from 367.8 billion RMB to 90.03 trillion RMB, according to the NBS or the National Bureau of Statistics (2018). China achieved an average annual GDP growth of 9.4% between 1979 and 2018 at constant prices, well above the 2.9% rate the world economy logged in the same period. The leap in the economy's global influence is evident: in 2018, China contributed to 27.5% of world economic growth, up 24.4 percentage points from 1978, the NBS estimates (Fig. 8.1).

According to the IMF, back in 1980, China was the seventh largest global economy and the size of the US economy was 9.4 times that of China.

Fast-forward to 2019, China is already the second largest economy, since 2010 when Japan surrendered its 42-year-old ranking in that position. Some economists have predicted that China's economy will surpass America's by 2030 and has pretty much caught up already in terms of purchasing power parity according to the World Bank.

China's entry into the World Trade Organization in 2001 helped it cement its status as the world's factory and largest trader. A recent report from McKinsey (2019) analyzed 186 countries, finding China to be the largest export destination for 33 nations and the largest source of imports for 65.

© The Author(s) 2020
C. Krosinsky, *Modern China*, https://doi.org/10.1007/978-3-030-39204-8_8

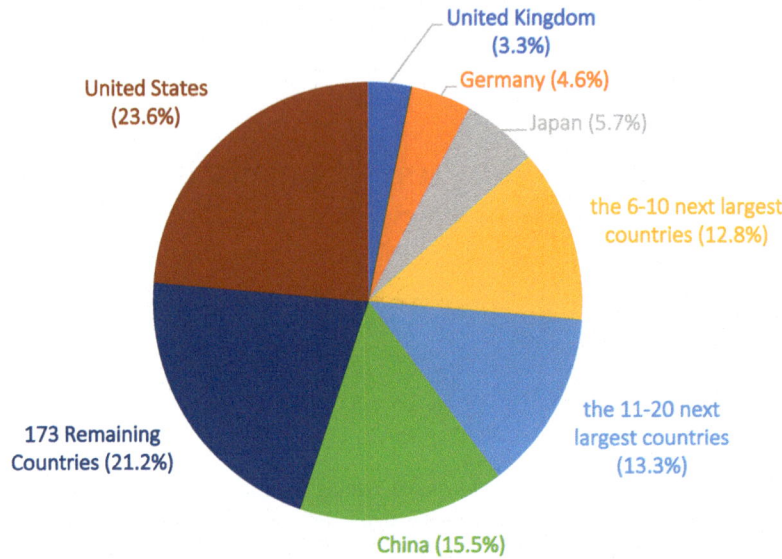

Fig. 8.1 Percentage share of the global economy. (Source: IMF)

In addition to its dominance in trade, China has also grown over the years to become a major player in global investment flows. From 2015 to 2017, it was the world's the second largest source of outbound foreign direct investment and the second largest recipient of inbound investment, according to that same McKinsey report.

In 1981, just three years after Deng's reform project was launched, almost 90% of Chinese people lived in extreme poverty under the definition used by the World Bank. By 2013, that number had dropped to less than 2%. According to the country's 13th Five-Year Plan, China will eradicate extreme poverty by 2020. Within 40 years, China raised an estimated 800 million people out of poverty (Fig. 8.2).

Not only is the typical Chinese person now not living in poverty, but many of them are in fact doing quite well. Per capita GDP grew by nearly 62 times from 1978 to 2018, while the US grew 5.9 times in the same period according to World Bank (Fig. 8.3).

In 1980, agriculture was a larger part of the Chinese economy than either industry (e.g. construction and manufacturing) or services (e.g. healthcare and education). Now, agriculture makes up less than 10% of the economy (Fig. 8.4).

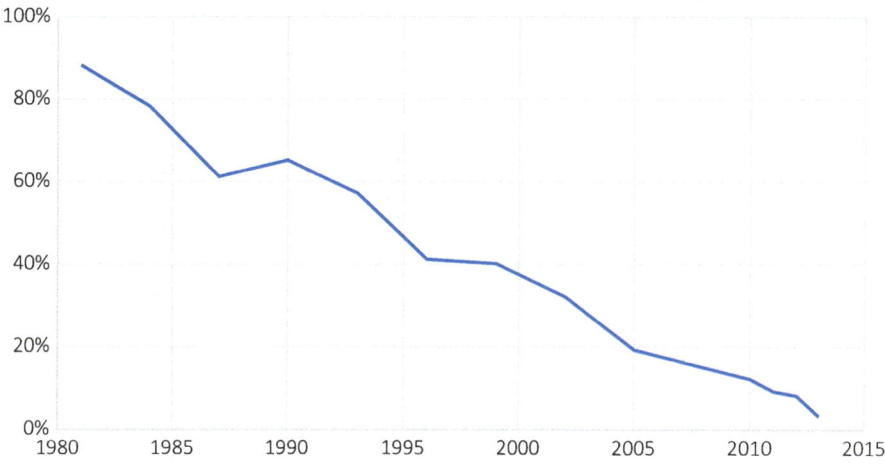

Fig. 8.2   China's extreme poverty rate. (Source: World Bank)

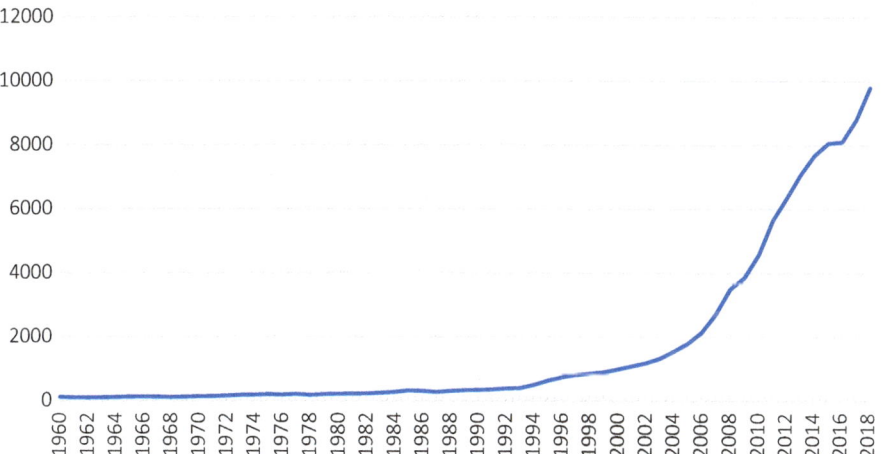

Fig. 8.3   China's GDP per capita (2018 US dollars). (Source: World Bank)

With a shift away from agriculture, Chinese people moved to the cities in droves. The share living in rural areas, which barely budged from 1960 to the late 1970s, fell precipitously after 1978 (Fig. 8.5).

In 1979, Shenzhen, the manufacturing hub just across the border from Hong Kong, had less than half a million people. In 1980, it became China's first special economic zone, allowing foreign investment into the city. It is now one of the world's biggest cities, with more skyscrapers built there in 2016 than the US and Australia combined. The city is emblematic of the rise of China's coastal metropolises (Fig. 8.6).

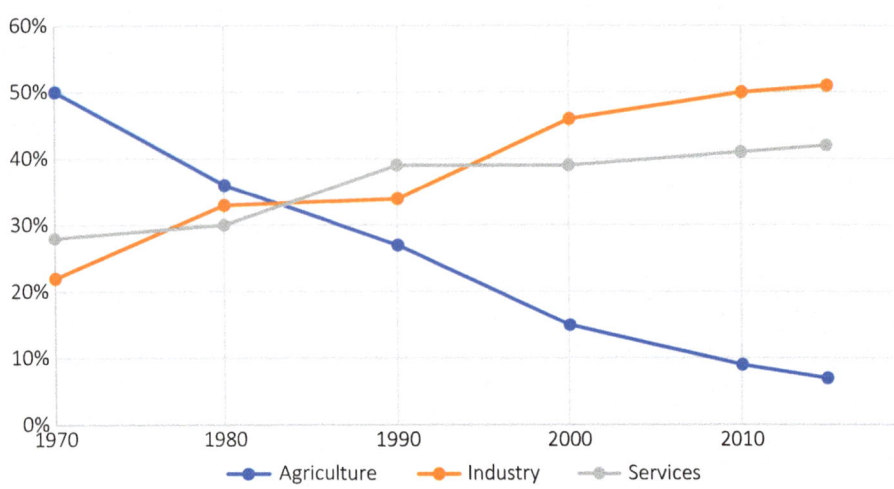

Fig. 8.4 Share of China's GDP by component. (Source: NBS, World Bank)

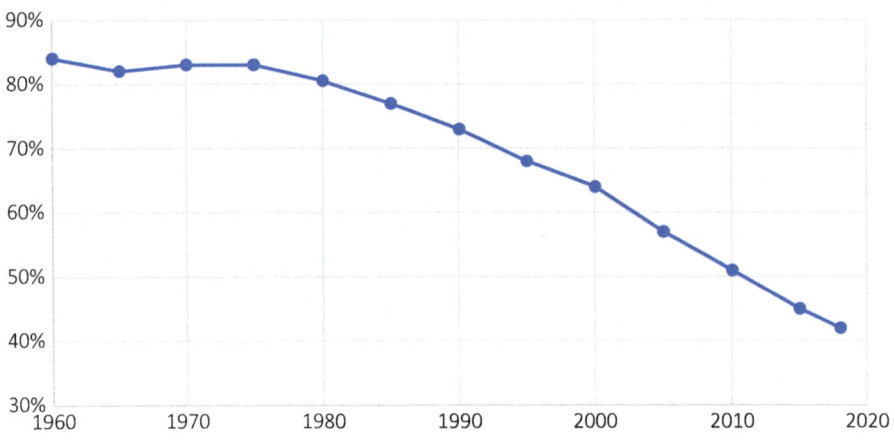

Fig. 8.5 Share of people in China living in rural areas. (Source: NBS, World Bank)

China's high-speed growth is not only demonstrated in its economy, but also on multiple other fronts.

In 2019, China launched 200,000 tons of naval vessels, including its first domestic aircraft carrier. At 300 warship hulls, the People's Liberation Army Navy (PLAN) is the largest navy in the world including aircraft carriers, cruisers, destroyers, frigates, corvettes, submarines and amphibious assault ships. The US Navy trails at 287 hulls, Russia has 83 and the UK 75. PLAN is expected to build another 150 naval vessels in the next decade, while most of the rest are expected to almost remain the same. Even if some of PLAN's

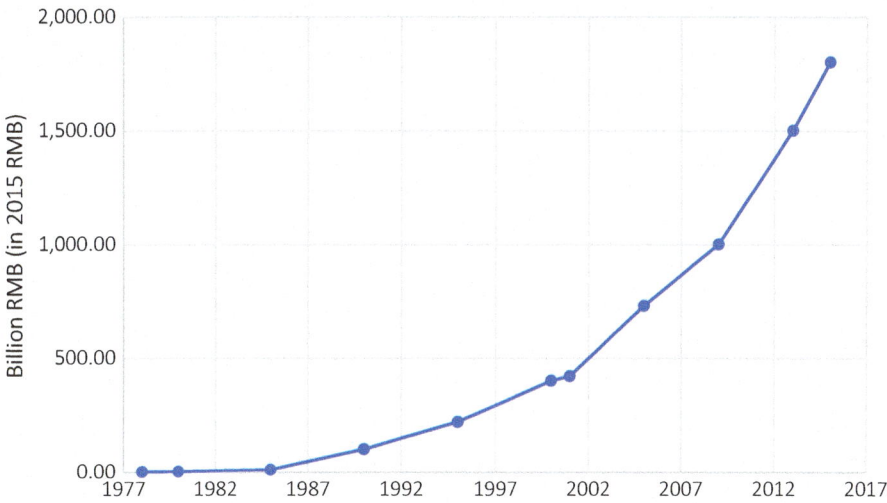

Fig. 8.6   GDP of Shenzhen, China. (Source: NBS)

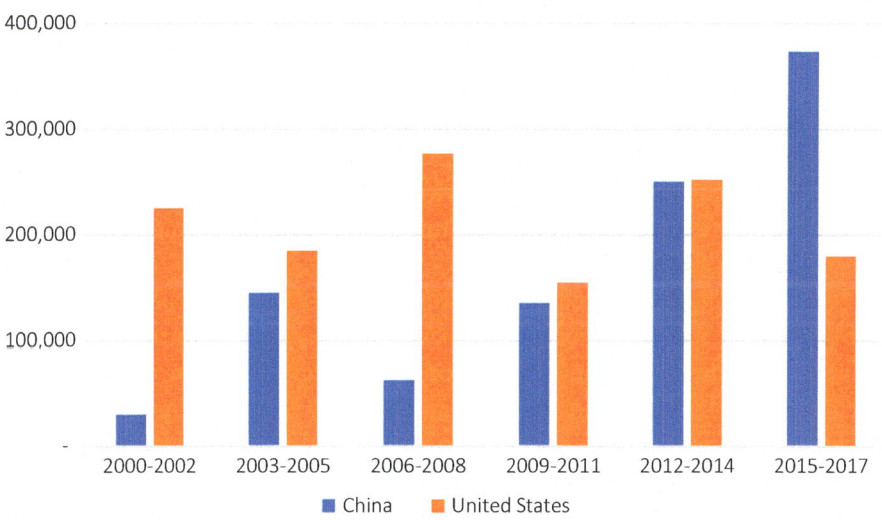

Fig. 8.7   Approximate full-load displacement (tons): Chinese and US naval vessels launched from 2000 to 2017. (Source: PLA Navy, Congress)

power is still lagging behind the US', its accelerating pace of innovation might allow it to catch up within the next 10–15 years (Fig. 8.7).

With its heavy-duty CZ-5 rocket launch on December 27, 2019, China has successfully launched 32 rockets in 2019, surpassing 27 launches by the US, 22 by Russia and 16 for the rest of the world combined. In the next two decades, China is committed to build its own space station, launch Mars explorers and send probes and astronauts to the moon. Its space program is only expected to accelerate.

"China is a sleeping giant. Let her sleep, for when she wakes she will move the world." Napoleon once famously claimed about the Central Kingdom.

Waking up, indeed.

A China Speed Metaphor: The High-Speed Railway (HSR)

The rapid development of China's high-speed railway system in less than two decades best symbolizes China Speed which has been enabling the country's rapid development over the past four decades. China's high-speed railways are known for speed, scale, convenience and comfort and are now the top choice for people on the move through cities. With the "Four South-North" and "Four East-West" high-speed rail network taking shape in China, zooming high-speed trains are changing the ways people choose to work and live.

In 1974, China debuted first-generation diesel locomotives to replace its steam engines. The trains were painted green with yellow stripes so people conveniently called them "Lù Pi Che" or "Green Skin Train." Yet the "Green Skin Train" was far from green: spewing black smoke, noisy, steamy hot in summer and freezing cold in winter, unreliable, and the average speed was a mere 48 km/h (30 mph).

Four years after the "Green Skins" went into service, China officially kicked off its Reform and Opening Up campaign, bringing the country to unprecedented rapid development. Huge labor forces migrating from rural to urban factories put a lot of pressure on the century-old railway system. Farmers from Sichuan province seeking jobs in Shenzhen would have to spend five days to get there, cramping themselves under seats, climbing on top of luggage racks or squeezing in toilets and in between cars.

After another 20 years, China deployed the electrified "Red Skin" trains to slowly replace the "Green Skins." Electrification was a huge step forward, complete with A/C, soft seats and a top speed of 120 km/h (75 mph) that was highlighted by a 15-hour "Depart in the evening, arrive in the morning" route between Beijing and Shanghai.

Recognizing the fact that the economy would not grow without robust transportation infrastructure, China continued to upgrade its locomotive technologies and spent heavily on building highways, airports and a brand-new high-speed railway (HSR) network.

By 2019, CRH trains were operating at a standard speed of 350 km/h (218 mph). Trips that normally took 15+ hours between Beijing and Shanghai now only take 4 hours and 18 minutes. In May 2019, a 600 km/h (375 mph) high-speed maglev test vehicle was rolled off the production line in Qingdao, marking a major breakthrough in the field of high-speed maglev technology in China.

In fact, China has already been operating the world's only commercial maglev line in Shanghai since 2006, at a top speed of 400 km/h (250 mph). It will not be surprising to see the country taking a leadership role in major transportation technology breakthroughs at even faster paces in the coming decades (Figs. 8.8 and 8.9).

What China takes 20 years to do other countries took many more decades to achieve (Fig. 8.10):

According to NBS, China added over 5000 km of high-speed rails in 2019, totaling 35,000 km (21,875 miles), more than two-thirds of the world's total high-speed railway mileage.

What's more surprising is that besides its higher and higher speed, China's HSR punctuality rate stays above 98% and with an average passenger load factor of 70–75%, carrying over 2.3 billion people in 2019.

The impact of China's HSR system is far-reaching.

- Over 60% of railway passengers now prefer HSR over the slower "Green Skins" and "Red Skins," accelerating the pace of payback for the huge

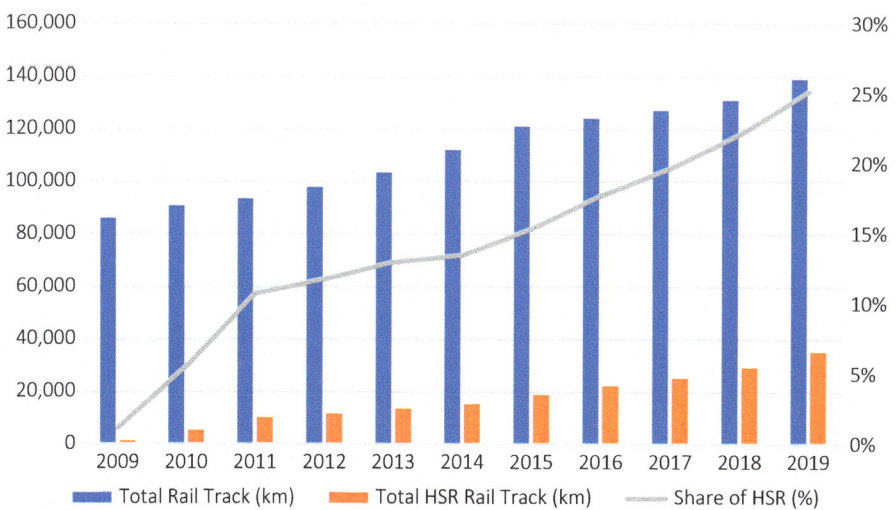

Fig. 8.8 China railway and HSR total lengths. (Source: NBS)

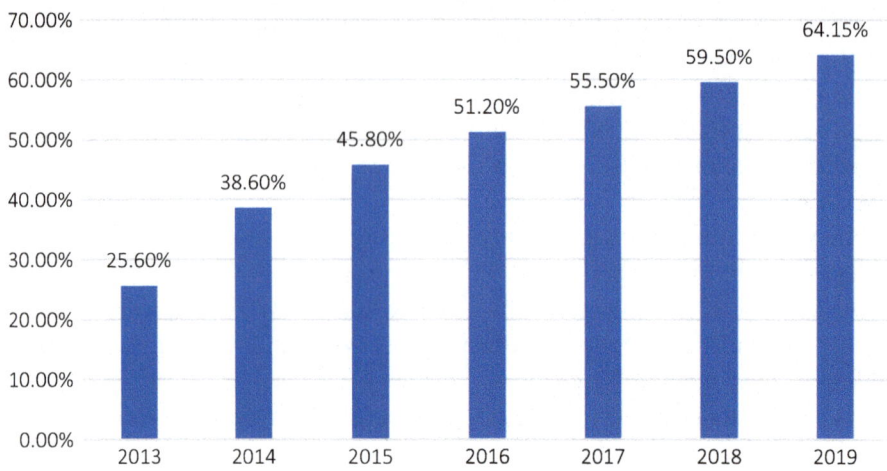

Fig. 8.9 Percentage of railway passengers taking HSR. (Source: NBS)

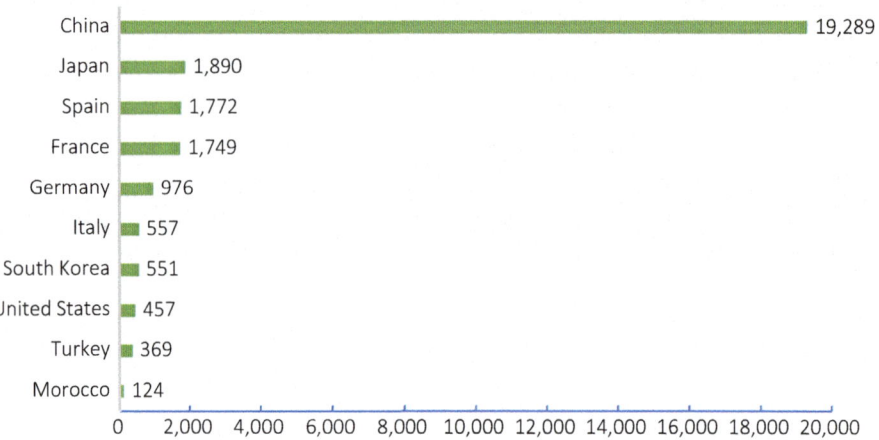

Fig. 8.10 Miles of high-speed rail track in operation by country, as of January 2019. (Source: World Railway Organization)

buildup cost. The Beijing-Shanghai HSR achieved net profit within three years of operation. To this day, there are at least six HSRs that have achieved net profitability.

• Faster speeds mean more people can work in high-paying big cities such as Shanghai, and live in lower-cost suburban areas such as Kunshan or Jiaxing, which are no more than 30 minutes by HSRs. Mega regional development plans such as the "Yangtse Delta Integration" plan, the "Greater Bay Area" development plan and the "Beijing-Tianjin-Hebei Integration" plan are all built upon and facilitated by the HSR system.

- Accelerating urbanization and improving poverty alleviation is also facilitated. Provinces and regions such as the remote Tibet and Xinjiang autonomous regions are now accessible through HSR. The network is even further expanding into some prefectures.
- Greater facilitation of the flow of products, information, capital and human resources is also enabled across regions. If the US is a country built on wheels, then China is a country run on rails.
- China is now the undisputed global leader in HSR technology. The first Smart Railway (SR), the new Beijing-Zhangjiakou HSR designed for the 2022 Winter Olympics, is officially in service as of December 30, 2019. Passengers do not need to print paper tickets or ID cards to take the train. The train features seamless 4G/5G coverage, full autonomous driving, facial recognition and automatic payment.
- Building the state-of-the-art HSR not only propels China to the crown jewels of smart manufacturing, and creating numerous sustainable jobs, but also significantly reduces the country's transportation carbon footprint.

The world has been amazed at the speed with which China has developed its railways. China is competitive worldwide in railway transportation infrastructure on the strength of its quality and production capacity, advanced technologies and delivery of value for money—all within a 20-year timespan. The result is a brand-new calling card for Chinese manufacturing.

How China Achieved China Speed

So how has China been able to pull off its signature China Speed from its economy to innovation to its military prowess in a relatively short time span?

According to Congressional Research Service Reports (Congressional Research Service Reports 2020), economists generally attribute much of China's rapid economic growth to two main factors: large-scale capital investment (financed by large domestic savings and foreign investment) and rapid productivity growth. These two factors appear to have gone together hand in hand. Economic reforms led to higher efficiency in the economy, which boosted output and increased resources for additional investment in the economy.

China has historically maintained a high rate of savings. When reforms were initiated in 1979, domestic savings as a percentage of GDP stood at 32%. However, most Chinese savings during this period were generated by the profits of State Owned Enterprises (SOEs), which were used by the central government for domestic investment. Economic reforms, which included the decentralization of economic production, led to substantial growth in Chinese household savings as well as corporate savings. As a result, China's gross savings as a percentage of GDP is the highest among major economies. The large level of domestic savings has enabled China to support a high level of investment. In fact, China's gross domestic savings levels far exceed its domestic investment levels, which have made China a large net global lender.

Several economists have concluded that productivity gains (i.e. increases in efficiency) have been another major factor in China's rapid economic growth. Improvements to productivity were caused largely by a reallocation of resources to more productive uses, especially in sectors that were formerly heavily controlled by the central government such as agriculture, trade and services. For example, agricultural reforms boosted production, freeing workers to pursue employment in the more productive manufacturing sector. China's decentralization of the economy led to the rise of non-state enterprises (such as private firms), which tended to pursue more productive activities than centrally controlled SOEs and were more market-oriented and more efficient. Additionally, a greater share of the economy (mainly the export sector) was exposed to competitive forces. Local and provincial governments were allowed to establish and operate various enterprises without interference from the government. In addition, FDI in China brought with it new technology and processes that boosted efficiency.

China's centralized and authoritarian political system also places a primary emphasis on facilitating long-term planning and unwavering execution.

The Five-Year Plan (FYP) is a series of social and economic development initiatives issued by the central government since 1953. The Party plays a leading role in establishing foundations and principles, mapping strategies for economic development, setting growth targets and launching reforms.

Planning is a key characteristic of socialist economies, and one plan established for the entire country normally contains detailed economic development guidelines for all of its regions. In order to more accurately reflect China's transition from a Soviet-style command economy to a socialist market economy (socialism with Chinese characteristics), the name of the 11th five-year program of 2006–2010 was changed to "guideline."

The FYPs also overlap presidencies. For example, Jiang Zemin held the presidency since March 27, 1993–March 15, 2003, under the eighth FYP (1991–1995), the ninth FYP (1996–2000) and the tenth FYP (2001–2005). Hu Jintao held the presidency from March 15, 2003–March 14, 2013, supervising the 10th FYP (2001–2005), 11th FYP (2006–2010) and the 12th FYP (2011–2015). Xi Jinping took over the presidency since March 14, 2013, and has since supervised the 12th FYP and the 14th FYP (2016–2020) and is overseeing the 15th FYP (2021–2025). Such overlapping ensures the FYPs get a smooth transition between administrations and that long-term goals get executed without major political swings and policy wastes.

People familiar with how Chinese companies operate often state that the prevailing business culture is one of utmost speed. A complete chain of suppliers facilitates innovations and is designed to maximize speed. Decisions that would take American and European companies weeks if not months to turn into action can happen faster in China where prototypes can be engineered within days. That's partially due to shorter physical distances between decision-makers and manufacturing facilities, but more than that it's an expression of a particular Chinese version of the "move fast and break stuff" attitude normally seen in Silicon Valley.

Market size can support Chinese innovations to quickly verify any product's market potential, ramp up volumes, drive down costs and, if successful, export overseas. This happens in almost all industries: e-commerce, electric vehicles, 5G and mobile phones, industrial robots and even AI doctors.

An almost universal presence of wireless internet, tech savvy millennials, politician's focus on longer-term achievements, a comprehensive manufacturing base, a low-cost logistics network, a highly sophisticated multidimensional transportation network, increasingly friendly capital markets and an increasing pool of highly educated talent, all of these factors contribute directly to the China Speed phenomenon.

Risks of China Speed

There are also, of course, areas of concern when the goal is to move as fast as possible and grow at all costs it perhaps goes without saying.

Four major categories of risk, all of which China continues to work on, but need further improvement include:

(a) Environmental deterioration, fossil fuel consumption and food safety concerns
(b) Shoddy quality observed, especially at earlier stages of China's rise
(c) Lax labor rights and unsustainable social and community impact
(d) IP protection

The good news of sorts is many of these problems are experiential for Chinese citizens, making finding answers a likely ever increasing priority for the government wanting to keep its growing middle class happy, but the problems are severe as detailed in Chap. 2.

China largely outsourced production from other countries, and so the fact that the country is the world's largest consumer of fossil fuel means that at least partial responsibility for those emissions is arguably in the West, where products made in China are often bought and consumed, and increasingly across Asia and the rest of the world as well. China becoming the world's factory means it has taken on the jobs and economic opportunity of production, but also that there are side effects generated such as local pollution of its air, land and water.

This partial responsibility makes an even more compelling case for increased cooperation so that the West can help China, and China can then help the rest of the world. Innovation such as the Internet of Things (Chap. 3) is helping advanced Chinese farms in creating traceable food for consumers to know specifically where ingredients came from. Social auditing of factories by groups such as Verite and Impactt helps ensure that minimum standards on labor conditions are in place. The cliché of Chinese goods being cheaply made is also starting to rapidly shift as quality in manufacturing is on the rise. China Speed pertains to not only the pace of its economy, but also the rate at which China learns and can learn how to make better products, treat its workers, help its communities recover from environmental damage and allow its businesses to develop and protect its IP.

Above all, these are all factors which further justify Western cooperation through investment which can:

(a) Demand better minimum standards of invested companies,
(b) Require certain parameters be delivered in return for debt and loans and
(c) Improve impacts on the ground with intentionality as per later chapters on impact investing.

Such a dynamic could create significant opportunity for Western investors while helping China improve conditions for its people, the ultimate win-win scenario perhaps that should be most encouraged.

What the World Can Learn from China Speed

Fast economic expansion has elevated people's living standards in China and boosted its economic clout globally; better rather than faster growth is the new trend as China seeks higher-quality development.

Many other countries seeking to economically rise can learn from what China has been through and continues to experience. Hopefully, China's transition can also become one that increasingly benefits local communities and global society so that other still developing nations can aspire to those eventual end goals as well.

China Speed as a term is also taking on new meaning as the country enters a new phase of development.

China Speed is now less about the breakneck pace of GDP growth, or the sheer velocity of building roads, bridges and skyscrapers. Instead, it's now more about how swiftly an economy of China's size can embrace a new development approach.

For starters, China Speed is propelled more than ever by technology and innovation.

A few clues on this front: a designed top speed of 600 kph for the country's newly minted high-speed maglev train testing prototype; the Tianhe-1 supercomputer that can compute in 1 hour what would have taken the entire Chinese population 340 years to process; a 5G network that can download movies within seconds.

Galloping technology advancement is underpinned by China's unprecedented spending on research and development, which jumped at an average annual rate of 20% between 1992 and 2018 to rank second in the world.

The speed of China's shift toward greener growth is equally impressive. China's per unit of economic output is obtained with 43.1% less energy consumption in 2018 than in 1953, and 11.4% less than in 2015. Instead of pursuing reckless industrial expansion, Chinese officials now show little tolerance for smokestack factories and energy waste, even if that means slower GDP growth.

China Speed in greening the Earth is leading the world and is visible from space. A study in February using data from NASA satellites revealed that China contributed to a quarter of the increase in global green leaf area since the turn of the century.

To observe it from the eyes of entrepreneurs, China Speed is increasingly relevant to how fast the country betters its business environment and opens up its market to foreign businesses.

As a result of China's reforms to expand market access and cut administrative red tape, the number of enterprises in the country mushroomed at an average growth rate of 16.9% annually from 2012 to 2017. A World Bank report ranked China 46th worldwide for ease of doing business in 2018, up 32 places from the previous year.

In particular, China is moving fast to share more development opportunities with foreign firms. The negative list for foreign access to business sectors is shortening year by year, new pilot free trade zones have been launched across the nation in just a few years and once heavily restricted domains such as finance are being opened up at a non-stop pace.

Behind the new face of China Speed is the country's all-out effort to pursue national rejuvenation, a vision that cannot be realized without a modernized economy that entails better quality, higher efficiency, more robust drivers of growth and opening up on all fronts.

By downshifting its GDP growth and demonstrating a new understanding of desirable speed, China is showing the rest of the world that it favors not economic dominance, but economic sustainability, which makes structural reforms and shared development a requisite in a highly connected global economy.

Recasting an economy as large as China's has taken time and courage, but it is a critical battle that China must continue to work on. The evolution of China Speed has proved how far the country has come and its efforts at greening finance are also worth closer consideration.

References

Congressional Research Service Reports. Accessed via EveryCRSReport.com, January 2020.

McKinsey. 2019. China and the World: Inside the Dynamics of a Changing Relationship. https://www.mckinsey.com/featured-insights/china/china-and-the-world-inside-the-dynamics-of-a-changing-relationship

National Bureau of Statistics. 2018. National Economic and Social Development Statistics Bulletin. http://www.stats.gov.cn/tjsj/zxfb/201902/t20190228_1651265.html

9

China as a Leader in Green Finance

Eleni E. Papapanou

Introduction

Over the past three decades, China has undergone a remarkable transformation, experiencing rapid industrialization and rising to secure its place as the second largest economy in the world. Naturally, such an impressive achievement was not accomplished without the accompaniment of several major costs, most notably to the environment and human health. Driven in large part by the need to address these resulting issues, the Chinese government created an array of overarching and far-reaching policy goals in 2012 which aimed to eventually establish the nation as an "ecological civilization." Less than a decade later, China certainly proved its ability to rise to its own challenge, distinguishing itself as both a pioneer and a persistent leader in green finance policy.

Ultimately, the creation of a well-ordered green finance system would enable China to enhance green investment return, reduce returns on polluting investments and increase both investor and consumer preferences for green assets. This shift in demand would in turn aim to mitigate—and potentially even work to reverse—the harmful consequences which have been brought on by such swift and unchecked industrialization, as well as fundamentally restructure the country's economic system so that it is better equipped to house more sustainable (i.e. both financial and environmental) growth and remain a worthy competitor in the future global economy.

According to the Green Finance Task Force's *Establishing China's Green Financial System*, providing the proper incentives necessary to stimulate such green investment and simultaneously reduce investment in polluting

© The Author(s) 2020
C. Krosinsky, *Modern China*, https://doi.org/10.1007/978-3-030-39204-8_9

industries would largely be accomplished through the utilization of the following linked strategies: Firstly, the return on investment of green projects must increase, requiring a decrease in financing costs and a substantial boosting of funds available for these projects. This would mainly be achieved by introducing structures and policies such as discounted interest rates, green bonds, green IPO, green ratings, green stock indices and mandatory disclosures. Conversely, there must be a drop in the return on investment of polluting projects, requiring that their costs and compliance charges are raised considerably. Means of doing so include the utilization of green insurance, environmental liabilities of banks, green ratings, green stock indices and mandatory disclosures. These shifts—along with the eventual creation of an active green investor network and the implementation of more effective educational programs in green consumerism—will work to improve investor, business and consumer awareness and responsiveness to green signals (Green Finance Task Force 2015).

Such steps play a crucial role in promoting environmental awareness and protection, in turn effectively "greening" the financial system—shifts which are fundamental to achieving the ecological society the Chinese government first set forth to create in 2012.

Unsurprisingly, the Chinese model of green finance policy has taken a top-down approach, with the government heavily involved in its promotion and implementation. The country's central bank, the People's Bank of China (PBoC), has defined green finance as "financial services provided for economic activities that are supportive of environment improvement, climate change mitigation and more efficient resource utilization" (PBoC 2016). In line with its support and extensive involvement in greening the economy, in September of 2016 the PBoC propagated the *Guidelines for Establishing the Green Financial System*, which addressed a range of priorities across banking, capital markets and insurance. A few days later, China introduced green finance as a topic to the G20 communiques for the first time in history.

A recent report found that China "arguably has been the most proactive country in the world in pursuing a coordinated and comprehensive approach to greening its financial system" (Gilbert and Zhou 2017, p. 1). This title has been achieved (and continues to be pursued) through a number of key strategies, including the introduction of green bonds, green credit, incentives for green investment, green ratings, mandatory disclosure, pollution pricing mechanisms and the creation of a carbon market. Government support for these initiatives has been undoubtedly crucial to China's success in adapting a wide range of green finance policies. However, the government does not pull enough financial weight to completely sustain the vitality of green investment on its own; as such, continuous and enthusiastic participation from the private sector is critical in continuing the transition to an entirely green financial system.

China has made remarkable progress over these past ten years, spurring international cooperation and conversation in addition to its individual progress: by introducing green finance policy as a topic worthy of discussion to the global economic community, it has managed to bring together emerging participants in the green finance market and establish itself as a leader of these conversations and initiatives. Though these changes did not occur overnight, nor are they anywhere near complete, China is a unique and important example worthy of examination when it comes to exploring the past trajectory and future potential of green finance policy.

G20 Guidelines: China's Journey to Green Finance Leadership

The year 2016 marked an instrumental year for China, in which the nation was able to propel green finance policy to the forefront of their larger economic policy. As the host of the 2016 G20 summit, China held the unique opportunity to embark on conversations exploring what it believed to be an emerging and critical issue, relevant both to its domestic economy and to the economy of the larger global community.

In January 2016, China established the Green Finance Study Group (GFSG), co-chaired at the time by the PBoC and the Bank of England, with the UN Environment Program (UNEP) acting as the secretariat. Given its establishment under the Chinese presidency, green finance was thus ensured for the first time, by its incorporation into the G20 agenda.

In August of the same year, the PBoC, along with six other government agencies and commissions, released its *Guidelines for Establishing the Green Financial System*. These aimed to establish a sound green financial system in China in order to "mobilize and incentivize more social (private) capital to invest in green industries, and to more effectively control investments in polluting projects" (PBoC 2016). Such guidelines were the first of their kind to be issued by any nation's central bank, and they represented a green financing mechanism suited to assist China's massive economy in an unprecedented transition toward a long-term sustainable structure.

More specifically, these guidelines focused on concrete policies which aimed to bolster the level of private capital funneled into green sectors and restrict investment in sectors which induced pollution and other negative environmental externalities. They chiefly called for action and policy change in seven distinct areas: green bonds, green lending, green development funds, green insurance, markets for pollution control rights, local government initiatives and international cooperation (PBoC 2016). Many of these areas are highlighted and explored further in this chapter as the most influential aspects of China's journey toward achieving its "ecological civilization."

Just five days after the PBoC's release of the guidelines, the G20 summit began in Hangzhou, marking the first time in G20's history that all heads of state settled on pursuing a common goal of supporting green finance. With the close of the summit, the GFSG released a *Green Finance Synthesis Report* which emphasized the integral role of green finance in sustainable development, identified the various challenges which remained when attempting to increase green financial flows and outlined seven key policy recommendations for nations which set out to construct environments for the optimal adoption of green finance (G20 Green Finance Study Group 2016). These included offering strategic policy signals and frameworks, providing clearer environmental and economic policy signals for investors regarding the strategic framework for green investment, promoting voluntary principles for green finance, expanding learning networks for capacity building, supporting the development of local green bond markets, promoting international collaboration to facilitate cross-border investment in green bonds, encouraging and facilitating knowledge sharing on environmental and financial risk and improving the measurement of green finance activities and their impacts. These recommendations were adjusted annually as the GFSG reevaluated both the committee's progress and remaining challenges and goals.

In addition to the policy recommendations explored, the report acknowledged three key challenges. Firstly, it highlighted the absence of clear definitions and guidelines of what truly constitutes green finance. Secondly, it recognized the general lack of adequate environmental information reporting and transparency among corporations. Finally, it noted the pressing need to determine how to properly and most cost-effectively internalize environmental externalities (G20 Green Finance Study Group 2016).

As such, the guidelines proposed by the PBoC and the first-time conversations held at the Hangzhou G20 summit served to clearly define 2016 as a key year for Chinese green finance policy, in which China acted not only to pioneer the significant restructuring of its own economic policy, but additionally to mobilize the international community in collaboration regarding actions necessary to solidify green finance as an integral aspect of sustainable development. By addressing the need for this economic transformation, acknowledging the existing relevant challenges and suggesting policy recommendations and guidelines on how to best tackle the transition, China undoubtedly has taken steps to instigate effective change and earn a leadership position in the area of green policy. Some of China's most significant developments which have proved crucial to the country's success in restructuring its economic system thus far are briefly described below.

Key Components of China's Green Markets

As aforementioned, successfully adopting a green finance policy as part of a nation's larger economic structure requires enthusiastic participation from public and private sectors alike. While the Chinese government and the central bank have clearly demonstrated their support by spearheading investments in such initiatives, they also have introduced a number of structures and policies which aim to incentivize the participation of the private sector as well.

Green bonds are perhaps the most well-known component of emerging green markets, and their introduction is an essential part of involving the private sector in the transition to a more sustainable financial framework. Green bonds are seen as attractive to investors for a number of reasons. Firstly, they represent a positive symbol in terms of their social value; with environmental social governance (ESG) and impact investing on the rise, there is a growing interest to invest in projects which promote positive externalities. Furthermore, green bonds in particular provide a unique opportunity for individuals who may otherwise hold no previous interest or experience in investing, but rather are attracted to the idea of using their capital to target specific ESG causes which align with their larger values or interests.

Essentially, green bonds are used to fund projects with positive environmental influences. China in particular has proven to perform remarkably in green bond marketing: in 2016, the nation became the holder of the world's largest green bond market, issuing RMB 230 billion (or $34 billion) for 40% of global issuance (Dr. Ma Jun, Brown China Symposium 2018). China today remains a leading player in the global green bond market, with the greatest amount of its green finance activity occurring in this sector. In 2019 alone, China's green bond market experienced $8.13 billion of activity, rising to make up 43% of the regional total (Hammond 2019).

Aside from symbolic attractiveness, green bonds offer a relatively short maturity (mainly between three to seven years) and high liquidity, maintaining the opportunity to be readily traded in secondary markets. Many green bonds are also tax exempt, encouraging solid investment returns. Moreover, they present a relatively low-risk manner in which to help promote ESG investment: rather than investing in individual environmental projects and enduring the accompanying risks and uncertainty, investing directly in green bonds sidesteps such complications. Issuers are additionally required to uphold a rigorous screening process for candidate investment projects, further reinforcing green bonds as a safe and strategic opportunity for potential investors (Green Finance Task Force 2015, p. 10).

Linked to green bonds is *green credit*. Green credit refers to the lending of capital for projects which meet certain standards of environmental criteria. Such lending falls under the umbrella of sustainable investing, aiming to reduce the environmental impact of expanding economies. Green credit is a vital component of China's green finance strategies, as the volume of its bank lending far exceeds its bond issuances. The balance of green loans in China has also seen fairly rapid growth: outstanding green loans in RMB and foreign currencies reached RMB 9.23 trillion ($1.37 trillion) by March of 2019, having climbed 4.3% just from the beginning of that same year. This figure amounted to 9.9% of total loans, highlighting a steady increase from previous years. Specifically, loan balances for projects concerning green transport and renewable or clean energy during this time came in at 4.1 trillion and 2.28 trillion RMB, respectively, corresponding to an increase of 4.8% and 1.7% from the beginning of the year (China's Green Loans Post Steady Growth in Q1 2019). Green financing has therefore been able to maintain steady growth as banks continue to be encouraged to lend more support to the budding green economy. By making funds for ESG projects readily available, China has been able to promote green economic growth and continuous business innovation while strategically managing potential risks.

The widespread existence of both green bonds and green credit in China indicates significant progress. However, they remain largely insufficient without certain complementary institutions and policies which help promote an economic environment most supportive of secure green investing. Examples of such enhancements include the *securitization of green assets* and the establishment of *green banks*.

Banks hold large amount of green loans on balance sheets, though much of these loans are not accessible by institutional investors. Securitizing these loans allows for their introduction to the larger green market. Asset-backed securitization aids banks and companies alike in freeing up capital for further lending by enabling them to sell existing loans to other investors in capital markets, essentially allowing assets to be turned into securities. By offering opportunities for investors and freeing up capital for originators, securitization works to promote liquidity in the market. Green projects therefore benefit from securitization as it allows for better access to capital at a lower cost; moreover, *green securitization* can help address low credit ratings at the issuer level in China. From a financial perspective, the securitization of green assets follows a process highly comparable to the securitization process required for any other sort of assets—the only major difference being that the originator must here use the money raised to fund green assets and projects. Currently, a number of strategies are being outlined to further grow a green securitization market capable of accessing international capital in China (Climate Bonds Initiative 2016).

The establishment and expansion of *green banks* is crucial to the creation of a sound economic environment supportive of widespread green investing. Green banks are established to encourage private investing in domestic green sectors, such as clean energy technology, low-carbon or climate resilient infrastructure and water or waste management—areas which, despite being commercially viable, have struggled to take significant hold in consumer markets. As such, green banks can help encourage growth in the return on green investment while reducing the investment risk and cost of private capital for green projects. In relation to the aforementioned efforts to securitize green assets, green banks can play a sizable role in their promotion; they have the ability to create and securitize portfolios of loans, in turn allowing investors to purchase a portion of the green bank's debt on the secondary market. The PBoC's *Establishing China's Green Financial System* extensively covers recommendations on how to best approach the creation of a green bank system, as well as the institution's major role in the future of the larger Chinese green economy (PBoC 2016). Since the report's emergence, China's banking system has visibly evolved—in terms of the number of green banks established, as well as the scale of green loan assets held by already established banks. For example, the scale of green loan assets increased from RMB 5.2 billion in 2013 to RMB 8.53 billion in 2017. China Development Bank, the Industrial and Commercial Bank of China (ICBC), China Construction Bank and the Agricultural Bank of China are among the highest in terms of RMB value of issuance of loans to energy-saving and environmental projects; similarly, the Industrial Bank of China, China Development Bank and the ICBC house the highest ratios of green loans (Baneman 2018).

Incentivizing the Growth of the Green Financial System

Successfully attaining the "ecological civilization" which China yearns for requires more than introducing a green bond and credit market along with a few accompanying policies. The government has therefore piloted a number of initiatives in order to further encourage the sale and utilization of sustainable oriented loans and equity within the financial system. While new incentives and frameworks are constantly being introduced or refined, the following are a few noteworthy examples of policies which China has implemented.

Throughout China, local governments have begun to offer subsidies for green projects. For example, in Guizhou (one of the five pilot zones chosen to promote green finance), different levels of financial aid get distributed based on potential projects' classification into one of three levels: dark green, green and light green (referring to the degree of environmental impact of these prospective projects). The government offers a 12%, 9% or 6% interest subsidy for these categories, respectively, in an effort to reduce the funding costs of green projects and in turn increase the return on equity (Dr. Ma Jun 2018). Such subsidies are ultimately introduced to attract more private capital into areas of green investment.

Simultaneously, China aims to reduce the return on investment of polluting projects by making them as financially unattractive as possible. In order to do so, the government is working to scale down their related subsides and raise the existing fines for pollution. Furthermore, increasing the cost and compliance hurdles necessary to finance these projects through policies such as lender liability and mandatory disclosure have proven to be an effective strategy, making investing in such projects a more cumbersome and thus less cost-efficient process (Dr. Ma Jun 2018). With these impediments woven into the green financial system, shareholders' expectations of returns on such investments will undoubtedly be lowered, thereby reducing the amount of capital funneled into these environmentally degrading projects as a whole.

Further incentivizing this transition is the incorporation of issues of sustainability and environmental impact into larger bank evaluations. In 2017, the PBoC introduced green ratings as part of their new macro-prudential assessment (MPA) framework. The MPA framework is essentially a scoring system that assesses banks' capital levels and monitors risks within the financial system (Dr. Ma Jun 2018). As such, the evaluation of a bank's green performance now serves as an integral component of its larger evaluation. Banks which maintain a high percentage of green loans, as well as a high percentage of green loan growth, receive a higher score. A higher MPA score can entitle banks to a number of privileges, such as higher rates on reserves held with the central bank, which further incentivize green investing and performance.

Mandatory Disclosure

Disclosure is another fundamental aspect of a strong green financial system, crucial to a successful partnership between the government, companies and potential investors in creating a more widespread demand for sustainable investment. For the government, this transparency allows for both the proper fining of polluting projects and the subsidizing of green ones. Simultaneously, requiring increased transparency causes companies to be more inclined to closely consider their environmental impact, over time growing to associate sustainability with broader successful performance. Investors too benefit from mandatory disclosure, with the readily available information regarding firms' green performance illustrating a clearer picture as to whether or not a company aligns with one's values or expectations. Ultimately, disclosing quantitative information is fundamental to properly assessing the ESG performance of corporations.

The lack of existing clear and honest information regarding a company's environmental impact was highlighted as a major issue in the GFSG's *Green Finance Synthesis Report* following the conclusion of the 2016 G20 summit. More specifically, the report noted the lack of disclosure of environmental information by companies and consistent/reliable "labeling" of green assets, the scattering of data among many government agencies and the financiers' lack of information about the commercial viability of green technologies all as significant barriers to a successful transition to a truly green financial system (Green Finance Study Group 2016).

Similarly, the PBoC's 2016 guidelines recognized the need for improvement in this area. In order to bring about change in as seamlessly a manner as possible, a three-step plan was designed. In 2017, all major polluters on listed markets were required to disclose environmental information. In 2018, a new semi-compulsory scheme for disclosure was introduced, in which listed companies were allowed the option to refrain from disclosing their impact, but were then required to explain their doing so to the market. By 2020, the plan expects that it will be mandatory for all listed companies to release information regarding their environmental impact (though in reality, it will take some time for this plan to function effectively). Moreover, the China Green Finance Committee is currently working to design a template for the contents of such disclosure, which include specific indicators such as CO_2, SO_2, NO_x emissions, as well as energy and water consumption for most sectors (Dr. Ma Jun 2018). The successful completion of this three-step plan will crown China as the only large economy to have introduced such environmental information disclosure requirements.

Another related effort has been led by the China UK Green Finance Task Force, which has set up a pilot program on climate risk and environmental information disclosure, with ten financial institutions (including China's largest bank, the Industrial and Commercial Bank of China, the Industrial Bank and the Asset Management Company of China) having volunteered to join. The participating banks have pledged to disclose information about climate and the environment ahead of the industry. A few of these Chinese banks have already come up with three-year action plans of their own, over the course of which they intend to release information regarding green loans and their environmental benefits, polluting ("brown") loans and their environmental impact and environmental stress testing (Dr. Ma Jun 2018).

Air Pollution Mitigation Mechanisms

In addition to working toward increasing environmental accountability among corporations more generally, China has also taken on more targeted approaches in order to tackle specific environmental issues. Air pollution is perhaps the most significant environmental challenge facing China today, exacerbated dramatically by the country's recent rapid economic growth. Air pollution poses a serious threat to human health, on average responsible for killing over 1.1 million people in China and costing the domestic economy 267 billion RMB each year (Kao 2018). However, it is also important to note that air pollution levels have recently declined. A key factor in initiating this change has been the increased regulation of the country's power sector. Such efforts have historically not received as much publicity as other attempts to curb emissions (namely, the creation of carbon markets); nevertheless, improvements in this sector serve as a prominent example of implemented policy which has brought about direct and tangible results.

Over the past decade and a half, the Chinese power sector has steadily increased emission limits and regulations. The first important standard was implemented in 2003, with the government requiring that scrubbers be put in SO_2 factories. Notable progress began to surface in 2006 with the announcement of the 11th five-year plan, where hard targets were put in place for SO_2 levels. In 2007, the State Council passed a law known as the "Reduction of the Three Ways." This law profoundly altered regulators' capacity to monitor SO_2 pollution, working to suppress tampering with SO_2 data collection at the political level, as well as to install appropriate monitoring equipment to enable frequent statistical inspections (Stoerk 2018). In 2013, China released the "Air Pollution Action" plan. This plan is regarded as perhaps the country's most influential environmental policy in recent years, helping China attain significant improvements in air quality by setting PM2.5 targets for key regions. PM2.5 refers to atmospheric particulate matter with a diameter of under 2.5 micrometers, harmful to human health in high levels. In order to attain these ambitious targets, a nationwide cap on coal use, divided among provinces, was imposed. The plan also banned new coal-burning capacities and sped up the use of filters and scrubbers (How China Cut its Air Pollution 2018). These measures were considered harsh, yet effective, distinguishing the plan from others with its imposition of an outright ban on polluting activities as opposed to a provision of incentives to clean up production.

Though new targets to decrease emissions are frequently released, proper enforcement is also required to ensure that such standards are truly being met consistently. Key to this enforcement are continuous emissions monitoring system (CEMS) spot checks, which keep factories accountable by adhering to these standards. Recent improvements in both technology and policy have made these checks a much more effective procedure, as inspections prior to these improvements were easy to evade: factories were generally aware of roughly when inspectors were coming, and if a factory had just undergone inspection, it was likely that they wouldn't have to entertain another visit for a while (given that these assessments were known to be time-consuming and costly). As such, the introduction of CEMS with telemetry—which initiated continuous monitoring 24/7—proved to be an extremely effective tool in increasing the accountability of factories.

However, it is important to note that the development and installation of such technology alone is not enough—proper *pollution pricing* has also played a crucial role in Chinese air pollution mitigation efforts. When the CEMS was first put in use, the fines for violations were too low, and local governments remained under pressure from local industries to turn a blind eye to violators. However, as fines were eventually raised to levels which proved to be prohibitive, the sector began to witness meaningful reductions in air pollution.

The effectiveness of these pollution pricing mechanisms rests in the way in which the country's power sector operates. In China, the grid operator must pay the power plant two separate prices: a base price and a pollution subsidy price. Since all prices in the power market are controlled, the prices the grid receives are unrelated to its payments. Given this, the system is essentially self-reinforcing: by hooking the grid up to CEMS, any time the power plant stops running its pollution abating equipment, the grid can stop paying the power plant the subsidy. The power plant therefore has an incentive to obtain the abatement subsidy (by continuously running pollution abating equipment), and the grid has an incentive to continuously monitor the plant (as to not pay extra money in subsidies to power plants failing to adhere to the standards in place) (Deborah Seligsohn, Brown China Symposium 2018).

Carbon Markets

In addition to efforts to mitigate air pollution levels as a whole, China has also made concerted efforts to address the need for decreased carbon emissions more specifically. China is the world's largest climate polluter, responsible for over a quarter of all carbon emissions. Without the country's approval of and participation in such initiatives, hitting worldwide climate-related goals remains nearly impossible; therefore, the nation's decision to pursue such targeted actions is extremely meaningful—and hopefully will prove influential as well, setting an example for other countries to follow suit and pursue similar efforts.

Despite China's generally top-down attitude to implementing green finance, the country has chosen to take a free-market approach to combating carbon emissions: though China is able to limit the overall level of emissions, economic freedom is granted to polluters in managing or reducing their own emissions by allowing them to buy or sell pollution permits within this market of emitters.

Following several years of regional pilot projects, the government announced long-awaited plans for a national cap-and-trade program in late 2017. These carbon markets were first piloted in Beijing, Chongqing, Guangdong, Hubei, Shanghai, Shenzhen and Tianjin, and represented 25% of China's total GDP. Since the pilot plan started, it is estimated that over 40.24 million metric tons of CO_2 have been traded. These early plans cover only the power sector, with expansion to other sectors such as petrochemicals, building materials and aviation expected to take place "when conditions allow," according to one translation of the announcement. Despite this first step being limited in scope, this market is by no means insignificant. China's cap is almost double that of the European Union's, and ten times the size of California's cap-and-trade system. This is due to the fact that China's power sector generates 65% of its electricity from coal and emits 3.5 gigatons (GT) of CO_2 annually. The carbon market therefore covers roughly 1700 emitters across the power sector, or one-third of China's total emissions (Bloomberg 2017). Though the country's carbon cap-and-trade system remains in a fairly nascent stage, the power sector's significant contribution to total carbon emissions and its general economy-wide importance has allowed this trade program to arise as a powerful policy tool which cost-effectively could cut carbon pollution and promote positive environmental change.

References

Baneman, Roger, ed. 2018. Green Banks Around the Globe: 2018 Year in Review. *Green Bank Network,* November 29. https://www.nrdc.org/sites/default/files/green-banks-year-in-review-2018.pdf

China Sets Out Scaled-Back Vision for Biggest Carbon Market. *Bloomberg,* December 19, 2017. https://about.bnef.com/blog/china-unveils-plan-for-worlds-biggest-carbon-trading-market/

China's Green Loans Post Steady Growth in Q1. *China Daily.com.CN,* April 28, 2019. http://www.chinadaily.com.cn/a/201904/28/WS5cc54bd2a3104842260b8e30.html

Establishing China's Green Financial System. *Green Finance Task Force,* April 2015. https://www.cbd.int/financial/privatesector/china-green%20task%20force%20report.pdf

G20 Green Finance Synthesis Report. *UN Environmental Programme Inquiry,* September 5, 2016. http://unepinquiry.org/wp-content/uploads/2016/09/Synthesis_Report_Full_EN.pdf

Gilbert, Sean, and Lihuan Zhou. 2017. The Knowns and Unknowns of China's Green Finance. *The New Climate Economy.* http://newclimateeconomy.report/workingpapers/wp-content/uploads/sites/5/2017/03/NCE2017_ChinaGreenFinance_corrected.pdf

Guidelines for Establishing the Green Financial System. *The People's Bank of China,* September 2, 2016. http://www.pbc.gov.cn/english/130721/3133045/index.html

Hammond, George. 2019. Asia-Pacific Issuance of Green Bonds Hits Record High of $18.9bn. *Financial Times,* October 28. https://www.ft.com/content/67d43332-f604-11e9-9ef3-eca8fc8f2d65

How China Cut Its Air Pollution. *The Economist,* January 25, 2018. https://www.economist.com/the-economist-explains/2018/01/25/how-china-cut-its-air-pollution2018

Jun, Ma. 2018. https://www.youtube.com/watch?v=QvOkQv3meGQ&feature=youtu.be

Jun, Ma, Deborah Seligsohn, and Xueman Wang. 2018. When Finance Goes Green: A Chinese Solution to Environmental Changes. https://watson.brown.edu/events/2018/when-finance-goes-green-chinese-solution-environmental-changes. Accessed 19 April 2018.

Kao, Ernest. 2018. 1 Million Dead and US$38 Billion Lost: The Price of China's Air Pollution. *South China Morning Post,* October 2. https://www.scmp.com/news/china/science/article/2166542/air-pollution-killing-1-million-people-and-costing-chinese

Roadmap for China: Using Green Securitisation, Tax Incentives and Credit Enhancements to Scale Green Bonds. *Climate Bonds Initiative,* April 2016. https://www.iisd.org/sites/default/files/publications/greening-securitisation-tax-incentives-credit-enhancements-green-bonds-en.pdf

Stoerk, Thomas. 2018. Effectiveness and Cost of Air Pollution Control in China. *Grantham Research Institute on Climate Change and the Environment,* November. http://www.lse.ac.uk/GranthamInstitute/wp-content/uploads/2018/08/working-paper-273-Stoerk-Nov2018.pdf

10

Modern Chinese Companies

Annie Phan and Cary Krosinsky

Introduction

Historically, the West has viewed China as a "borrower" of ideas and innovations from developed industries and countries. However, this perception has undoubtedly changed in recent years, with China now establishing itself as a leader in technology and innovation. In 2017, China began taking over Forbes's "Midas List," a ranking of the world's most successful venture capitalists, and as such this marks an era in which Chinese technology companies are exerting a rapidly growing influence on the modern global economy (Fannin 2018). Housing advanced capabilities in areas such as machine learning, artificial intelligence and deep learning, Chinese companies are mastering techniques and capabilities allowing them to fully compete on modern technology. China possesses a trio of large companies, namely, Huawei, Alibaba and Tencent, which have managed to conquer the global economy at a rapid speed, garnering significant attention from the US and the rest of the world.

Huawei

Founded in 1989 in Shenzhen, China, by Ren Zhengfei, Huawei Technologies was originally a reseller of affordable telecom switches created in Hong Kong for small city hotels. In an age where state-owned enterprises ruled the Chinese economic landscape, it was no easy feat for Huawei to gain the trust of its country's companies and users. However, with the help of China's Open Door Policy, the company was able to generate $250 million in revenue within ten years.

© The Author(s) 2020
C. Krosinsky, *Modern China*, https://doi.org/10.1007/978-3-030-39204-8_10

Today, Huawei dominates the global 5G market. While global technology companies are still scrapping to launch their first 5G smartphone, Huawei has long been ahead of the curve, having first developed its own 5G technology as early as 2009. By 2017, the company had put $1.4 billion of investment into 5G research (Huawei Press 2019).

In 2016, it successfully launched its 5G product line, earning it the reputation as the one and only "true 5G provider" (ibid.). Huawei was able to master the art of 5G not only through massive investments but also by cultivating thoughtful ideas for the use of its products. In terms of its technological capabilities, the company has achieved leading system performance due to its extensive experience in decoupling core networks, bearer networks and base stations. Simultaneously, it has worked to establish an extensive network with more than 186 industrial partners worldwide, further helping incubate its 5G business. As a result, Huawei managed to successfully build an ecosystem for 5G significantly before its competitors, becoming the only company in the world able to offer 5G end-to-end products and solutions. Huawei is as such a global mass producer of high-quality, high-standard 5G smartphones, having shipped over 200 million units in 2018 (ibid.). By 2019, it had overtaken Apple, becoming the world's second largest manufacturer of smartphones just behind Samsung.

More than just a smartphone manufacturer, Huawei has also established 15 research institutes, 36 joint innovation centers, 20 international standard organizations, and spent over $15 billion on R&D, all contributing to Huawei's ability to lead just about every possible modern technology movement (ibid.). The company has been crowned the leader in cloud storage and standardization, the producer of the fastest and best smartphones and the first ever world producer of AI chips. Huawei seems potentially capable of producing its own "Midas List," with almost everything it touches turning into digital gold.

Though the world knows Huawei as its No. 1 telecom supplier and No. 2 phone manufacturer, the current US administration tends to view the company as more of an enemy. Over the course of 2019, Huawei has received a series of bans and allegations from the US, with the Justice Department accusing Huawei of intellectual property theft, obstruction of justice and fraud related to the alleged evasion of US sanctions against Iran. The Department of Commerce's Bureau of Industry and Security's Entity List includes Huawei as a target, with the company's products and services banned from the US communication network. It remains unclear how Huawei will be affected by pressure from the US longer term, but its prowess at innovation is hard to deny.

Concerns on privacy are certainly not limited to Chinese companies as concerns regarding Facebook and other Western organizations are also increasing.

While the US's focus remains on Huawei, Tencent and Alibaba are publicly traded large companies with market capitalizations of over half a trillion US dollars each, which hold significant command over the growing Chinese digital landscape. Alibaba, on the one hand, rules e-commerce, with online marketplaces servicing well over 500 million active customers, while Tencent reigns over gaming and messaging, with its extremely popular application WeChat serving over 1 billion account holders.

Alibaba resides in Hangzhou, not far from Shanghai, while Tencent is headquartered in Shenzhen as part of China's south. Their competition and interests aren't limited to mainland China, but instead extend globally, where both companies have spent billions of dollars backing up small yet promising top-tier start-ups in regions where large young populations and burgeoning smartphone penetration reign. These two companies continue to race to be number one in the world's fastest-growing digital economies deploying interesting and distinct strategies in the race to succeed.

Open Sesame: How Alibaba Discovered the Treasure Trove of e-Commerce

Alibaba, now the largest e-commerce company in the world, is known as the "Amazon of the East" and is also perhaps that company's most direct and notable rival. Founded in 1999, Jack Ma collaborated with 18 other technology pioneers to create a wholesale internet marketplace. Alibaba was first created as a website that functioned as an e-commerce marketplace solely for Chinese consumers, but has since gone on to compete with the largest e-commerce players everywhere. After receiving $35 million in venture funding from Goldman Sachs, Softbank and Fidelity, Alibaba launched itself as the new shopping hot spot for commerce-starved Chinese shoppers and quickly prospered by tapping into young Chinese shoppers emerging in the face of the country's growing economy. Just four years later, Alibaba's efforts expanded considerably as the company launched three related tools: a C2C online retail marketplace known as Taobao.com, Aliwangwang, an instant messaging tool for online shoppers and sellers, and Alipay, an online payment platform of the new digital age. In 2005, the company's success was further boosted as it secured a formidable business ally: the Chinese government. Thriving on the government's fear of foreign invasion, Alibaba was free to roam as policymakers restricted internet control from foreign e-commerce giants, conveniently helping the company position itself as the Asian leader of e-commerce. By 2014, it had officially evolved into a technology unicorn, with a $25 billion IPO, well positioned to compete with global companies such as Amazon and eBay (ibid.).

Now a king of e-commerce, Alibaba continues in its conquest by investing in burgeoning start-ups, a strategy for global expansion that allows the giant to dominate more global business segments. Alibaba is famous for its operation-heavy investment style, focusing on companies that can create partnership opportunities and synergies within its pipeline. By 2018, it was estimated that Alibaba generated around $6.4 billion annually in return from its investments (Geromel 2019). Its favorite non-Chinese destinations are India and elsewhere across Southeast Asia where technology, innovation and young populations are surging just like they once had in China.

Alibaba's (and the world's) most valuable subsidiary is Ant Financial, at approximately $150 billion (Wu 2019). As Alibaba's online payment service provider and fintech subsidiary, Ant Financial offers a suite of services aimed at providing inclusive finance to Chinese citizens through mobile payments, savings accounts, personal investing, lending and credit scoring. Though officially established in October 2014, Ant Financial's inception actually began in 2004 as Jack Ma developed Alipay, which initially functioned as Taobao's (renamed TMall in 2012) payment system to support then Taobao's growing consumer e-commerce base (ibid.). In six short years, Alipay skyrocketed into a network with over 200 banks, 270 million total users and a daily transaction volume of over 1.2 billion RMB in China (ibid.).

Through this, Ant Financial was born. Taking advantage of the 2013 Chinese government's guidelines on establishing private capital and banks, Ant Financial created the Online Merchant bank of Zhejiang, aiming at servicing 10 million SMEs over the next five years. It also partnered with Paytm, a prominent Indian e-commerce payment system and digital wallet, and has since established a strong collaborative force to exchange knowledge and skills. This began the age of acquisition for Ant Financial, which was then quickly followed by its investment in Thailand's Ascend money (ibid.). Today, Ant Finance has grown into an empire of 1 billion customers and holds many formidable weapons: MYBank, an online microfinance lender that had lent out more than $290 billion in just four years of existence, Alipay, Asia's largest online transaction service that now operates in 54 markets and 27 currencies, and Ant Financial Cloud and Ant Financial Technology, a suite of AI products and services that have been used at over 100 banks, 60 insurers and 40 asset management firms and security brokers ("Ant Financial: How a Bug Took On the World").

Tencent: "Ten Cents," Yet Worth Billions of Dollars!

Despite its humble name "Tencent," the technology giant is now worth $500 billion, having recently overtaken Facebook as the world's most valuable social media company. Only requiring 18% of total revenue to come from online advertising compared to its Western rival's 98%, Tencent's monetization potential makes it arguably the most formidable unicorn of the three Chinese tech giants (Buche and Cantale 2018).

Co-founded in 1998 by Huateng Ma, or Pony Ma, Tencent was initially a free PC-based instant messaging service named OICG (later renamed QQ). Since its establishment, Tencent has maintained an eccentric yet powerful growth strategy. First receiving investment from South African media giant Naspers, Tencent initially generated revenue only from value-added services, such as its premium users subscription fee on QQ, smartphone and PC-based gaming, and advertising. Through its video game publishing division known as Tencent Games, the company also began working to develop its own games, with some such as Honors of Kings becoming global sensations.

Years later, Tencent's business has extended far beyond the confines of social media and gaming. In 2005, it launched a C2C auction site named PaiPai.com as well as TenPay, a Chinese version of PayPal (ibid.). Later in 2006, it launched the search engine Soso.com, which later evolved into Sogou Search (ibid.). In 2007, the company invested over RMB 100 million to establish the Tencent Research Institute, China's first research powerhouse dedicated to internet technologies (ibid.). Tencent continued to launch a number of services in subsequent years, highlighting the company's endless potential in internet software expansion. However, the most notable of Tencent's services is its all-in-one social media platform: WeChat (ibid.).

Since its inception in 2011, WeChat has grown to be the most powerful internet platform in the world. With over 1 billion monthly active users, the site has brought Tencent billions of dollars in revenue (ibid.). Originally born as the social media app Weixin, WeChat transformed just six years later from a simple social media app into an all-in-one platform (ibid.). After rolling out over 1 million mini-programs which allowed smartphone users to access mobile apps directly on the application without needing to download them individually, Tencent was able to attract over 980 million monthly active users (ibid.). Today, the power of WeChat is endless, facilitating individuals to fulfill all of their daily needs through a single app: they can, for example, hail a cab, buy movie tickets, order food delivery, pay utility bills or send money to friends, all through incorporated mini-programs. WeChat is essentially transforming the lives of consumers and businesses alike, creating a new way to do business for advertisers, and for subscribers to communicate, buy and sell merchandise and exchange information.

Tencent holds the strongest position in the gaming industry of the three tech giants, housing a portfolio of 34 companies which include big names such as Singapore Sea, Sweden Paradox Interactive, France Ubisoft, England Frontier Developments and Korean GoPets. Yet Tencent's real ingenuity lies in its ability to remain flexible and agile in the age of political and economic conflict. Amidst rising trade war tensions with America, Tencent has proven able to diversify, moving away from the US and shifting its focus more toward territories closer to home. As such, it invested a total of $1 billion in Southeast Asia's growing economies in 2019, while committing only $450 million to US interests (Wang 2018).

What Next?

While Huawei struggles to deal with US tariffs, Alibaba and Tencent remain largely unaffected. In fact, in July 2019, Alibaba announced that it had opened up its online platform to allow American companies to trade with small and midsize business buyers globally, declaring direct competition with American companies such as Amazon and Shopify. Meanwhile, Tencent announced a recent strategic partnership with Roblox, an American online gaming company with more than 90 million players. Together, the companies aim to establish a joint venture company with an initial focus on education to teach coding fundamentals, game design, digital citizenship and entrepreneurial skills. Based in Shenzhen, the joint venture will create opportunities for local Chinese developers to leverage the global Roblox ecosystem, with the ultimate goal of bringing Roblox to China (Perez 2019).

After much back and forth, it seems as though increased partnership between Chinese technology companies and the US may become more of a possibility with a "Phase One" trade deal agreed early in 2020. For example, the current administration began issuing licenses to allow some companies to restart tech sales to Huawei in November of 2019, indicating a potential willingness to ameliorate past tense relations (Whalen et al. 2019).

Regardless of how negotiations play out going forward, Chinese technology giants will indisputably continue to expand with or without the accompaniment of US and Western cooperation. We would like to think there is space for cooperation and collaboration as we go forward especially on the societal challenges we all face.

Opportunities for success are becoming clearer. Note for example that four shareholders in a major Chinese supplier of batteries for electric vehicles amassed a fortune of $17 billion for their efforts (Metcalf and Yi Mak 2020). The biggest risk of all for global investors may be missing out on such opportunities.

References

Ant Financial: How a Bug Took on the World. 2019. Asia Money, September 26. https://www.euromoney.com/article/b1h7mtyfd5d8lg/ant-financial-how-a-bug-took-on-the-world

Buche and Cantale. 2018. The Story of Tencent's Rise to the Top of the Social Media World. *World Economic Forum,* February 14. https://www.weforum.org/agenda/2018/02/how-tencent-became-the-world-s-most-valuable-social-network-firm-with-barely-any-advertising

Fannin, Rebecca. 2018. Midas List 2017 Credits 16 China VCs And 6 Chinese Unicorns for Making the Top 100 Rankings. *Forbes,* April 6. https://www.forbes.com/sites/rebeccafannin/2018/04/06/midas-list-2017-credits-china-vcs-and-unicorns-for-impact/#2c6801dc705e

Geromel, Ricaardo. 2019. As Tech Cold War Looms, Chinese Internet Giants Like Alibaba and Tencent Tackle Emerging Markets. *Forbes,* June 17. https://www.forbes.com/sites/ricardogeromel/2019/06/17/as-tech-cold-war-looms-chinese-internet-giants-like-alibaba-and-tencent-tackle-emerging-markets/#2192e4185ee0

Huawei Press. 2019. An Overview of Huawei 5G: The Battle Over 5G Commercial Devices Is Coming. *Huawei Press,* February 25. https://Consumer.Huawei.Com/En/Press/Media-Coverage/2019/An-Overview-Of-Huawei-5g/

Metcalf, Tom, and Pei Yi Mak. 2020. These Billionaires Made Their Fortune by Trying to Stop Climate Change, January 22. https://www.bloomberg.com/features/2020-green-billionaires/

Perez, Sarah. 2019. Eyeing an Entry into China, Roblox Enters Strategic Partnership with Tencent. *Techcrunch,* May 29. https://techcrunch.com/2019/05/29/eyeing-an-entry-into-china-roblox-enters-strategic-partnership-with-tencent/

Tencent. Popular Timelines. https://populartimelines.com/timeline/Tencent

Wang, Yue. 2018. China's Tech Giants Turning Away from the US Amid Escalating Trade Tensions. *Forbes,* September 25. https://www.forbes.com/sites/ywang/2018/09/25/chinas-tech-giants-turning-away-from-the-u-s-amid-escalating-trade-tensions/#74f50d7c10a1

Whalen, Jeanne, Joseph Marks, and Ellen Nakashima. 2019. US Approves First Licenses for Tech Sales to Huawei. *The Washington Post,* November 20. https://www.washingtonpost.com/technology/2019/11/20/us-said-approve-first-licenses-tech-sales-huawei/

Wu, Julia. 2019. A Brief History of Jack Ma's Ant Financial – The $150B Unicorn. *HackerNoon,* August 6. https://www.searchnewworld.com/search/search2.html?partid=snschbng&p=Wu%2C+%E2%80%9CA+Brief+History+of+Jack+Ma%27s+Ant+Financial+-+the+%24150B+Unicorn%E2%80%9D&subid=446

11

Dynamics Emerge on ESG and Sustainable Investment in China

Justin Kew and Cary Krosinsky

Growing investor attention on ESG especially in Europe has started now shifting to China. The inclusion of Chinese A-Shares into the MSCI index has been a major driver for more company disclosure in particular extra financial information demanded by investors from Europe.

On top of demand from European investors, China also acknowledges that to build a resilient society and economy, the country needs to look after the welfare of the society and environment. Building an inclusive world as is seen with its Blue Sky Policy demonstrates China's focus on not just monetary profit, but also an increased focus on how profit and value creation can also connect to positive change. As with its economy and policies, when China decides to move in a specific direction the entire boat is steered to move in that direction with a fast pace. European and American economies take decades to realize the importance of stakeholder value creation; the Chinese economy only takes a few years to do so.

As Chinese companies are increasingly under pressure to be transparent on their operations, there are certainly cautions that need be taken on this. The first step most companies have taken was to understand how ESG ratings, provided by various rating agencies, are constructed. Companies may start to use a box ticking approach to disclose documents required by these rating agencies. The risk lies where companies do not change the way they operate but use ESG as a box ticking exercise through production of various documents—a process of "greening a company." There are certainly a lot of benefits to having a high ESG rating, one being overweight in an ESG index, while the other being included in mutual funds as an end result of ESG screening processes.

© The Author(s) 2020
C. Krosinsky, *Modern China*, https://doi.org/10.1007/978-3-030-39204-8_11

China has the opportunity to be a leader in ESG, whether it is at the corporate or at the investment level. ESG ratings, by the nature of their methodology, are constructed without adjusting for company size, geography and stage of growth of the company. The "materiality" map of ESG ratings are predominantly based on index industry classifications adjusted for nuances on types of businesses at times. Being a young yet large with rapid growth economy and through its companies, China is able to share with the world that ESG is about understanding how the management of non-financial factors can affect financial factors. In other words, ESG is about the quality of a company's business and their management. A company that has top quality in both aspects would look after their stakeholders and focus on total value creation to remain competitive and a market leader in the long term.

It is very easy to ask companies to disclose various things to just to improve ESG scores; however, high ESG scores do not necessarily help with social inclusion growth or climate change mitigation.

We have already seen Chinese companies electrifying their steel production, cement production within which the majority of European producers are still using coal, electrifying their transport system and expanding their renewable power supply, just to name a few. China, being the factory of the world, where the EU and the US has outsourced their dirty production to China, is rapidly changing their economic model for a cleaner environment. While it is easy to be pointing fingers at China on their high CO_2, however, the driver of this high CO_2 is from the demand for products from Europe and the US. However, this is also changing, as European companies and some in the US are under pressure to reduce their upstream scope 3 carbon footprint, which means they are looking for products that have gone through a cleaner production process.

Hence another reason for China to remain relevant, competitive and continue to be the biggest exporter of goods to the world, China's businesses are under pressure to be transparent on their governance, social and environmental factors. These factors are looked at by procurement teams within companies in North America, Japan and Europe in particular during their supplier assessments. The flexibility of Chinese businesses, and their eagerness to innovate and react fast would mean China would not take long to surpass the rest of the world again, to become the leader this time in sustainable business. This will then lead to China's ability to export their clean business model to other parts of the world in particular other nations that are not as advanced, or that are suppliers to China.

The next few chapters contain case studies of investment strategies that are emerging in the country including from mainstream investors such as one of China's largest in ChinaAMC (Chap. 13), which now actively engages with

Chinese companies, seeking to adapt and adopt some of the better sustainable investment strategies from Europe, working as they have, for example, with Dutch fund manager NN Investment Partners. This case study stands as an excellent example of how cooperation works well. Also profiled is a long-standing expert on navigating Chinese companies in East Capital (Chap. 15).

Other Chinese investors such as Harvest Fund Management (Medium 2019) are also working on related active portfolio approaches. The largest index providers including FTSE and MSCI are ramping up work on related data for the construction of passive options for investors looking to tilt toward sustainability as the country's companies are hopefully only going to increase their responses to these challenges and opportunities.

Impact investing also continues to emerge, often focused on improving the quality of people's lives and we look at a number of examples in Chap. 14, namely, Ehong Capital and the work of the large private equity manager TPG, one of a number of leading investors we were proud to feature at our successful January 2019 event on the Future of Sustainable Investment in China (Sustainable Finance Institute 2019). In later chapters we look at trends in infrastructure investing and green bonds in China, including Chinese investments and interactions with overseas countries and partners. Progress, potential as well as risks to manage are unfolding now across all asset classes.

We begin with a look at the US China Green Fund (Chap. 12), which was also featured at our event, and as was championed originally by former US Secretary of the Treasury Hank Paulson, a prime example of cooperation through investing which could set a path for more mutually beneficial ways to work together on sustainable and impact investment in China.

References

Ford Foundation Website. https://www.fordfoundation.org/our-work-around-the-world/china/
Sustainable Finance Institute. 2019. Sustainable Finance and Its Future in China. https://mp.weixin.qq.com/s/6vl5kvllx90lHV9KdIwmNQ. Accessed 6 Jan 2020.
The Asian Banker. 2019. Harvest Fund Focuses on Ideas That Deliver Sustainable Returns to Investors. https://medium.com/@theasianbanker/harvest-fund-focuses-on-ideas-that-deliver-sustainable-returns-to-investors-d03e05648f7b. Accessed 6 Jan 2020.

12

The US China Green Fund

Annie Phan

The US China Green Fund is a market-driven private equity firm focusing on environmental and social challenges across China through innovative US-China cross-border mechanisms. Even during an age of exacerbating tensions, the US China Green Fund managed to actively facilitate a successful partnership between the two countries bringing them together to help develop and encourage environmental and social opportunity. The fund's design attempted to utilize a unique blend of featuring to global investors both a US based fund and a China based fund, positioning it to share relevant technologies where possible while also avoiding currency related challenges that might emerge.

History, Philosophy and Strategy

Established in 2015, with the support of the Paulson Institute, the US China Green Fund was born as a contributor to China's private sector efforts to help China raise $1 trillion annually to combat environmental pollution in the nation (Paulson Institute). The US China Green Fund was started thanks to committed efforts from the US and China leading up to the Paris Climate Agreement, and on the back of Chinese President's Xi's 2015 visit to the US. Its forefathers included former US Treasury Secretary Henry Paulson, founder of the Paulson Institute, a US China relations think tank, and Vice Premier Liu He, who heads China's Office of the Central Leading Group for Financial and Economic Affairs (Price, "US-China Green Fund Kicks off Next Stage of Investments in China's Low-Carbon Transformation"). The two founders later tapped Bo Bai, an MIT PhD who was leading Asian energy investments for Warburg Pincus, to head the fund (ibid.). Bo served as Vice Chairman, Chief Executive Officer and Founding Manager Partner of the Fund together with Chairman and Managing Partner Xu Lin and the fund continued to attract useful allies. The Paulson Institute, one of the top think tanks dedicated to fostering the US China relationship, continued on as its non-commercial advisor. The Environmental Defense Fund helps the fund track and manage its impact on climate emissions, energy savings and other climate goals (ibid.).

Stage One: Conquering the Chinese Market

On the China side, through its $430 million subsidiary Renminbi (RMB) fund (Dowling, The US China Green Fund Brings Western Tech To China's Environment), the US China Green Fund invests in growth-stage businesses that have deep access to channels in China to maximize environmental impact through innovative technology, improved business strategies and partnership expansion. One of the fund's flagship investment strategies is maintaining a hands-on and engaged relationship with its investments. CEO Bo Bai shared that the firm dedicates itself to "30% pre-investment, and 70% post-investment management" (ibid.). In an emerging economy like China, this grassroots approach seems to work well to groom and foster its investments.

In an attempt to "accelerate China into a low carbon environment" (ibid.), the fund delineates a two-stage strategy. During stage one, it invests in Chinese companies that "open trusted channels into major Chinese markets for the cleantech transformation of agriculture, housing, building, manufacturing, transportation and small businesses" (ibid.). The fund emphasizes not on the ability of companies to offer environmentally friendly technology but rather their channels, relationships and the ability to leverage resources around them to deliver solutions. In return, it offers companies its know-how and expansive local connections in China, giving them access to a market where even the largest of foreign companies struggle to navigate in China's constantly changing economic landscape and obscure regulations. Drawing on this bottom-up approach, the fund plans to approach companies close to the source of pollution to influence their decision-making processes.

One of its most recent notable investments in the Chinese market was $70 million in Huitongda in December 2017, a start-up that provides rural retailers with merchandising and marketing tools that generated $5.24 billion in revenues in 2018 (US China Green Fund website). Huitongda caught the eye of the US China Green Fund for its online network of more than 100,000 mom-and-pop shops that reach about 50 rural Chinese families representing a third of China's vast rural population through offering safer fertilizers and pesticides, solar mini-grids, electric vehicles and other green products to farmers and agribusinesses (ibid.). Immediately, right after the US China Green Fund made its offer, Alibaba chimed in with $717 million, also desiring to add such an opportunity to its portfolio. Shortly after Huitongda, in June 2018, the fund also secured investment in property management operator Chang Cheng Property Co Ltd. to jointly develop green and smart communities (ibid.).

Prior to Huitongda and ChangCheng, the fund had invested in a plethora of other innovative green tech Chinese start-ups, including New Starting Point, a dormitory rental and services company for blue-collar workers in the urban service industry; Hos Joy, an energy-efficient integrated home improvement solutions service provider; and Capital Heat, a centralized waste heating company ranging from industrial facilities to district heating (ibid.). Its first ever investment in January 2017 was in the Chinese firm East Low Carbon, which performs efficiency upgrades to hotels, hospitals and other buildings. East Low Carbon used a UK water-based cooling system for computer data centers, Cooltera's products, to cool data centers that are proliferating in China.

Stage Two: Helping West Meet East

During stage two, the fund aims to bring Western-based cleantech companies to the green tech-hungry market of China, a market that is prioritizing green tech. The effort is led by Doug Cameron, the fund's Senior Managing Director and Investment Partner. Elaborating on how the fund can achieve this goal, Doug shared plans to raise $1 billion for a second RMB-denominated fund to expand investments in Western firms with proven clean technologies and distribution channels with a goal of bringing them to the Chinese economy (Price 2019). Determined to debunk the notion that "in the US venture community green or cleantech investments often equate with money-losing investments," the fund hopes to bring US and Chinese investors together to create efforts that transform the perception of cleantech investments in the West, thereby influencing China as well (Dowling 2019).

In doing so, the fund relies on heavy research initiatives to ensure sound investment strategies and efforts, particularly through the US China Green

Technology Research Institute. This helps the fund not only source and screen potential investments but also hone its goal of "assessing whether potential investments are mature, more innovative than what already exists in China, and applicable to the Chinese market" (ibid.). As opposed to its investment strategy in the Chinese market in which majority investments are prioritized, in foreign investments the fund focuses more on "finding great technologies in the West that could grow to be even bigger, stronger companies if they were able to tap into the Chinese market," per Doug Cameron (ibid.). As such, the Institute screens for companies not with impressive financial performance but rather mature and proven green technology that can be replicated for the Chinese market.

Using a combination of research and advisory tools, the Institute provides the fund with technical expertise for identifying viable green technologies applicable in the Chinese market, helping it overcome previous green funds' mistake of investing in companies that possess impressive but not applicable pipelines relevant to the Chinese market. Through analysis of industrial technology, support for integration of technological solutions and guidance to contractors, architects and real estate companies, the Institute seeks to provide complete solutions to helping the Fund guide its Western investments on how to use and deploy green technologies effectively and how to best replicate them in the emerging and complex economy of China (ibid.).

A notable example was its July 2017 $750 million efforts in establishing Four Rivers (Liao 2019), a fund that aims to restructure and upgrade the Chinese steel industry, in collaboration with Hwabao Investment Corp, WL Ross & Co. LLC and China Merchants Finance Holdings Co. Further, in October 2019, it established strategic investment partnerships with a distributed solar PV producer and an intelligent parking service provider to create a rural e-commerce network that distributes green energy and agricultural products to village consumers (US China Green Fund website).

Though there exist differences among its investment strategy in the Chinese and Western market, one philosophy the fund has maintained across its portfolio is its value-added investing strategies. Even with Western investments, the fund seeks to supply them beyond just providing capital: "If we invest, we want to make sure that our channels to markets in China are valuable for the company. With every investment we make in China, we improve our understanding and our market access in China. So it's a dynamic situation," Cameron expressed (ibid.).

Amidst rising trade war tensions between the two countries its investment focuses on, the fund remains relatively immune, raising the question of how can it achieve and maintain such balance. In response to our questions, the US China Green Fund stressed that the firm's dual mission is to "improve the bilateral relationship" on top of "addressing environmental pollution through market-oriented means and generating sustainable returns" (Dowling, "The US-China Green Fund Brings Western Tech To China's Environment"). To achieve this mission, it maintains a politically neutral stance and distances itself from affiliations tied to governmental influence. According to CEO Bai, any investment that the fund makes "needs to make sense without government subsidies" (ibid.). As such, when looking at potential state partnerships, the fund does not move forward with government partners that are not fully committed to partnerships or building teams and supporting technology development. It especially wishes to distance itself from officials who only wish to come in with politically charged agendas as well as from companies in similarly politically involved sectors. It not only survives the eye of political storms but is also part of a larger effort to avoid wiping out cordial relationships and potential collaboration between the two giant nations to tackle global environmental challenges.

A Greener Future for China, America and the World

The Paulson Institute recently announced that regarding the future, the US China Green Fund will focus on four key areas: "Clean Energy & Energy Efficiency, Green Manufacturing & Environmental Protection, Green Consumption & Services, Green Mobility & Smart Logistics" (Paulson Institute 2019). Drawing on these pillars, the fund will continue fighting for cross-continental efforts to combat environmental challenges in China and the world. With its unique investment strategy and philosophy, the fund continues to play a sort of peacemaker role alongside the currently complicated US-China's economic and political relationship. Though it is unclear whether trade tensions will cease, the US China Green Fund will not halt its efforts to reconcile at times opposing global forces to create a greener, more sustainable planet and improve societal conditions on the ground, helping solve what is often seen as a dilemma between financial gain and social good. The US China Green Fund is combating one social norm at a time to ensure that sustainability can be achieved in China, which hopefully can be taken to a global scale.

References

About Us. US-China Green Fund Homepage. http://www.uschinagreenfund.com/home/aboutus/index.html

Dowling, Savannah. 2019. The US-China Green Fund Brings Western Tech to China's Environment. *Crunchbase,* November 1. https://news.crunchbase.com/news/the-u-s-china-green-fund-brings-western-tech-to-chinas-environment/

Liao, Rita. 2019. This $550M Fund Is Bringing Green Tech from the West to China, Despite Trade Tensions. *TechCrunch,* March 1. https://techcrunch.com/2019/02/28/us-china-green-fund/

Price, Dennis. 2019. US-China Green Fund kicks off next stage of investments in China's low-carbon transformation. *Impact Alpha,* March 5. https://impactalpha.com/u-s-china-green-fund-kicks-off-next-stage-of-investments-in-chinas-low-carbon-transformation/

US-China Green Fund Turns Two. 2019. Paulson Institute, January 30. http://www.paulsoninstitute.org/the-green-scene/2019/01/30/u-s-china-green-fund-turns-two/

13

Case Study: ChinaAMC

Cary Krosinsky

China Asset Management Co., Ltd. ("ChinaAMC"), was founded in 1998, the same year as the birth of China's asset management industry. Headquartered in Beijing, the company is one of the largest asset managers in China, with approximately 1 trillion RMB asset under management.

ChinaAMC signed the UN Principles for Responsible Investment (PRI) in March 2017, becoming the first full-service Chinese asset management company to join the organization. It is also the first Chinese asset manager that embeds ESG function directly into the investment team. The company's systemic ESG integration commenced in 2018, starting with several select actively managed equity products of its QFII clients, accounting for approximately 20 billion RMB.

In September 2018, ChinaAMC became a supporter of TCFD (Task Force on Climate-Related Financial Disclosures), an international initiative supported by nearly 800 companies globally. The company is also the first Chinese investor that supports the Climate Action 100+ (CA100+) to promote climate-related information disclosure in China.

ChinaAMC has integrated ESG philosophy into the whole investment process of our qualified foreign institutional investor (QFII) investment team. Following the PRI's suggestions on ESG integration, the company has developed a six-step ESG integration process, including determining sustainable investment objectives, fundamental ESG analysis, ESG portfolio management, ESG risk management, active engagement with listed companies and regular reporting. The framework ensures that ESG issues are considered at every moment of investment. ChinaAMC believes the focus on ESG issues can promote sustainable growth for Chinese companies and generate alpha for investors in China's semi-efficient market.

© The Author(s) 2020
C. Krosinsky, *Modern China*, https://doi.org/10.1007/978-3-030-39204-8_13

Using Fundamental Insights to Complement Factor-Driven Models and Universal Frameworks

As quantitative back-tests in ESG research may yield useful insights, ChinaAMC is applying factor-driven models as a tool to determine the significance of ESG key issues. The use case of ESG key issues and observations may reveal contrasting results from global norms but still generate useful fundamental insights. Certain key issues may require additional market developments to become material. For example, appropriate level of management compensation may incentivize executives to enhance company profit generation, which aligns with shareholders' interest and reduces agency costs. However, the result was counterintuitive—the factor only passed tests for the consumer sector, which may indicate that companies producing and selling consumer goods rely more heavily on management's strategy compared to industrial and energy companies. In this case, management risks should be weighted more within the corporate governance pillar for this industry. The quantitative model retrospectively refreshes our perspectives in measuring management's impacts.

However, quantitative analysis and the construction of quantitative analysis are highly dependent on the quality of data. When the quality of data is a concern, fundamental research and insights may be used to complement the lack of data coverage or inaccuracies. After all, it is ultimately the economic considerations of ESG issues that impact financial performance. Besides, although some globally recognized frameworks provide universally applicable analytical structures for ESG assessment, they cannot offer sufficient evidence to distinguish Chinese companies due to lack of full awareness of China's economic development status and local business environment. As such, ChinaAMC's in-house ESG fundamental framework was developed and is necessary for the analysis of material, China-focused and sector-specific ESG issues.

Take real estate as an example. Third-party data may not be sufficient to analyze the specific issues in the industry. ChinaAMC supplements the research with detailed and localized analysis. Being aware that the majority of Chinese real estate companies are involved in off-balance sheet financing and profit shifting which significantly embezzles the stakeholder's benefit, our research team adds more tools to capture such activities. As shown in Table 13.1, our adjusted ESG scores reflect more perspectives of Chinese real estate (RE) companies' essences and estimate potential risks of tunneling, which can better help portfolio managers to avoid governance risks and make stock selection.

Table 13.1 Evaluating Chinese real estate companies

	Company A	Company B	Company C	Company D	Company E
Market cap (billion RMB)[a]	297.92	180.28	154.56	86.27	83.18
Third-party ESG rating	BB	BB	BBB	BB	B
ChinaAMC add-ons					
Pledge of shares	●●●	●●●●	●●	●	●●
Financial sustainability	●●	●●●	●●	●●	●
Off-balance sheet financing	●●●	●●●	●●●●	●●	●●●●
Accounting governance	●●●	●●●●	●●	●●●●	●●●●
Potential profit shifting	●●●●	●●●●	●●●	●●●●	●●
Total adjusted scores	6.73	7.14	6.49	5.87	5.82

[a]●●●●: first quartile in peers, ●: fourth quartile in peers. Information is as of September 30, 2019

To conclude, picking out the most significant ESG-related performance drivers enables us to screen stocks more efficiently. Based on the initially selected stock pool, we also consider other ESG and fundamental factors that are not quantified or included in the screening model to further incorporate comprehensive analyses.

ESG Integration in Risk Management for Downside Protection

Risk management is an integral and critical part of the investment process. Starting in 2018, ChinaAMC began to implement a firm-wide risk management screening system for ESG controversies. Key words were monitored on local regulators and reputable media sources and are captured and mapped to companies in the stock pool, and risk flags were sent to related portfolio managers and analysts for further analysis. The investment staff then provide feedback on the controversies to the risk management team who decide whether to temporarily exclude the stock.

In 2019, the ChinaAMC risk team observed an announcement by Beijing Municipal Ecological Environment Bureau alleging that a public company was replacing qualified pollution-control devices with inferior alternatives and may face a significant penalty. ChinaAMC's ESG team and research analyst was immediately alerted of this scandal. Subsequent research showed that the faulty engines were produced by the company's outsourced supplier and the company was not liable for the fines. However, this also reflected the company's inability to implement stringent quality controls throughout its supply chain, which in turn makes the company susceptible to similar reputational risks and legal costs in the future. It is insights like this that help the portfolio management investment research teams to enhance their understanding on invested companies.

Exercising Active Ownership Through ESG Engagement

As a supporter of TCFD and CA100+, company engagement plays an important role in ChinaAMC's ESG integration program. ChinaAMC's participation in collaborative engagements with public companies in China has yielded valuable insights for investment managers. Since 2018, ChinaAMC has had numerous conversations with Chinese industry leading companies in food and beverage, oil and gas, construction material, healthcare and manufacturing sectors. These senior-level meetings between investment managers and company executives were highly constructive and involved in-depth conversations on enhancing ESG disclosures and sustainability practices. In addition, engagement enables constructive dialogues to be had with companies, improves their understanding regarding sustainability issues and improves the quality of ESG disclosure. In a collaborative engagement effort on one of China's major coal miners and power generators, ChinaAMC recently engaged with members of the CA100+ group to strengthen with the company's carbon emission control and relevant information disclosure. Interactions with the firm's executives have been informative about the firm's technological advancements toward energy efficiency and pollution reduction, as well as yielded valuable insights on their plans toward adhering to China's commitment toward the Paris Agreement. As a result of the collaborative efforts, the firm has decided to report to the Carbon Disclosure Project ("CDP") for the first time in 2019.

Besides bottom-up efforts in promoting the ESG information disclosure of listed companies, ChinaAMC also engages with authorities in order to facilitate the ESG integration from a top-down perspective. In 2017, ChinaAMC joined the China Green Finance Committee. In the following year, the company became one of the only two Chinese asset managers in a new private group of UK and Chinese financial institutions to pilot TCFD reporting, which was established by the City of London Green Finance Initiative, China

Green Finance Committee and the PRI. In April 2019, the group participated in drafting the *Guidelines of Financial Institution Environmental Information Disclosure* for A-share listed companies. In this way, the company hopes to assist in directing and regulating ESG information disclosure in China.

As one of the pioneers in China's sustainable investment industry, ChinaAMC continues exploring the best practice of international ESG investment methods in China and is dedicated to bridging the gap between investors and listed companies. We believe the approach of ESG is not only a mainstream trend that is taking place in this immature market, but also an effective way for alpha generation. Although market awareness and data quality are still worrying, we are confident of the future of ESG investment in China given the positive result of our research and the fruitful return of our strategy.

14

Case Study: Ehong Capital and Measuring Impact in China

Kara Huang and Cary Krosinsky

Introduction

Established in Shanghai in 2007, Ehong Capital is a Chinese social impact private equity and venture capital fund, arguably the first in the country, whose primary mission remains fostering the creation of direct social impact. Its founding partners began their journey with Project HOPE, which developed a Chinese public service aimed to bring more schools to lower socioeconomic communities in rural areas of China (Huang 2012). Project HOPE began in 1989 and still strives today to improve China's education quality and availability including through the expansion of improved nutritional knowledge as well. Project HOPE has achieved significant accomplishments; by the end of 2004, it financed the education of over 3 million students (Liu 2004). Project HOPE has been considered one of the more successful non-governmental, public welfare projects in China.

In 2012, Ehong Capital engaged in a more explorative role in what later became known as impact investment, specifically through engaging with portfolio companies to improve the thoroughness and standardization of their ESG practices. In 2018, Ehong Capital began to actively invest in impact in China, acting as limited partners to foundations to form an impact fund, called Ehe Impact Fund (Fang 2019). In 2019, Ehong Capital partnered with a professor at the Shanghai Institute for Finance to develop an "Impact Measurement and Management" framework by participating in fieldwork on the invested companies of Ehong Capital. The Ehe Impact Fund, based on a risk classification system partnered with the Shanghai Institute for Finance, garnered support from both the private and the public sector, and was the first of its kind to be created in China.

© The Author(s) 2020
C. Krosinsky, *Modern China*, https://doi.org/10.1007/978-3-030-39204-8_14

Recently, Ehong Capital was awarded the coveted 2017 Annual Investment Institution Award of China Social Enterprise and Impact Investment. Largely because of its early start in the Chinese impact investment industry, and comprehensive dedication to quantifying meaningful measures of impact wherever possible, Ehong has gained recognition in China and among investment professionals from around the world. Guided by a selection of the UN's Sustainable Development Goals, Ehong Capital is one of the earliest practitioners of Chinese impact investing with potential for expansion.

Investment Philosophy

Ehong Capital is committed to a "double-bottom-line" principle, whereby financial returns and social impact are equally important goals. Understanding that quantitative and material evidence of impact is necessary in the current state of development for ESG analysis, Ehong measures and tracks metrics such as emissions reduction and the number of people impacted in categories of "vulnerable groups" and quality of education.

At the start of their investment process, Ehong approaches the wide category of social impact firms with a bottom-up approach. There are three criteria that must be met in order to be seriously considered as a sound investment.

The first is innovation; Ehong looks for an innovative business model or technology that makes a company's approach to solving widespread issues not only special, but specific. Second, the solution that the company presents must be a commercial one. It is in their belief that a social enterprise with limited services cannot have a meaningful breadth of impact. Therefore, the scalability of a solution is necessary for impact to be observed and felt at a broader, public scale. Lastly, Ehong attempts to identify company founders with an innate mindset of social responsibility and entrepreneurship. If founders are too focused on profitability and financial aspects, it can hinder the potential for truly new and successful social enterprises. After an investment is made, Ehong works with its portfolio companies in testing, improving and measuring impact at all stages of their lives: pre-investment, post-investment and exit (Fang 2019).   Ehong Capital focuses on what its investment team thinks are the most relevant and problem-ridden industries in China: sustainable agriculture, health and elderly care, energy and environmental protection, and quality education.

Sustainable agriculture identifies specific issues like improving farmers' salaries, ensuring food safety, developing the industry and ecology/sustainability. *Health and elderly care* refers to expanding coverage in China, improving the quality of life for the increasing number of elderly people and making public medical resources more efficient. *Energy and environmental protection* is more straightforward, defined as carbon emissions reduction, improving recycling practices and moving toward more affordable clean energy. Lastly, *quality education* is defined as quality, equitable and life-long education. Ehong believes that there is significant growth potential for impact investment in China. According to their projections, by 2030, the four industries that Ehong specializes in will reach a market size of $10 trillion.

Case Study: Zhejiang Lvkang Medical Care

Though over 50% of Ehe Impact Fund's AUM is invested in portfolio companies in the quality education category, a recent investment in the health and eldercare sector demonstrates Ehong's dedication to diversifying their array of portfolio companies. Zhejiang Lvkang Medical Care, the medical service company that Ehong invested in, has a goal of providing and improving available nursing care to the semi-disabled and disabled elderly. Ehong has a strong conviction that Zhejiang is positioned as the pioneer in the long-term care industry in China and demonstrates the potential to grow based on the current state of medical service trends (Fang 2019).

The investment thesis relies on a few important criteria. First, there is very strong demand for semi-disabled and disabled nursing care. Second, the exploration of the medical trend service has the potential to be scalable. Lastly, there is strong medical background among the founders of the company and they demonstrated personal experience and strong social responsibility surrounding the medical care industry. The decision to invest was deeply rooted in these three aspects that Ehong identified.

Most of Ehong's time is spent in the post-investment stage, where there are five key areas that are focused on. First is strategic planning, where the investment team helps the portfolio company streamline a strategy. At this stage, Ehong guided Zhejiang to position to a disabled/semi-disabled-only service and encouraged the company to change their business model to a "light asset business model" to focus on the service provider aspect. The second area is financial and social KPIs (key performance indicators). Ehong helped set a three-year revenue target, set a goal gross rate they determined fit and streamlined the medical insurance component. Third, to improve the state of corporate governance, Ehong sent a team to collaborate with the company on the ground, to help execute the KPI plan and to organize periodical meetings to analyze results month-by-month. Fourth, industry relations are essential for peer-to-peer comparisons. Ehong helped establish a strategic development committee for industrial results in an effort to garner support and resources from the medical service industry and to ensure that they provide stellar services. Lastly, Ehong aids with financial services, which take form in refinancing, and applying and securing bank loans. The post-investment process is extremely intensive and at this stage Ehong can demonstrate their value-add to the portfolio companies' operations and strategy (Fang 2019).

After Ehong's 2014 investment in Zhejiang, its revenue doubled, and in 2020, Zhejiang is projecting a revenue of over $20 million. As for social impact, the company improved its reach from servicing 3000 semi-disabled or disabled elderly in 2014, to cover over 100,000 elderly at home after expanding their business model to a home care service. The impact has been truly significant and impactful on both a financial and a social front, underscoring the ability and potential investment has to improve the biggest public issues China faces today.

Measuring and Investing in Positive Impact in China

Investors who want their money to make a positive difference want more than anything to see a demonstration of that positive impact (Wilshire Associates 2017).

Can that be accomplished given the wide variety of ESG issues that are manifesting across categories of risk and opportunity? Not easily. First of all, everything basically has both a positive and a negative impact and so the main opportunity is to measure a net positive impact but there have been some decent attempts to figure out how to answer this important question.

Early movers on this include KPMG and their attempts at calculating "True Value," such as can be seen in their work with Safaricom (Krosinsky et al. 2017), demonstrating how the company created something on the order of ten times the societal value above and beyond the financial profit the company made by providing access to cellphones to the average Kenyan, allowing them in many cases to run a business efficiently for the first time. Such calculations require estimating environmental damage from doing a normal course of business alongside the social benefits, creating a net score; in this case the telecommunications company in question is seen to be creating a net positive benefit for society and shareholders alike.

Such work helped inspire the more recent work of the TPG Rise Fund, now managing $4 billion per the TPG website, making it the largest impact investment vehicle in the world (Barron's 2019), and which uses their Impact Momentum of Money (IMM) calculation, built upon the work of KPMG and the idea of calculating positive net impact.

IMM involves a six-step evaluation process (Harvard Business Review 2019), which includes:

1. Assess the relevance and scale of the potential significance of the impact of a particular investment
2. Identify target environmental and social outcomes on a thematic basis
3. Estimate the economic value of these outcomes for society (using what is seen to be an academically rigorous, relevant and reliable study)
4. Adjust for risk (TPG here calculates what they call an Impact Realization Index on a 100-point scale, up to 60 points available based on the perceived quality of the impact study and its direct relevance to the product in question, 10 for the context, 10 for the income bracket [is impact being delivered to those most in need?], 10 for relative product or service similarity and 10 for the likelihood of projected use of the product or service)
5. Estimate the terminal value (a particularly cool feature as most private equity manager by design hold investments only for a few years in most cases. IMM accounts for the impacts of investment even after they are sold to others)
6. Calculate the social return of every dollar spent

A specific example of such an investment is Dodla Dairy which produces fresh milk from over 200,000 smallholder farmers across rural southern India. With projected sales of 2.6 billion liters of milk over five years, Rise estimated that investments in Dodla would increase farm families' annual incomes by 73%, from $425 to $735, creating both financial profit and societal benefit. Credit Suisse is another impact-focused institution, which cites the case of investments by blueberry farmers in China, where impact investments have not only helped bring farmers out of poverty but also helped catalyze an industry which is now lucrative and expanding; such approaches have been useful in countries such as China that have been successfully achieving higher degrees of poverty alleviation.

Another example would be to suppose a company invested $25 million to launch a line of low-cost eyewear for rural residents of developing countries, and its research leads to an estimate of $200 million in social benefits, based on increased customer productivity and income. An investor can simply divide $200 million by $25 million, with the eyewear generating $8 in social value for every $1 invested and IMM expresses this as 8X.

Such an approach can allow a fund manager to measure and report on its net positive impact.

In China, many societal goals can be potentially addressed through investment in such a manner.

Such goals include:

- Poverty: it is aimed to be eliminated by 2020
- Air: cities must achieve pollution index below 100 for 80% of the year by 2021
- Water: 80% of major waterways to meet tier 3 standard by 2020
- Soil: 90% of contaminated land to be treated 2020
- Healthcare reform: one clinic and one medical service center for each community with a population over 30,000

Examples of potentially measurable net positive impacts per sector which can be tracked and reported include:

- Education: Increased attendance in schools and specific increases in academic performance
- Energy: Increased number of households with reliable access, increased percentage of clean energy used in regions and increases in the number of good jobs
- Financial services: Levels of access to financial services and improvements to financial resiliency
- Food and agriculture: Higher crop yields, lower crop loss and increased farmer margins and income stability
- Health: Increased rates of care in various demographics and improved health status
- Technology: Increased digital connectivity and improvements in business productivity

The TPG Rise Fund website lists two investments in China as of January 2020, both in the realm of providing access to financial services to those less well off. The two investments are in CPFA, which works on increasing access to finance to the some 500 million people not served by traditional banking systems or non-bank institutions, and Du Xiaoman Financial, which uses artificial intelligence and aims to add 10 million users in 2020 presently unbanked.

References

Barron's. 2019. How TPG's Rise Fund Invests in Energy. https://www.barrons.com/articles/future-returns-how-tpg-growths-rise-fund-invests-in-energy-01569953521. Accessed 6 Jan 2020.

Ehong Capital Awarded as 2019 Impact Investing Venture Capital of the Year. 2019, December 19. Retrieved December 20, 2019, from http://www.ehongcapital.com/en/2019/12/19/blog11en/

Fang, Wei. 2019. Personal Interview, December 7.

Harvard Business Review. 2019. Calculating the Value of Impact Investing, January. https://hbr.org/2019/01/calculating-the-value-of-impact-investing. Accessed 6 Jan 2020.

Huang, T. 2012. Improving Children's Nutrition in Rural China, December. Retrieved December 20, 2019, from https://www.projecthope.org/improving-childrens-nutrition-in-rural-china/12/2012/

Krosinsky, Cary, and Sophie Purdom, et al. 2017. Chapter 16, *Sustainable Investing: Revolutions in Theory and Practice*. London: Routledge.

Liu, Fei. 2004. 15 Years of Project Hope (希望工程15年). Retrieved December 20, 2019, from http://www.edu.cn/20041119/3121055.shtml

TPG Rise Fund Website. https://therisefund.com/. Accessed 6 Jan 2020.

Wilshire Associates. 2017. Where's the F in ESG. https://wilshire.com/Portals/0/consulting/Perspectives/Wilshire_Wheres_the_F_in_ESG_2018-03.pdf. Accessed 6 Jan 2020.

15

Case Study: East Capital

Kara Huang

Introduction

Founded in 1997, East Capital was established as an independent, specialty asset manager in Stockholm, Sweden. Known for its fierce focus in frontier and emerging markets, East Capital began its global investments in Russian and Baltic equities, and from then on expanded into the rest of Eastern Europe, Central Asia, East Asia and both global frontier and emerging markets. Today, the investment firm manages just under 4 billion EUR in public equity funds, real estate funds and separate accounts for a broad base of international clients.

Since its beginning, though it did not formally call its analysis "ESG," East Capital considered responsible governance as central to their operations and investment processes. Similar to KYC (Know Your Customer), KYO—Know Your Owner—is a principle that East Capital abides by when performing due diligence in potential investments (Hirn 2019a, b).

East Capital's Founding Partner and Chief Investment Officer, Peter Elam Håkansson, emphasizes that maintaining conversations and connections with company management and observing operations themselves is at the core of East Capital's pre-investment and portfolio management process.

The Chief Sustainability Officer and Founding Partner, Karine Hirn, shares an anecdote that demonstrates the power and importance of consistent, in-person meetings with management teams: in the winter of 1998, she and her colleagues sat down with the management team of a pipe manufacturing company in St. Petersburg, Russia (Hirn 2019a, b). Karine recalls it being so cold in the conference room that she had to keep her coat on. In general, the

© The Author(s) 2020
C. Krosinsky, *Modern China*, https://doi.org/10.1007/978-3-030-39204-8_15

meeting went well, with the company management noting that business is going well, and new clients were coming in. After the meeting concluded, the East Capital team casually asked the reason it was so cold indoors and was told that the company was having a cash crisis as clients resorted to barter trade, and could not pay its electricity bill. Rather than cash payments, the company was even paying dividends in sugar! For East Capital, there has always been value outside of simply reading a company's financial statements on Bloomberg.

Since its inception in 1997, East Capital has continuously integrated more ESG analysis into their investment process, because it believes that not only is a company's ESG standing central to a company's quality, but it also can mean life and death for a company's profitability and operational efficiency; that is, it is the company's sustainability per se that the investment teams are assessing.

East Capital's Investment Universe and Spotlight on Frontier Markets

Extractive mining in Africa, oil and gas in Russia, and so on, present threats to climate change, but also represent an opportunity to put money in companies that will be pioneering responsible alternatives and improvements in those businesses (Hirn 2019a, b). East Capital views frontier markets as "next-generation" emerging markets. These markets specifically should be similar to emerging markets in economic growth, income levels and the development of capital markets, regulatory environment and liquidity.

When it comes to the investment process, East Capital's investment universe begins with countries in the MSCI Frontier Markets Index, which includes countries like Vietnam and Bangladesh in Asia, Kuwait and Morocco in the Middle East North Africa region, Nigeria and Kenya in Africa, among other countries in Eastern Europe and South America (Hirn 2019b). Identifying secular trends, meeting in-person and on the ground and conducting thorough, in-house research is at the core of the investment process.

Environmental, Social Governance

Though the analysis of governance and various environmental and social factors have been central to East Capital's investment process, it was formalized in 2016 with a scoring system, with the integration of particular SDG metrics added in 2017. Following a thorough regular screening for controversies among portfolio holdings, and negative screening for involvement in vice industries, and so on, East Capital's scoring system encompasses their own ESG analysis, which has approximately 60 questions, with a focus on corporate governance. Portfolio managers and analysts might score companies in different ways, and "calibration calls" are done with the Chief Sustainability Officer in order to challenge analysts to be objective and thorough. In these more contested points of scoring—where the team sees possibilities for improvement—East Capital takes the opportunity to engage with the company, and remains open in giving feedback, collaborating with other investors and participating in initiatives.

Because of its focus in less developed markets, East Capital cannot rely on external ESG data (usually unavailable, and often misleading when available) and must look at ESG through its own lenses. There are many challenges when conducting ESG analysis for emerging and frontier countries, such as low quality of financial reporting, a lack of materiality analysis, board composition not supportive to minorities, majority shareholders not passing the KYO test. At the same time, these countries are in a stage of transition when regulations and reforms can have a huge impact and where such risks can be properly addressed. East Capital views investing in underdeveloped or lower developed countries as an opportunity to help achieve meaningful improvement (Hirn 2019b), both at corporate and at regulators' levels.

East Capital, being founded in Sweden, has developed a specific approach to sustainable investing, which offers a unique and effective perspective. At the inaugural Bloomberg Sustainable Investing Conference in Bangkok in October 2019, Hirn joined a panel where she emphasized three pillars of the Nordic approach of sustainable investing, which East Capital holds close to their investment process and ESG analysis: collaboration, transparency and engagement.

The model for investing, especially in Northern Europe, is extremely open and collaborative. For example, the four Swedish pension funds have an ethical council, whereby shareholders appoint an appropriate set of people to sit on boards of listed companies, "diminishing the risk 'ownerless companies'" (Hirn 2019a, b). Additionally, Swedish Investors for Sustainable Development, or SISD, is a network where major Swedish asset owners and managers come together to address the 2030 UN Agenda, and the UN SDGs. SISD has been an inspiration for the recently launched and UN-backed "Global Investors for Sustainable Development." East Capital is an active member of SISD as well as other associations and investor-led initiatives such as API in Russia, ACGA in Asia, BICG in the Baltics and Climate Action 100+. It is also a strong supporter of the CDP disclosure campaign.

The second aspect of Nordic investing is transparency. Sweden, in addition to the other Northern European countries, typically ranks consistently high on the Corruption Perceptions Index. Hirn claims that this is largely because of a Swedish principle, *offentlighetsprincipen*, whereby public access to official documents has existed since the eighteenth century and is a part of the Swedish constitution. Thus, Swedish state-owned enterprises were among the first in the world to adopt Global Reporting Initiative (GRI) reporting, which was enacted as the global standard for sustainability reporting in the late 1990s.

Lastly, and demonstrated by East Capital's origins and investment process, engagement is at the core of the Nordic investing approach. As Hirn states, this push for engagement from asset managers in Sweden extends even to the individual investor level; 64% of Swedes think that it is preferable to personally choose investment funds for their occupational pension. East Capital does not engage simply to check a box either; it strives to make areas of engagement "as specific, measurable, and achievable as possible" (Hirn 2019a, b).

These three pillars of Nordic investing are at the core of East Capital's investing philosophy. East Capital views ESG factors as *risks*, but also as *opportunities* for it to push companies to improve, and investors to push companies to improve.

Case Study: Solar Power

East Capital views frontier and emerging markets as places with inherent potential for future growth, in both financial return and innovative solutions. A recent article by East Capital's Head of Asia, Francois Perrin, details how China has been a fierce leader in the clean energy transition in recent times. In 2018, China maintained its dominance as the largest solar power installation market for the sixth year in a row. The cumulative solar power generation capacity grew at CAGR of 88%. Because of a favorable regulatory and policy environment built on the implementation of the China Blue Sky Anti-Pollution plan and particulate matter (PM) reduction targets, and the continuous decline in costs of solar power technologies, China was able to rapidly grow this market (Perrin 2019).

The "grid parity policy" refers to the point at which alternative energy costs the same or less as conventional energy sources like fossil fuels; this has major implications for China itself, with grid parity achieved in an increasing number of provinces. In the article, Perrin discusses how he views the solar energy pivot to the cheapest energy resource as spilling over to emerging markets as of now in places like India, the UAE, South Africa and more to follow shortly thereafter.

As returns for solar energy projects in China have the potential to reach 8–10% in the medium term, East Capital "continues to favor Chinese manufacturers over Chinese solar developers" because of market dominance and the potential for further consolidation (Perrin 2019). East Capital will be watching markets in India, South Africa and the Middle East for future investments in solar developers that might benefit from China's lowering cost of production.

References

Hirn, Karine. 2019a. The Nordic Approach of Sustainable Investing, November 17. Retrieved November 20, 2019, from http://www.linkedin.com/pulse/nordic-approach-sustainable-investing-karine-hirn/
———. 2019b. Personal Interview, November 21.
Perrin, Francois. 2019. Frontier Markets Through the ESG Lens: Specialist in Emerging and Frontier Markets: East Capital, June 25. Retrieved November 20, 2019, from http://www.eastcapital.com/Look-East/News-articles/Articles-2019/Frontier-markets-through-the-ESG-lens/

16

Additional Considerations Including China's Belt and Road Initiative

Cary Krosinsky

China's recent investment initiatives include expanded relations with many countries especially through its ambitious *Belt and Road Initiative* (BRI) and this could be a blessing or a curse; in fact, the future direction of the BRI has a great bearing on the future of the planet. Chapter 17 goes into detail on the significant investment infrastructure China has been building on infrastructure investment, Chap. 18 describes how China has been interacting with countries on the ground and some of the challenges and opportunities this presents and Chap. 19 focuses on China's rise as a leader on issuing Green Bonds.

China's BRI could prove problematic in a number of ways or it could be a mechanism for positive change. Criticisms have included wasteful spending and poor work quality (Guardian 2019), that it could be a form of "debt trap diplomacy" and either that promised local jobs haven't always manifested or that Chinese employment was a requirement of some contracts (Foreign Policy Research Institute 2019). But arguably most important is the impact BRI-related investments and lending could have on locking the world into a climate-changed future.

A recent Brookings Institute article by Simon Zadek (Brookings Institute 2019) argued that infrastructure may represent half the sources of new carbon emissions in the coming few decades alone and most of the world's infrastructure that will exist by 2050 has yet to be built so the opportunity and the imperative to build better is clear as is the risk of getting this wrong.

British economist Sir Nicholas Stern of the London School of Economics recently said: "The more than 70 countries that are signed up to the *Belt and Road Initiative* have an average GDP of around one third of that of China. If they adopt China's development model, which resulted in a doubling of

© The Author(s) 2020
C. Krosinsky, *Modern China*, https://doi.org/10.1007/978-3-030-39204-8_16

China's greenhouse gas emissions in the first decade of the previous century, it would make the emissions targets in the Paris Agreement impossible" (Yale Environment 360 2019).

A five-point green finance roadmap was announced as a result by the ClimateWorks Foundation (ClimateWorks Foundation 2019) in conjunction with Tsinghua University and Vivid Economics on the back of such concerns in September 2019 calling for the following steps:

1. The Development of Belt and Road Country Capabilities: We propose establishing an international platform, possibly hosted by the UN, to support the intensive development of green finance across B&R countries and to meet the rapidly growing demand from these countries.
2. China Action on Outward Investments: Extending China's green requirements to its investment in the Belt and Road Initiative. This should involve applying mandatory environmental assessment requirements for Chinese investments in B&R countries.
3. International Green Investment: Promoting the adoption of green investment principles by global investors, the process of which has already been initiated by China and the UK's Green Investment Principles (GIP) covering investment in B&R countries. GIP membership should be further expanded.
4. Carbon Transparency: Given that infrastructure investments in B&R countries will have a defining impact on global carbon emissions in the future, it is imperative to improve disclosure of the climate impact of these projects.
5. International Climate Coalition: We propose to build a coalition among various international, regional and bilateral collaborative schemes, with a view to more effectively advancing low carbon and climate-resilient investments in B&R countries.

In 2018, over 40% of BRI lending in the power sector was still involving coal (CSIS 2019) and estimated investment in the BRI is roughly $1 trillion (Nicholas Institute 2019).

The BRI needs to be steered in a green direction, which we see as just one more argument for the necessary cooperation imperative and related success that can come from further collaboration.

References

Brookings Institute. 2019. The Critical Frontier, Reducing Emissions from China's Belt and Road. https://www.brookings.edu/blog/future-development/2019/04/25/the-critical-frontier-reducing-emissions-from-chinas-belt-and-road/. Accessed 5 Jan 2010.

ClimateWorks Foundation. 2019. Decarbonizing the Belt and Road Initiative. https://www.climateworks.org/wp-content/uploads/2019/08/BRI_Exec_Summary_v10-screen_pages_lo-1.pdf. Accessed 5 Jan 2020.

CSIS. 2019. Greening or Greenwashing the Belt and Road Initiative. https://www.csis.org/analysis/greening-or-greenwashing-belt-and-road-initiative. Accessed 5 Jan 2020.

Foreign Policy Research Institute. 2019. Unequal Sequal: China's Belt and Road Initiative. https://www.fpri.org/article/2019/08/unequal-sequel-chinas-belt-and-road-initiative/. Accessed 5 Jan 2020.

Nicholas Institute, Duke University. 2019. Belt and Road Initiative. https://nicholasinstitute.duke.edu/project/belt-and-road-initiative. Accessed 5 Jan 2020.

The Guardian. 2019. China's Belt and Road Initiative Criticised for Poor Standards and 'Wasteful' Spending. https://www.scmp.com/news/china/diplomacy/article/3014214/chinas-belt-and-road-initiative-criticised-poor-standards-and. Accessed 5 Jan 2020.

Yale Environment 360. 2019. How China's Big Overseas Initiative Threatens Global Climate Progress. https://e360.yale.edu/features/how-chinas-big-overseas-initiative-threatens-climate-progress. Accessed 5 Jan 2020.

17

China's Integrated Policy, Market and Technology Offering for Sustainability

Sebastian Sheng

Building infrastructure and maintaining a healthy ecosystem are complex and costly activities, especially for a country such as China that seeks economic growth, infrastructure modernization and environmental protection all at the same time. Nonetheless, by examining broader strategies and alternatives, China has opportunities to create more sustainable value for each investment made. As China progresses toward its Ten-Year Plan through 2025, lessons can be observed on how it has guided its development strategies which can essentially be summarized under two overarching principles: (1) decision-making in approaching sustainability issues that applies a rigorous evaluation and governance structure on the policy, finance and technology aspects, uncovering savings and increasing performance; (2) expanding the number of both traditional and non-traditional options that can help to achieve its social and environmental goals more efficiently and effectively. Before starting, a few words about what this chapter is not. China's development strategy, in the form of "13th Five-Year Plan," or "Manufacturing 2025," is the name given to a dynamic, heterogeneous distribution system through which its resources are budgeted to a variety of social and economic activities which include poverty elimination, multilateral trades, manufacturing modernization and of course infrastructure and environmental sustainability, among many others. This chapter is not a balanced overview of its comprehensive "Ten-Year Plan"; rather, it is a targeted look at the instruments used by China and the underlying principles which guide their approaches to infrastructure management.

A late bloomer in industrialization and the subsequent industry transformation to the service-based economy, China has been catching up and is now at the edge of addressing climate change and sustainable infrastructure

© The Author(s) 2020
C. Krosinsky, *Modern China*, https://doi.org/10.1007/978-3-030-39204-8_17

with an integration of strategic feasibility studies, green finance, P3 and technological innovations that has created the possibility for increased positive impact through how it deals with sustainability, waste, energy and infrastructure. Putting investments in these solutions to work has been China's optimal strategy to accelerate climate change while performing better infrastructure development risk management. Because of harnessing the private sector, connecting nations with its "Belt Road Initiative" and fusing sustainable innovations with finance and technology—sustainable development and management is starting to happen. Not only China, but every market, organization, nation and every individual could be affected for the better.

Challenges and Progress

Mauricio Macri, Argentina's President and this year's host of the G-20 summit, has stated "sustainability is a core value that should serve as a unifying framework to meet economic, social and environmental goals." Indeed, growing pressure to create smart and sustainable infrastructure has manifested itself, especially in developing countries like China where high-density urbanization, unregulated car-based transport and coal-fired power plants wreak havoc on the environment. A united front among global governments to expand well-developed infrastructure, and focus on doing so without contributing to the mounting environmental issues, has been established through milestones such as the UN Sustainability Goals in 2015. Additionally, social awareness has been awakened across virtually all societies including China; yet it is safe to assess that insignificant contributions have been made to truly ameliorate current challenges.

As one of the fastest growing economies, China has been demonstrating a strong top-down investment-led growth model to the world. The central government has a strategic infrastructure plan to support its own national economic growth and rapid urbanization. Contrary to its Western counterparts operating within levels of segregation of power and fiscal management, China, or more specifically the Communist Party itself, has set high priorities and provided direct investment for building out the infrastructure framework, such as China's national road network and high-speed train system have demonstrated. Massive development of physical infrastructure has resulted in sustained economic growth and increased international competitiveness. The Chinese government is aware of the long-term costs of environmental damage to the Chinese economy and of the potential of the undeveloped inner provinces. Leadership across all levels took the chance to accelerate the country's development when stimulus was most needed to compensate for the lack of international growth. For example, in 2009, 40% of China's total activity resulted in furthering infrastructure development. Meanwhile, the lack of practice in operating and managing the system in a sustainable way over the past few decades has caused deforestation, atmospheric corrosion, water pollution, among other natural damages—serving as an example of economic issues prevailing over environmental and societal costs. Adding to these challenges is the daunting statistic that China's peak population will move forward from 2028 to 2023, with more than 60% of that population living in cities.

China understands that if it doesn't strip away political and economic interests to implement workable guidelines, the gap between infrastructure demands and unprecedented pressure to protect its environment will continue to widen. Indeed, there are a range of considerations to be addressed—at the core of which lie the economic and political implications behind policymaking. Ever since President Xi came into power, "accountability" has been a central theme that has permeated through governments, state-owned enterprises to nowadays even large-sized private institutions—this "forcible" approach in cracking down on corruption, exerting peer reviews and encouraging whistle-blowers has in fact effectively addressed political and economic interests more transparently. Even so, practically speaking, the government realizes that there is and has been no single solution to a broad issue such as climate risk or deteriorating infrastructure. Nevertheless, a wave of innovations and reforms in policies, market mechanisms and disruptive technologies have been under way in China applied to stimulate conversion from a fossil fuel-based economy and infrastructure to cleaner, greener and more sustainable alternatives, which have benefited from China's unique governance and operational structure.

Market Mechanisms with Political Implications

The need to address economic and political implications behind policymaking within all governmental bodies is mandatory. Despite headline-grabbing sound bites about "green governments and policies," climate change or healthy infrastructure has had a relatively low profile among the coalition of all levels of governments or public institutions in China over the past few years. The phrase "we're all in this together" and a well-known saying by President Xi that "clean water and green mountains are mountains of gold and silver" have been used, to an extent, to put on propaganda for the benefit of public perception or to justify other programs of unpopular public sector cuts—which is unsurprisingly a universal phenomenon across nations. Seemingly, underlying values of smart and sustainable infrastructure are widely recognized; in practice they are poorly considered. China's "nationwide carbon emissions trading scheme" has been a long-awaited proposition to curb surging greenhouse gas emissions that is running behind schedule. First tested back in 2013, regional pilot programs were carried out to force firms in industries such as power, cement and steel to cut emissions or purchase carbon permits to cover their annual allocations. Positive results were well received: accumulated trade volume from China's seven pilot regional carbon trading schemes (Beijing, Tianjin, Shanghai, Chongqing and Shenzhen, as well as the provinces of Guangdong and Hubei) reached 6 billion RMB ($863.9 million) by 2018, up from 4.7 billion RMB in 2017, according to the Ministry of Ecology and Environment. However, the replacement of the regional pilots with a nationwide emissions trading scheme has been phased in slowly, mainly as a result of (1) the need to obtain massive and accurate data, (2) the necessity to put in place new laws and regulations, as well as (3) a bureaucratic reshuffle that has hindered the work plan timeline. Outlined in 2017, a three-step process toward creating the market are inclusive of a first phase focused on developing systems for data reporting, registration and trading, a second stage on mock trading of carbon credits to test the effectiveness of the market and a final stage for the execution of spot trading.

Given the regulatory restructuring with respect to the Ministry of Ecology & Environment taking over climate duties from the National Development & Reform Commission, China has, nonetheless, been closely monitoring the outcome of the emissions trading system—its massive scale could be an important force in shaping global trends and spurring a faster transition toward green energy. The market, covering more than 1700 companies across the power and utilities sector, bears the potential to manage about a quarter of the world's carbon emissions. A true step-by-step execution: China understands that for the success of this market to happen, it needs to draw lessons from preceding experiments such as the EU's carbon market which was up and running for about three years before it was proposed. A lack of data accuracy could lead to surplus of allowances which then keeps pricing compressed, which effectively goes against the goal of keeping the cost of pollution high. All in all, this "slow" but stable start epitomizes China's desire in action to enforce on emission control and its important step in creating sustainability.

Public-Private-Partnerships (PPP)

Akin to other countries, China has resorted to PPP as an alternative public procurement tool to facilitate its effort in infrastructure development and management. PPP represents a newer form of financing infrastructure projects where governments work with the private sector to combine external capital with government funding and incentives, ideally generating revenue from the resulting projects to help defray project costs. From early stages of adoption when PPP's output was trivial compared to the total amount of public investment in China, to recent years when PPP has delivered substantial economic and social benefits crucial to future development, China has effectively set up mature financial and regulatory frameworks that promote PPP expansion over the next few years. The establishment of a PPP network was an initiative proposed by the China PPP Center of the Ministry of Finance at the Fourth Asia-Pacific High-Level Dialogue on Financing for Development in 2017. The goals of the PPP network are to (1) promote the exchange of experience among Asia-Pacific countries, (2) improve infrastructure development in the Asia-Pacific region and (3) help achieve the 2030 Sustainable Development Goals of the United Nations.

This network will also bridge communication among domestic organizations, institutional investors and foreign development agencies by giving practical support to Chinese enterprises for participating in PPP and infrastructure projects in these countries, thus motivating these organizations to pursue international cooperation under the Belt Road Initiative (BRI). As such, the network is one of the key initiatives in transforming the BRI into high-quality and sustainable development according to President Xi. Overall, the Chinese government has shown an active stance in encouraging and supporting the participation of private investors in the provision of healthy and sustainable public infrastructure and services.

According to a top Chinese economic advisor, as at the beginning of November 2019, China had nearly 7000 PPP projects under way that amount to a total investment of about 9 trillion RMB (equivalent to about $1.28 trillion). Among projects being financed, urban infrastructure, social affairs, transportation and ecological environment protection represent the bulk of the use of proceeds, accounting for approximately 90% of the total investments—a characterization at the core of the PPP model: aligning public and private markets with societal goals.

In Guizhou province, a relatively more underdeveloped area in China, Zhenxin Kindergarten was the first project that adopted this PPP model in carrying out school construction. By virtue of the cost-effectiveness and innovation underlying PPP, the goals of building new education facilities and increasing educational resources were achieved in a balanced and time-efficient manner.

In addition, the second stage of the Nanming River Water Environment Comprehensive Project is another example that applies a PPP approach by combing a Build-Operate-Transfer (BOT) model with a Transfer-Operate-Transfer (TOT) model. By adopting the approach of "local treatment, local reuse," it was able to save approximately 1.1 billion RMB in investment into the pipe network collection system and 158 million RMB in ecological water transfer costs each year. Ever since, the Nanming River has successfully transformed from a "sewage river" into a "landscape river," becoming a landmark of the capital city Guiyang. Lastly, the 89-kilometer-long expressway from Guiyang to Wengan of the Guizhou province is still by far the longest suspension bridge with a steel-truss structure across the mountainous areas of Asia. In this project, the PPP model effectively took advantage of social capital in the design, construction and operation of the bridge, and greatly enhanced project efficiency in creating an economic zone that expanded the coverage of Guiyang and facilitated robust economic and social development.

18

China's Investment in the Rest of the World

Jimena Terrazas Lozano

China, since 2014, has become the third biggest source of foreign direct investment in the world. Through its *Belt and Road Initiative*, China has managed to catalyze major infrastructure projects that would otherwise not likely to have been started in Africa, Europe and Asia. Furthermore, China has agreements in place and contracts to invest in many Latin American nations. Inevitably, as a result, Chinese foreign direct investment is helping shape the global economy and this chapter will examine such Chinese investment through a sustainability lens, looking at several case studies of China's recent interactions with a variety of such countries.

We will explore Chinese foreign direct investment in Africa and Latin America, as part of the *Belt and Road Initiative* and the CLASII (China-Latin America Sustainable Investing Initiative) showing how China has facilitated sustainable development in some of the more marginalized areas in the world. This will allow us to contextualize how successful Chinese foreign direct investment (FDI) has been in several developing nations, in contrast to a case where this has been less successful, namely, in Mexico, with suggestions of possible projects in countries such as Mexico which could further benefit from Chinese foreign direct investment in the immediate future.

In the mid-2000s, as China began to implement its "Go Out" policy, which encouraged Chinese enterprises to invest in foreign nations, a set of environmental and social guidelines appeared to ensure a more responsible and sustainable way of investing. Among the most important guidelines were the Green Credit Directive (2012), encouraging banking institutions to conduct "complete, thorough and detailed" analysis before engaging in any project; the Guidelines for Social Responsibility in Mining Investments Abroad

© The Author(s) 2020
C. Krosinsky, *Modern China*, https://doi.org/10.1007/978-3-030-39204-8_18

(2014) required companies to get informed and non-coerced consent from communities affected by mining operations; the Guidelines for Environmental Risk Management for China's Overseas Investment (2017) required Chinese companies to conduct environmental assessments, thoroughly analyzing the environmental costs and benefits and including this knowledge in their investment decision-making process; and the Standardization of Banking Services Enterprises to Go Out and Strengthen the Guidance of Control and Risk Prevention (2017) urged Chinese companies to establish complaint response mechanisms to deal with conflicts that arise and acknowledged individuals, communities, non-governmental organizations and other stakeholders involved or affected by operations (Garzon 2018, p. 17).

However, such guidelines challenged three principles that had typically characterized Chinese foreign direct investment. First, Chinese banking institutions were previously not required to have their own social and environmental standards. Under the new guidelines, they were required to engage in socially and environmentally responsible investing. Second, these institutions used to follow a "non-interference" principle, where they would only engage with the host country's government but deny participation in the decision-making processes to non-governmental organizations, communities and individuals. Third, a "deferential approach" meant that Chinese companies were only required to follow the host country's legislation but had made no further commitments beyond that (Garzon 2018, p. 10). These new guidelines now instead urged Chinese banking institutions to try to maximize welfare and minimize environmental degradation during their operations.

While these guidelines set a better precedent, they remain legally non-binding. Chinese investing is still far from perfect and such guidelines often exist in theory but are not implemented in practice. For this reason, host countries have come up with treaties, legislation and supervising organizations of their own to ensure more environmentally and socially mindful practices.

Chinese-led infrastructure projects in several nations in Africa and Latin America are worthy of further review in this regard. Projects in the eastern hemisphere are part of the *Belt and Road Initiative*, while projects in Latin America are part of CLASII (China-Latin America Sustainable Investment Initiative). In the case of African nations, the focus will be on two of the countries officially added to the Belt and Road route: Egypt and Kenya. Peru will also be examined as a case study in Latin America. These case studies seek to analyze Chinese foreign direct investment in the developing world and how it has often been a powerful tool to promote sustainable development.

Chinese Foreign Direct Investment and the Belt and Road Initiative

In 2013, Chinese president Xi Jinping announced what would become one of the most complex development strategies of the twenty-first century. The *Belt and Road Initiative* (or "One Belt One Road," as it directly translates from Mandarin) was and remains an economic strategy to connect China to other world economies through an ambitious infrastructure network. Some economists consider this modern "silk road initiative" one of the largest development plans in modern history. One Belt One Road has connected Europe, Central Asia, East Asia and Africa through railways, roads, power grids, pipelines and ports, creating a terrestrial and maritime economic route. Ultimately, China intends to integrate the economies of all countries connected by One Belt One Road to create a multinational production chain that would facilitate policy coordination, financial integration and technological exchange within countries. Furthermore, leading this initiative would position China as an economic and political hegemon in the international community.

One Belt One Road connects 67 countries, representing cumulative GDP of $2.1 trillion, almost a third of the global economy (ZiroMwatela and Changfeng 2016, p. 11). While many emerging economies will benefit from the infrastructure projects that China intends to build, the Chinese government has strategically picked some nations based on geography and resource production to provide foreign direct investment. These infrastructure projects include dams, railways, power plants and ports, among others. Chinese foreign direct investment could be used to meet the 17 sustainable development goals. For example, it is expected to help with poverty alleviation (SDG 1), improve access to clean water and sanitation (SDG 6), provide clean and affordable energy (SDG 7), enhance economic growth and employment (SDG 8) and develop industry and infrastructure (SDG 9).

These characteristics of Chinese investment in the *Belt and Road Initiative* are consistent with the principles of ESG and sustainable investing. However, some of these projects have been highly controversial due to the environmental damage or disruptions to national sovereignty that they caused. The following case studies will analyze Chinese foreign direct investment through a sustainability lens, exploring both the benefits and the limitations of each project.

Egypt

Egypt is perhaps one of the most important Chinese allies in One Belt One Road. Controlling the Suez Canal allows Egypt to control maritime trade between the Indian Ocean and the Mediterranean Sea. Egypt also connects Central Asia and the Middle East to the rest of Africa. Unsurprisingly, Egypt is the only African nation that has become an official signatory of the One Belt One Road memorandum.

The core projects that China intends to develop in Egypt is expanding the Suez Canal over the next decade, establishing an economic zone in the region and building a new administrative capital 45 km east of Cairo. These projects will require Chinese investment of $230 million and $45 billion, respectively. Moreover, the Chinese National Bank gave $1 billion in loans to the Egyptian Central Bank and $700 million to the Egyptian National Bank. Aside from the enormous contribution to economic growth and infrastructure development, the development of a new economic zone and enlargement of the Suez Canal is expected to create over 10,000 new jobs and increase other opportunities related to sustainability and development.

Along with the expansion of the Suez Canal, the Chinese and Egyptian governments also developed the Suez Canal Economic Zone, a world class trade hub along the banks of the newly expanded Suez Canal. All imports crossing through this zone are 100% exempted from duties and sales taxes (Suez Canal Economic Zone General Authority 2019, p. 4). What makes this area attractive is that it is strategically located in the main trade route between Europe and Asia, controlling approximately 8% of all world trade. The Suez Canal Economic Zone has several investment opportunities, including infrastructure, technology, automobile assembly, textiles and agri-business and Information Technology and Communications (ITC) and services. The Suez Canal Economic Zone is controlled by the General Authority of the Suez Canal Economic Zone, comprising Egyptian and Chinese experts on trade. In accordance with the Egyptian Law for Economic Zones of Special Nature (No. 83 for 2002 and amendment in 2015), companies can be 100% foreign-owned as long as they are registered and licensed as Egyptian joint stock companies, allowing them to repatriate 100% of the profits in the currency of their choice. To promote employment opportunities for Egyptian workers, the percentage of foreign employees working in each company cannot exceed 10%. Similarly, all companies are required to conduct an environmental assessment, which is reviewed by the SCEZ General Authority in partnership with the Egyptian government to ensure transparency and accountability.

The renewable sector along the Suez Canal is becoming one of the most popular investment options, given its potential for solar and wind farm development. This could have a powerful impact in reducing carbon emissions and pollution. According to their sustainability report, "The Suez Canal Economic Zone's sustainability goals are maximizing energy, water and waste efficiencies, managing developmental impacts, balancing built environment and biodiversity values and achieving best practice in urban and built design." They have also committed to 100% transparency and disclosure and have created an Environmental Committee that meets regularly to ensure compliance with environmental policy and the maximization of sustainable practices.

The SCEZ has become an economic, political and sustainability milestone in modern world history. Imagine the New Suez Canal, completed with Chinese financing and managed by a Chinese company, as the gateway between Europe and Asia. While Egypt's privileged geographical position made it an ideal candidate to receive foreign direct investment, the Suez Canal Economic Zone has set a precedent more generally demonstrating that it is possible to promote economic growth and be environmentally and socially responsible.

Kenya

As one of the fastest growing economies in Africa, Kenya is a key ally in the development of One Belt One Road projects. According to the World Bank, Kenya has a GDP of $63 billion and has experienced an economic growth of 6.1% in 2019 (World Bank 2019). In recent years, China has invested billions of dollars in infrastructural projects in Kenya.

Among such core projects are improving the Mombasa port, building a new high-tech port in Lamu and building a railway system connecting Mombasa, Nairobi and land-locked nations. The railway, perhaps the most important infrastructure project in Kenya, was expected to cost $25 billion with 90% of the project financed by the China Exim Bank. Building the port in Lamu is expected to cost $27 billion. These projects worth over $50 billion represented roughly 90% of Kenya's annual GDP.

China's investments in Kenya are likely to have countless impacts on poverty alleviation, boosting economic growth, developing infrastructure, improving access to water and energy in marginalized communities, improving mobility, among others. However, China also benefits greatly from these projects. The railway is expected to connect Kenya to Ethiopia, Rwanda and Burundi, which are exporters of raw materials to China with other projects connecting the South Sudan and Uganda to Kenya, which have been hindered in recent years by the Sudanese civil war and other armed conflicts in the region.

So far, it would seem like One Belt One Road investments in Kenya are a success and ideal examples of sustainable investment; however, these projects have several limitations in terms of interference with governance and environmental damage. The railway is expected to cross through the Tsavo East National Park and the Nairobi National Park, which serve as a natural reserve to the eastern black rhino and the African elephant, among many other endemic species. Splitting their ecosystem could severely impact migration routes, reproductive success and conservation efforts. Moreover, the construction of the standard gauge railway has displaced many Masai communities and the government had to pay millions of dollars in compensation to encourage these groups to relocate (Kushner 2016). Masai pastors have also protested the low wages that Chinese companies are offering for unskilled labor in the construction of the infrastructure projects.

The main company in charge of building the standard gauge railway in Kenya is China Communications Construction Company. According to their Environmental, Social and Governance Report, "the Company has set up a set of integrated management systems, including quality governance system, environmental management systems and occupational health and safety management systems based on international standards" (China Communications Construction Company Ltd. Social Responsibility Report 2018). They have committed to ambitious ESG goals, including reductions in emissions, lowering pollution, reducing energy consumption, supporting governance in partnering nations, complying with national and international legislation, full transparency and disclosure and supporting the One Belt One Road initiative. In practice, however, its methods are questionable, with the displacing of indigenous populations and jeopardizing endemic and endangered fauna, which is inconsistent with sustainable investment principles.

Despite the limitations of the project, China was and is still willing to invest in Kenya due to its richness in natural resources.

Chinese Foreign Direct Investment in Latin America: CLASII

Despite the recent deceleration in China's economic growth, Chinese investment in Latin America is on the rise. In 2016, Chinese loans to Latin American nations accounted for $21 billion and foreign direct investment accounted for

$10.3 billion, making the country a key player in support of Latin American economies.

However, most Chinese foreign direct investment and loans in Latin America have focused on resource extraction, as well as creating the necessary infrastructure to export raw materials. As Latin American governments continue to sign more agreements to develop infrastructure, particularly construction of hydropower plants and the extraction of oil and minerals, more environmental and social problems are likely to arise.

Given some troubling experiences with Chinese investment in the region, as well as other developing nations, Latin American countries pushed for the creation of CLASII. This initiative intends to improve the implementation of policy related to environmental and human rights as pertaining to Chinese loans and foreign direct investment. Ultimately, it seeks to promote environmental protection and sustainable development in Latin American nations. CLASII is also in charge of investigating companies and projects and providing debriefs to evaluate the viability, benefits and risks of each project that China intends to start in the region.

CLASII was created by the Bank Information Center (BIC) in Washington DC in 2014, and was based on principles of international environmental law. CLASII published the first educational tool in Spanish to inform about Chinese environmental and social guidelines and how to demand compliance in the foreign direct investment realm. The handbook "Manual Legal Sobre Regulaciones Ambientales y Sociales Chinas para los Prestamos e Inversiones *en el Exterior: Una Guia para las Comunidades Locales*" (Environmental and Social Regulations on Chinese Loans and Foreign Direct Investment: A Guide for Local Communities) has been translated to English and Portuguese and might soon be translated to other indigenous languages of the region.

CLASII has also organized workshops and mediated dialogue between NGOs, communities and Chinese companies and supported non-governmental groups in drafting petitions and complaints to address important issues related to human rights and the environment.

Peru

Fishing is the second most important economic activity in Peru after mining. According to the United Nations Food and Agriculture Organization (FAO), Peru produces approximately 30% of the world's fish flour. Fisheries primarily capture anchovy, which is used to produce flour and oil. Between 1970s and 1990s, fisheries experienced a decline in anchovy due to overharvesting. In

1992 the Peruvian government, for the first time in its history, began to regulate the amount of fish that different companies could harvest. It implemented a quota system, given increasing demand for anchovy and the increasingly short fishing seasons each year.

The implementation of individual quotas of fish forced leading companies in the market to optimize harvesting techniques to minimize bycatch. In accordance with the "Capture Limit per Embarkation Law," total sustainable catch was divided among companies that could not exceed their quota unless they bought another company's quota permits. This system is called "individual transferable quota."

China Fishery Group is a Chinese enterprise, controlled by the Pacific Andes International Holdings Ltd. China Fishery Group exports primarily to China, where demand for fish flour is on the rise. CFG Investment Peru SAC, representing China Fishery Group, was established in Peru in 2006. CFG Peru is among the top seven fisheries in Peru which control 70% of all fish production. To meet China's growing demand for fish flour, CFG wanted to expand its production, but given quotas in place this was not possible. The Chinese enterprise then decided to buy other fisheries to absorb their rights to harvest fish. In 2013, CFG Peru bought 99.1% of Copeinca, one of the largest fisheries in Peru, and the main exporter of fish flour. CFG paid $802 million for Copeinca, receiving most of its fishing quota. CFG went from having 6.2% of the total fishing quota to having 16.9%, placing it above Tecnologica de Alimentos SA, the company with the largest quota up to that point in time. Currently, China Fisheries Group has bought 33 Peruvian fishing companies and continues to increase its rights to harvest fish.

According to their sustainability report, CFG Peru follows a model of sustainability and social responsibility to ensure that it has a positive impact on the Peruvian economy, society and environment. In 2013, CFG Peru received the Friend of the Sea Certification. This means that the company is in compliance with the FAO Guidelines for Ecolabelling and Fishery Products and that the company has reduced ecosystem impact and managed fish stocks within the maximum sustainability yield. The company incurred 80 infractions during 2013 due to bycatch over 5% or over 10% of undersized juvenile catch. However, they were transparent about it and explained that it is often beyond their control whether they catch bycatch or juvenile fish. To further improve sustainability standards, they modified the drying process. They transitioned from direct fire drying to steam drying, which is considerably less polluting. CFG Peru also invested $15 million in La Planchada Plant to be able to utilize the energy released in one process to fuel another. Now the steam used for drying is also used in production processes, thus saving 40 gallons of diesel per ton of fishmeal produced. They have also installed scrubber systems to remove particulates during drying processes. Since CFG operates within the limits of the Paracas National Reserve, they have ensured that their activities do not interfere with conservation efforts in the reserve. They make sure to respect the perimeter boundaries of the reserve and do not ever fish in protected zones.

As part of their community investment project, CFG Peru has developed the "Family Nutrition Project" where they donated to schools, offered conferences and workshops to families and children to increase awareness about healthy eating and started the school program "Conciencia Ambiental" where they teach middle school children about sustainability and conservation. These projects have helped with achieving sustainable development goals 2 (zero hunger), 3 (good health and well-being) and 4 (quality education). Lastly, they partnered with Caritas Peru to offer technical training to marginalized communities to increase qualifications and employability.

Mexico

In 2014, China loaned $22 billion to Latin American countries, more than all of the loans issued by the Interamerican Development Bank and the World Bank combined in the region. Between 2003 and 2012, Chinese FDI in the world grew at an annual rate of 38% reaching $87 billion by 2012. However, despite China's growing presence in international finance, Chinese foreign direct investment in Mexico still plays a secondary and rather small role.

Compared to other Latin American nations, Mexico receives a small percentage of Chinese FDI entering Latin America. Mexico received an underwhelming amount of 0.05% of all Chinese FDI in the world and 0.36% of Chinese FDI in Latin America and the Caribbean. Between 2003 and 2012, Mexico received FDI from 102,079 enterprises, averaging almost 7300 companies per year as compared with 968 Chinese enterprises investing in Mexico, an average of 69 enterprises per year with 80% of all Chinese FDI in Mexico received through only 11 transactions.

The following section will analyze Huawei and First Automotive Work Group Corporation (FAW), two of the more significant Chinese companies, and their investments in Mexico. It will also discuss incidents that have negatively impacted Chinese investment in Mexico including the cancellation of the Mexico-Queretaro train and the cancellation of the New Mexico City

International Airport, NAICM. The point of these case studies is to illustrate why Chinese investment in Mexico has been low, despite Mexico's economic potential. While the first two cases show that investing in the country can be successful, the last two show why Chinese firms often feel distrustful of investing in a country such as Mexico.

Huawei

Among the successful precedents of Chinese foreign direct investment in Mexico is Huawei. As per Chap. 10, Huawei is a global enterprise started in China, specializing in science and technology development related to communications. In 2012, it became the biggest company in the world providing network infrastructure, telecommunications and multimedia solutions and currently specializes in manufacturing and sales of telecommunications equipment and related services both at a national level (in China) and internationally.

Huawei was established in Mexico in 2001 with merely four employees (two Mexican and two Chinese). Surprisingly, it is currently the number one provider of the three main telecommunications operators in Mexico: Telcel, Telmex and Iusacel. They also cater their services to several companies, ranging from private enterprises, to government organizations like the Instituto Mexicano de Seguro Social (Mexican Institute for Social Security), Comision Nacional del Agua (National Water Commission) and PEMEX (Mexican Petroleum). They established a manufacturing center in Guadalajara, Jalisco, in partnership with Flextronics, taking advantage of Mexico's comparative advantage in assembly lines. Similarly, they established 15 science and technology centers in Mexico City. With an initial investment in Mexico of around $50 million, Huawei currently receives gains of $1 billion annually.

Huawei has established a solid market in several Latin American countries, including Brazil, Peru and Argentina. Despite complex and unstable relations with Mexico, however, Mexico's geographical location makes it a desirable partner. Mexico is one of the fastest growing economies in the region, able to provide a growing domestic market. Its proximity to the US allows for easy access to the American market, and is an efficient way of avoiding tariffs imposed on Chinese exports since Mexico is part of the North America Free Trade Agreement, NAFTA. Lastly, it is easy to export products from Mexico to other countries in Central and South America. Nevertheless, Huawei faced a major challenge when establishing in Mexico. People were somewhat distrustful of Chinese enterprises with American fears of China spreading far enough south to hinder Mexico-China relations and, combined with preconceived beliefs that Chinese products would be of low quality, Mexicans did not always feel comfortable acquiring Huawei phones and services. This did not stop the company, now well established in the country, making important profits and playing a key role in telecommunications.

In 2014, Huawei invested $50 million in developing a third Regional Monitoring Facility in Queretaro (the other two are in China and Russia). Likewise, by 2014 the Mexico Supply Center became a hub of logistics and production, providing products and services to 42 countries in the region, including the US, Canada, Colombia and Ecuador, among others. It seems like Huawei will continue to expand and develop in Mexico in years to come.

Despite a highly successful trajectory, Huawei has had some bumps in the road and limitations while operating in Mexico. Mexico's low human capital and technology skills meant Huawei had to invest more money than expected to train local workers. Moreover, they had to import several components for manufacturing that were already domestically produced in other manufacturing centers. For this reason, Huawei has been strongly criticized for focusing on Mexico as a geographical ally and as a place where they can get cheap labor for their assembly lines only, while maintaining investment in human capital development relatively low.

Despite the criticism, Huawei has made serious attempts to contribute to Mexican society and comply with environmental and sustainability standards. They donated high-tech core switches to the Universidad Nacional Autonoma de Mexico (UNAM) and to the Instituto Tecnologico de Estudios Superiores de Monterrey (ITESM). Likewise, they have provided workshops and training in both universities through the Huawei Authorized Network Academy. They often organize competitions and offer scholarships to students interested in telecommunications and technology. During the earthquake in September 2017 in Mexico City, Huawei opened Global Centers for Assistance where technicians worked to recover telephone lines and provided assistance so people could connect with each other after the catastrophe. They also partnered with the Mexican Red Cross and Fondo Fuerza Mexico to donate food and medical supplies to people who had been affected. Their Flextronics Guadalajara headquarters received in 2019 the Gilberto Rincon Gallardo Inclusive Business Award for inclusive policies and practices. The Mexico City headquarters ranked #3 of 500 in the Transparencia Mexicana Index (Mexican Transparency Index), acknowledging their work on fighting corporate corruption and improving disclosure (Huawei Sustainability Report 2018). They also partnered with Mexican Laboratoria Coding, a program targeted at empowering young women interested in pursuing science and technology-related careers by providing mentorship, scholarships and other opportunities. This strategy has contributed to reaching the fifth Sustainable Development Goal, gender equality.

At an environmental level, in 2018 Huawei, in partnership with Flextronics, planted more than 6800 trees in Mexico. They are also striving for minimum waste operations and receiving LEED (Leader in Energy and Environmental Design) certification for all their buildings. Huawei is also striving for ambitious emissions reductions and has already started advancing toward their goal, receiving R2 certification for its efforts.

Huawei is certainly a successful example of FDI in Mexico; however, it remains one of the few cases in which Mexican-Chinese investment relations went smoothly. It is important to focus on the strengths of this project to make sure that future investments and relationships can be as successful.

Giant Motors Latin America and FAW

Another instance of successful Chinese investment in Mexico is the partnership between Giant Motors Latin America and Chinese truck manufacturing enterprise FAW.

The FAW was founded in 1953 as part of the first Five Year Plan. The Soviet Union supported China to start this company, which currently employs more than 130,000 people worldwide, has expanded to 70 countries and receives annual revenues of $26 million. FAW is the world leader in manufacturing heavy trucks, controlling 22.7% of global production in 2010.

FAW began its strategic partnership with Giant Motors Latin America (GML) in 2006. From that point on, GML chose to use the brand "FAW Trucks Mexico." Giant Motors Latin America was a 100% Mexican-owned enterprise, founded in Ciudad Sahagun, Hidalgo. When the partnership first began, it was merely a business strategy. FAW had close to no experience in the international market and allowed GML to use its brand indiscriminately. Several years later, as the brand became increasingly popular at a global scale, FAW held GML to better quality and stricter environmental standards. FAW overcame several limitations to facilitate production and assemblage in Mexico. Shipping necessary parts to assemble trucks was one of the greater challenges they faced. Auto parts would arrive several months later, rusty and often damaged. In recent years, they have managed to overcome this challenge.

While it might be surprising for a big company like FAW to be interested in partnering with and investing in a small enterprise such as GML, FAW actually benefited greatly from their cooperation. It gave FAW experience in investing abroad, relevant for the brand to expand to other countries. FAW also used Mexico as an entrance gate to the Latin American market and has been able to expand to other countries in the region since then. Free trade agreements that Mexico had previously joined were also useful for FAW. This, in combination with Mexico's proximity to the US, allowed for easy exporting to the US and Canada. This is the reason why FAW encouraged GML to use the "Hecho en Mexico" (made in Mexico) certification. GML also benefited greatly from receiving Chinese investment. They have expanded to almost every state with 20 agencies and 10 service centers.

In recent years, FAW Mexico has committed to minimizing its negative impact on the environment. This could be extremely relevant, given that vehicle pollution is one of the main pollutants in Mexico, particularly in densely populated urban areas. Heavy trucks are one of the main contributors to air pollution, smog, ground level ozone and particulate matter, which can negatively impact public health. Manufacturing more efficient diesel motors could considerably reduce air pollution in the nation. In 2012, FAW Mexico developed the GF-900 Ecotruck, which uses Euro IV technology to minimize emissions and utilize diesel in a more efficient way. One of their most recent models, GF 250, uses new technology to maximize fuel efficiency. Their GF 7000 uses a technology called ISF, which reduces emissions up to a Euro V level, making it one of the most efficient of its kind.

According to their sustainability report, FAW Mexico is fully up to date with environmental, ecological and security legislation. They have received Centro de Investigación y Asistencia Técnica del Estado de Querétaro (CIATEQ) and Meusnier certificates, which acknowledge their efficiency and effective disposal of waste. They have fully accredited the Euro IV, Centro de Investigación e Innovación Tecnológica (CIITEC), Programa de Promoción Sectorial (PROSEC) and Normas Oficiales Mexicanas (NOM) norms for acceptable carbon emissions from their vehicles and passed the Extreme Performance Test (EPT).

They are committed to full transparency by receiving audits from the Secretary of Environment and Natural Resources (SEMARNAT) and advertise themselves as a socially and environmentally responsible enterprise. Up to date, they have complied with 100% of NOM norms and received the NOM-044 certificate from PROFEPA, the organization in charge of implementing legal compliance with environmental rules in Mexico, for their outstanding performance. Despite belonging to a pollution-intensive industry, FAW Mexico has managed to follow a more sustainable and environmentally responsible path.

Just like Huawei, FAW is one of the few instances in which Chinese investment in Mexico has been successful. The case of FAW is very unique, since it is actually a Mexican-owned firm, cooperating with a Chinese firm; however, it is a good example of how successful financial cooperation between Chinese and Mexican enterprises can be while also focusing on sustainability improvement.

Chinese Investment in Mini-Hydroelectric Plants

In May 2018, the Secretary of Energy in Mexico, Pedro Joaquin Coldwell, met with China's Vice-Minister of Science and Technology, Huang Wei, and Mexican Sub-Secretary of Energy Transition, Leonardo Beltran Rodriguez. Together, they signed the agreement on Mexico-China Cooperation on Sustainable Hydroelectric Energy (Cooperacion Conjunta Mexico-China sobre Energia Hidroelectrica Sustentable). With this agreement, the Secretary of Energy (SENER) established that Mexico is open to Chinese foreign direct investment in any activities related to sustainable hydroelectric energy production (Secretaria de Energia 2019). The Mexican government hopes that this will be one of the first steps to help Mexico transition to cleaner sources of energy and achieve its goal of producing 40% of energy used in the country from renewable sources.

Joaquin Coldwell admitted that he hopes this agreement will incentivize foreign direct investment from other countries in Mexican sustainable projects, particularly those related to innovation, science and technology. As part of the energy transition project, Mexico has already established five Innovation and Clean Technology Centers to develop technologies to help the nation meet its goals. He also added that Mexico will be doubling government investment on clean technology by 2020.

After discussing different possibilities, Chinese and Mexican representatives decided that the most viable option was to build thousands of small hydroelectrical plants throughout Mexico. Currently only 17% of energy production in Mexico comes from hydroelectric power. Investing in further technological development would also increase human capital and develop expertise. However, General Electric's director in Mexico, Marco Vera, expressed concerns for this plan. He believes that Mexico should diversify its energy sources, instead of focusing exclusively on hydroelectric energy, as current Mexican President Andres Manuel Lopez Obrador has planned. He also said that Mexico should develop alliances between the private and public sector, rather than depending on Chinese foreign investment to promote sustainability in the country (Solis 2018). Moreover, he claims that Chinese investment in hydroelectric technology in other developing nations has negatively impacted the environment and communities involved.

Furthermore, there are several logistical limitations to the energy transition agreement that several enterprises and organizations have pointed out. According to the Secretary of Energy, producing a megawatt/hour with wind power or solar power in Mexico would cost around $20, while producing the same amount of energy with hydroelectric power would cost between $44 and $47 (Solis 2018).

Another limitation to the project is the current state of hydroelectric plants in Mexico. The nation has 62 hydroelectric plants, most of them in Chiapas, Michoacán, Nayarit and Jalisco. However, these plants are in a terrible condition and need considerable investment to repair their infrastructure. If operated correctly, these plants could produce 12,140 MW, but the previous administration neglected their maintenance and focused on natural gas.

Despite the evidence, Andres Manuel Lopez Obrador still believes that hydroelectric power is "Bueno y barato," good and cheap, so investment will continue to grow in future years. This will also be a unique opportunity to bridge relations between Mexico and China after several past incidents that negatively impacted relations and investors' confidence. Hopefully, this will set a precedent to foster further Chinese involvement in sustainable development in Mexico.

Failed Instances of Chinese Investment in Mexico

From previous case studies of Chinese foreign direct investment, it can be seen that Chinese sustainable investment not only is a viable option to countries such as Mexico but could also be highly beneficial to both parties. The aforementioned case studies portray Mexico-China investment relations as mostly effective and fruitful. However, in recent years, investment relations between the two countries have gone through difficult periods.

Increasing cartel violence, high corruption levels, low investment confidence, political tensions between Mexico and the US and the lack of strong institutions to protect property rights are just some of the many limitations Chinese investors have encountered in Mexico. Mexican enterprises and consumers also seem to be distrustful and fearful of Chinese companies and their products.

The next two cases will present instances that have deterred Chinese sustainable investment in Mexico. These cases were controversial and had a negative impact on China-Mexico relations, while also deterring other forms of sustainable investing in the country.

Tren Mexico-Queretaro

After being elected President of Mexico in 2012, Enrique Pena Nieto announced the construction of two major infrastructure projects that would strengthen the Mexican economy and would attract sustainable investment from abroad. One of these projects was the construction of a high-speed train connecting Mexico City to the City of Queretaro. This train would also connect four states through a 212-km-long rail.

The Mexican government initially invested 40.7 billion pesos and opened a competition where different companies both from Mexico and abroad submitted their project proposals. Several Chinese-owned companies decided to enter the competition, investing a total of $2 million in conducting environmental impact and economic assessments in the area. On November 3, 2014, the Secretary of Communication and Transport finally announced that the competition had been won by China Railway Construction Corporation. For the construction of the high-speed train, they would partner up with four Mexican companies: Gia, Prodemex, GHP and Teya. The environmental assessment conducted by China Railway Construction Corporation showed that the train operations would produce considerably less carbon emissions than the thousands of cars traveling between Mexico City and Queretaro every day. Furthermore, since Queretaro and Mexico City are within the Metropolitan Area of Mexico City, one of the biggest urban spots in the world, no natural ecosystems would be harmed by the project. The only negative environmental impact that the construction of the train might bring would be population growth in the outskirts of the urban area. This is a common phenomenon that has been exacerbated as infrastructure development is able to connect marginalized areas in the outskirts of the city to more economically productive zones.

However, three days after announcing the winners, the Mexican government announced that they would reopen the competition. Journalist Carmen Aristegui published an article, exposing that President Enrique Pena Nieto owned a $7 million house, constructed by Grupo Teya, one of the Mexican companies that had won the high-speed train construction competition (Aristegui 2014). After the alleged corruption scandal, several participating companies demanded that the Mexican government reopen the competition. In January 2015, however, the Mexican government announced the cancellation of the project due to rising oil prices and their negative impact on the Mexican economy. China Railway Construction Company demanded that Mexico pay a fine of $600 million for cancelling the contract and for the alleged corruption.

This incident helped make 2015 a historically low point for China-Mexico relations. In order to compensate for the failed investment attempts in the country, the Mexican government announced that they intended to collaborate with Chinese companies to construct the Nuevo Aeropuerto Internacional de la Ciudad Mexico, an airport that would be among the most sustainable in the world. Little did they know that this promise would also end in failure.

Mexico City New International Airport (NAICM)

When announced in September 2014 by President Nieto, the NAICM became the biggest infrastructure work in Mexico in over a century and the largest sustainable project in Latin America at the time. News that Mexico would start constructing what was deemed as "the most sustainable airport in the world" soon spread through the world. The NAICM became a sign of success in the sustainable investing field in the region, showing that it was possible to promote economic development while also protecting the environment. The development and engineering plans were conducted by the consultancy company Arup Group Limited. The architectural project was designed by Norman Foster (who also designed the Beijing Capital International Airport) and the Mexican architect Fernando Romero (who designed the Soumaya Museum in Mexico City). The financial strategy was under Grupo Aeroportuario de la Ciudad de Mexico, GACM, a state-owned company owned by the Ministry of Transportation. GACM held a 50-year concession to build, develop, operate and manage NAICM.

This airport would substitute the Benito Juarez International Airport, the busiest and one of the most unsustainable airports in Latin America. The NAICM architects were building using LEED (Leader in Energy and Environmental Design) standards and planned to achieve LEED V4 Platinum certification, an award given to buildings that are highly sustainable and do not make an impactful contribution to carbon emissions. When the Mexico City Airport Trust issued $6 billion of green bonds to finance the construction of the new airport in Texcoco, the investor community welcomed a green issuance from a sector that hadn't been linked to sustainability and the green financial markets before. This project soon became the biggest sustainable project in Latin America.

The NAICM had a sustainability strategy divided into three parts: environmental protection in the surrounding areas, sustainability standards on the construction itself and social welfare for the Texcoco community. The GACM implemented the Institutional Environmental Program which aimed to mitigate environmental damage, start reforestation projects, protect endemic fauna and flora, monitor water quality for Texcoco Lake and surrounding water bodies and prevent any accidents related to waste disposal. During the construction of the NAICM, this program reforested over 500 hectares and has aided in the protection of the white tail hare, the castellano rabbit, the cincuate snake and the Alicante lizard, all endemic species to the Valley of Mexico. Regarding the sustainability standards part of the project, the NAICM would become the first airport in the world to receive LEED certification. Engineers working on the project were committed to thorough waste management and energy efficiency both during the construction and once the airport started operations. Lastly, regarding social well-being, the project was expected to improve living standards in the east part of the city, creating thousands of employment opportunities in a highly marginalized area.

After the Mexico-Queretaro train fiasco, President Enrique Pena Nieto welcomed Chinese investment for the NAICM, hoping to amend China-Mexico relations. Beijing officials expressed their interest in the project and announced that they would discuss the possibility of investing in the new airport. However, Pena Nieto's administration was about to come to a close.

In July 2018, Andres Manuel Lopez Obrador (AMLO) was elected President of Mexico. After an informal referendum, AMLO announced that he would cancel the construction of the Mexico City New International Airport. He claimed that the land to construct the airport had been expropriated from indigenous and marginalized communities in the surrounding areas without previous consultation regarding the construction of a new airport. Moreover, the airport would be constructed over the Texcoco Lake, a sacred place for the indigenous groups of Central Mexico.

Unsurprisingly, the green airport bonds underperformed the market by as much as 200 basis points in November 2019, right before AMLO took office. The cancellation of the airport had a negative impact on market confidence and brought hard criticism to the Mexican government. Eventually, the government decided to launch a buy-back project capped at $1.8 billion of the $6 billion outstanding. While this project placated investor's concerns, the green evaluators were not pleased with the alternative project of constructing the NAICM in Santa Lucia. Moody's lowered its green bond assessment from GB5 (highest score) to GB1 (lowest score), noting that the proceeds (40% of scoring) no longer constituted qualifying environmental projects. S&P withdrew its green evaluation report, given that the project had changed so much from what it initially was before AMLO's presidency.

The cancellation of the NAICM set an ominous precedent on sustainable investing in Mexico. However, many people considered that while the airport would be a world example of environmental sustainability, interfering with indigenous governance and affecting marginalized communities would make the project inadmissible for some sustainable investing indexes. The Texcoco airport is currently more than half-way built, negatively impacting Texcoco Lake's ecosystem, and the government has just started to build a completely new airport facility in Santa Lucia.

The cancellation of the NAICM also affected international investor's trust in Mexico. After so many investment failures, China stopped perceiving Mexico as a potential ally or as a regional hegemon. This perception has heavily affected their willingness to invest in the country.

Potential Investment Opportunities for China in Mexico

Based on negative experiences that Chinese investors have had in Mexico, it becomes clearer why China is investing less in the country relative to other Latin American nations and relative to Mexico's economic power and potential. However, positive experiences with companies like Huawei and Sinohydro show that it is possible to have successful financial relations between the two countries. While AMLO's presidency has been interpreted as a negative omen for investing in Mexico, the current president has announced several infrastructure projects that could benefit from Chinese investment for their development.

President Andres Manuel Lopez Obrador has announced projects to be completed during his administration including the Tren Maya (Mayan Train). While the OECD and other environmental organizations have strongly opposed some of the announced projects due to their potential negative environmental impacts, AMLO is set on completing these infrastructural works in the next few years. Working with Chinese companies that have a reputation for developing infrastructure in less developed countries, while minimizing environmental damage, could benefit Mexico under these circumstances. In this section we will explore how Chinese companies could aid Mexican companies in completing infrastructure projects and how this could strengthen China-Mexico relations.

Tren Maya

The Tren Maya or Mayan Train is a 1525-km railroad in Mexico that would traverse the Yucatan Peninsula, connecting Mayan archaeological sites in the states of Chiapas, Tabasco, Campeche, Yucatan and Quintana Roo, with a total of 15 stations. It will be constructed using the National Fund for Tourism

Development and it is estimated to cost $7.4 billion and allow for the transportation of 8000 passengers daily. However, an alternative estimate conducted by a public policy think tank declared that the train would cost $25.3 billion, supported by the 90% cost overrun of the Mexico-Toluca railway project (Barragan 2017).

While the Tren Maya expects to run with 100% emission-free locomotives, the negative impacts to the Mexican rainforest during its construction and operations are a factor to consider. The Tren Maya will cross though the Calakmul Biosphere Reserve. Calakmul is the largest rainforest reserve in the country, occupying a considerable area of the state of Tabasco. Proceeding with the construction would threaten endemic species such as jaguar, puma, tapir, white lipped pecari, saraguato monkey, spider monkey, king vulture and the Mexican crested eagle. Moreover, the construction of the rails would require the cutting of thousands of trees, including mahogany and cedar, which are necessary to maintain the ecosystem equilibrium. The construction of train stations along the route would also facilitate irregular human settlements in the middle of the rainforest, causing pollution and disturbances to the natural environment.

The rails would also interfere with biological corridors which facilitate species migration between Center and North America. Jaguars depend on these corridors to expand their ecological niche and, according to the National Alliance for Jaguar Conservation, 2000 jaguars (approximately half of all jaguars living in the wild in Calakmul) would be threatened by the project.

While the Mexican government announced that they are currently working on an environmental impact assessment, they will be starting the construction concurrently. President Lopez Obrador claims that he has already received the rainforest's approval to construct the Tren Maya through a shamanic ritual in which he communicated with the rainforest itself. This project, as it currently is, is not an environmentally responsible form of investment.

Given the risks to the environment that this project poses, Mexico would benefit greatly from working with a company that has already developed railway projects in similar ecosystems and which has successfully conducted environmental impact assessments. China Railway Construction Corporation is one of the main participants of the *Belt and Road Initiative*. It has successfully developed projects in Zambia, Ghana, Angola and Indonesia, among other nations. It has extensive experience building railways in rainforest ecosystems following environmental legislation to minimize negative impacts to ecosystems. Opening the Tren Maya project to Chinese investment could be extremely beneficial to Mexico. First, the country would benefit from the expertise of other enterprises to promote sustainable development and protect the Yucatan ecosystem. Second, this would be a perfect opportunity to amend relations with China, positioning Mexico as an ally and an ideal candidate for foreign direct investment.

Conclusion

Judging from how successful Chinese foreign direct investment has been in enhancing sustainable development in developing nations, there are opportunities to expand on this in countries such as Mexico. Controversial political issues and project cancellations have led to Mexico-China relations becoming stressed at times but there is now much to learn from and, especially as China continues to quickly learn and adapt, there are many opportunities for China to work with more countries together toward sustainable development in the immediate future.

References

Aristegui, Carmen. 2014. La Casa Blanca de Enrique Pena Nieto. *Aristegui noticias.* Retrieved December 2019, from https://aristeguinoticias.com/0911/mexico/la-casa-blanca-de-enrique-pena-nieto/

Barragan, Sebastian. 2017. China Reclama a Mexico 11 mil millones por cancelacion del tren Mexico-Queretaro. *Aristegui noticias.* Retrieved December 2019, from https://aristeguinoticias.com/2211/mexico/china-reclama-a-mexico-11-mil-millones-por-cancelacion-del-tren-mexico-queretaro/

China Communications Construction Company Limited. 2018. Annual Report. H Share. Retrieved December 2019, from http://en.ccccltd.cn/investorrelations/announcement/201904/P020190430666124841547.pdf

Garzon, Paulina. 2018. Handbook on Chinese Environmental and Social Guidelines for Foreign Loans and Investments: A Guide for Local Communities. *Bank Information Center.* Retrieved December 2019, from https://bankinformationcenter.cdn.prismic.io/bankinformationcenter%2F5ff4145c-ceaa-4760-85b6-67397e3a220d_handbook+on+chinese+e+%26+s+guidelines+for+foreign+l+%26+i+2019.pdf

General Authority for Suez Canal Economic Zone. 2019. The Suez Canal Economic Zone. Retrieved December 2019, from https://www.sczone.eg/

Huawei Investment & Holding Co., Ltd. 2018. Sustainability Report. Retrieved December 2019, from https://www-file.huawei.com/-/media/corporate/pdf/sustainability/2018/2018-csr-report-en.pdf?la=en

International Development Association. 2019. World Bank Group. Retrieved December 2019, from https://ida.worldbank.org

Kushner, Jacob. 2016. Controversial Railway Splits Kenya's Park, Threatens Wildlife. National Geographic. Retrieved December 2019, from https://www.nationalgeographic.com/news/2016/04/160412-railway-kenya-parks-wildlife/

Secretaria de Energia. 2019. Gobiernos de Mexico y China firman acuerdo de cooperacion conjunta sobre energia sustentable. Gobierno de Mexico. Retrieved December 2019, from https://www.gob.mx/sener/articulos/gobiernos-de-mexico-y-china-firman-acuerdo-de-cooperacion-conjunta-sobre-energia-hidroelectrica-sustentable-157790?idiom=es

Solis, Arturo. 2018. Mexico no puede depender solo de energia hidroelectrica. *Forbes Mexico*. Retrieved December 2019, from https://www.forbes.com.mx/mexico-no-puede-depender-solo-de-energia-hidroelectrica-ge/

ZiroMwatela, Raphael, and Zhao Changfeng. 2016. Africa in China's One Belt, One Road Initiative: A Critical Analysis. *Journal of Humanities and Social Sciences*. Retrieved December 2019, from http://content.csbs.utah.edu/~mli/Econ%20 5420-6420-Fall%202018/Zhao-Africa%20in%20Belt%20and%20Road%20 Initiative.pdf

19

China as a Leader on Green Bonds

Nimish Garg and Cary Krosinsky

In addition to being a leader in both green finance policy and infrastructure investing, China has also become a leading issuer of green bonds. Having seen its first green bond created in 2015, China has gone on to issue over $36 billion of green bonds in 2016 alone, accounting for both 39% of total global issuance and seven of the ten largest issuances. Today, China is the second largest green bond country in the world (Ken 2018).

China's central government and municipalities are both highly focused on promoting and issuing green bonds. As such, all regions of China (aside from the Northeast) have issued green bonds. For example, Beijing aims to almost double its subway lines to 1000 km by using green bonds as financing. Municipalities can and do also provide incentives. For example, loans for green finance in Jiangsu have interest rates subsidized by 30% per Sean Kidney, head of the Climate Bonds Initiative (Zengkun 2019).

Private companies also contribute to the boom in green bond issuance, in part due to a strong push from the central government. For example, China allows banks and businesses to borrow from the central bank at a lower rate and receive subsidized interest payments of up to 12% of the interest rate. Banks, in particular, can bundle their existing green loans into a new bond with a longer duration, lower risk and lower interest rates, allowing them to issue even more new bonds.

Increases in regulation and the growth of private, municipal and national contributions have helped encourage financial centers from around the world to tap into the growing green bond market. For example, in 2018, the China Construction Bank listed a $561 million green bond on the newly formed Luxembourg Green Exchange, making it the first Chinese institution to do so

© The Author(s) 2020
C. Krosinsky, *Modern China*, https://doi.org/10.1007/978-3-030-39204-8_19

Table 19.1 Five largest green bonds issued by China over the past three months

Name	Amount issued ($)	Issue date	Maturity	External review
Bank of China	2,000,000,000	Oct-19	Oct-21	N/A
China Construction Bank	1000,000,000	Oct-19	Oct-22	N/A
China Construction Bank Corporation	500,000,000	Oct-19	Oct-22	N/A
China Development Bank	412,480,000	Nov-19	Nov-22	N/A
Bank of China	350,000,000	Oct-19	Oct-22	N/A

Source: Climate Bonds Initiative (2019a, b, c)

(Morris 2019). In 2019, the FTSE Russell also launched its Chinese Green Bond Index, dedicated to specifically tracking Chinese green bonds (FTSE Russell 2019).

Depicted in Table 19.1 are five of China's largest green bonds issued over the past three months.

Outsider Access to Chinese Green Bonds

Although international investors have begun to consider China's green bonds, Chinese capital markets have historically been difficult to access for foreign investors and there is still a lot of room for growth. In 2017, only 6.6 of the $38.6 billion of Chinese bonds were issued abroad. Currently, there are three ways that international investors can invest in Chinese green bonds.

First is the Bond Connect program, a mutual market scheme that allows Chinese investors to invest in overseas markets and vice versa. Prior to Bond Connect, foreign investors needed to go through a lengthy process to open an account with many restrictions; this was the case largely because authorities wanted to control the monetary policy and the exchange rate of the RMB.

Second would be through the Direct China Interbank Bond Market (CIBM Direct), launched by the central bank in 2016. Bond Connect is more practical for outside investors, as they can conduct account opening, trading and settlement in the offshore market while the whole process is completed in the onshore market with CIBM Direct. Bond Connect is more centralized than CIBM Direct, in which investors must rely heavily on onshore bond settlement agents. Overall, Bond Connect improves operational efficiency by shortening the approval process (Invesco 2017).

The *third* way would be for Chinese issuers to list their bonds offshore, as exhibited by the Luxembourg exchange example. This is the fastest process of the three, but is limited to Chinese offshore bonds. It gives Chinese banks access to foreign currency and lower interest rates (as some countries' bonds have lower interest rates, allowing Chinese banks to proportionally decrease their interest rates in these countries) (Yao and Larsen 2018).

China's Future

While there has been increased interest from international investors in Chinese bonds, there still remain a number of challenges to achieving scale. These challenges include understanding how Chinese green bonds differ from the Green Bond Principles, which are widely viewed as the international green bond standard, and further opening up China's capital markets to facilitate foreign investment in green projects across the country.

China's 2017 Green Progress Report suggested that 3–4 trillion RMB (~$600 billion) should be directed to green investments annually in order for China to meet its environmental goals (银行_财经_中国网). Given the scale of this targeted investment, the transition to greening China's bond market must happen more quickly. To remedy such issues and meet its environmental goals, China is working to both develop clearer legislation and build international initiatives.

In terms of legislation, the Green Finance Committee of China is collaborating with the EIB to match its green bond standards to worldwide standards. This should allow investors to apply their existing knowledge to the Chinese market, making them feel more comfortable with the investment process. In November 2017, the Committee completed the first step—providing a framework to compare the Chinese Central Bank's standards to those of the EIB. Next, the NDRC will go through a similar process to standardize enterprise bonds (银行_财经_中国网).

China's *Belt and Road Initiative*, outlined in previous chapters, will also lead to fixed investment that can be financed by green bonds, further providing methods to "green" the Belt Road Initiative (BRI) (Ken 2018).

By sector, most recently, 44% of green bonds were dedicated to renewable energy, 25% to clean transportation (increasing further per the Climate Bonds Initiative, always check their website for latest trends on Chinese green bonds), 11% to agriculture/forestry, 10% to water, 9% to infrastructure and 1% to waste management (Oguh and Tanzi 2019).

How Much Is Enough

By 2019, annual issuance of global green bonds reached just over $250 billion and the total value of green bonds recently exceeded $1 trillion in total (Climate Change News 2018). The market is poised to grow, as green bonds still constitute a relatively small part of the $110 trillion global bond market, and regions such as Europe alone are predicted to need hundreds of billions of dollars of bonds per year to reach emission targets set during the 2015 Paris Agreement negotiations. Experts believe that by the early 2020s, worldwide annual issuance of green bonds will reach $1 trillion per year, more than six times the current levels (Climate Bonds Initiative 2019a, b, c).

Green Bond Processes

The Green Bond Principles recommend that bond issuers provide information about the process for project evaluation and selection, use of proceeds, management of proceeds, impact reporting and second party verification. Processes for project evaluation and selection provide more detail, giving information on the specific projects that fit the use of the proceeds category chosen, the criteria used for determining environmental impact, and so on. Use of proceeds entails choosing specific categories which each green bond will support, such as renewable energy or pollution prevention. Management of proceeds offers more details about the monetary component of the bond, such as how much of the bond will be used for refinancing old projects versus how much will be used for new project finance. Reporting provides an annual update of how the funds have been used, and what impacts have been made so far. Separate verification makes sure that the green bond issuer is following guidelines that are in the spirit of a green bond (Municipal Securities Rulemaking Board 2018).

Benefits of Issuing and Buying Green Bonds

Although issuers need to develop impact reports and pay for a second opinion to confirm that a green bond is truly green, benefits can outweigh the cost of such assurance. Green bond issuers can highlight the green nature of such assets, potentially useful for marketing and attracting environmentally conscious investors, in turn encouraging further demand during investor roadshows (Climate Bonds Initiative 2019a, b, c).

On the flip side, investors can earn tax-exempt income through green bonds, experience personal satisfaction for helping on environmental challenges and young investors in particular can see the impact of longer-duration investments throughout the course of their lives. Green bonds can also at times have a higher dividend than might have otherwise been assigned due the high demand for green bonds (which can lead to lower borrowing costs and expenditures) (Kenny 2019). Moreover, green bonds are an alternative source of investment, are arguably good hedge vehicles of sorts and can mitigate risk in portfolios. They also allow institutional investors to accommodate client requests and can provide geographic diversity, risk mitigation and positive impact.

Challenges with Green Bonds

Despite the positives green bonds can offer, the fact that green bonds are a relatively new construct can also bring challenges. Although green bonds are growing quickly, there could be liquidity challenges to overcome when investors look to exit positions from what are somewhat nascent green bond markets. Furthermore, in spite of the creation of green bond standards, these standards are voluntary and can sometimes be misconstrued by certain issuers. For example, although a bond issuer could state that the bond proceeds will be directed toward renewable energy, in reality, proceeds could be used for nuclear power; though such an investment technically "fits" the bond's claim, it can also be controversial.

Furthermore, even if bond issuers follow the Green Bond Principles (they can also follow other international principles such as the Green Loan Principles), the criteria used for second opinions can widely differ across providers. Overall, there is still work to be done as regards standardizing green bond frameworks, including in China. There is also a conundrum of sorts, whereby there is a clear desire to increase the flow of capital to green bonds more generally, yet ensuring such bonds are truly green, and not "greenwashed," comes with additional cost. Finally, some claim that green bonds can yield lower returns than standard bonds, though this is debated (Moskowitz 2019).

Types of Green Bonds

The four main types of green bonds are use of proceeds bonds, asset-backed bonds, project bonds and pure play bonds. Use of proceeds bonds are issued by large, investment-grade issuers, used solely for a group of green projects.

These constitute the majority of green bonds issued to date. Asset-backed bonds are offered by pools of smaller assets for smaller projects, such as leases for rooftop solar panels. Project bonds are issued for a specific green project, such as a large wind farm. Finally, pure play bonds are issued by companies that deal exclusively in environmentally based projects. All bonds issued by these companies are green by definition (Bank of America 2017).

Conclusion

Ultimately, green bonds are making a useful impression but still have further room to grow to fully achieve and help create adequate levels of sustainability. In China, the future is bright for green bonds. Chinese authorities are working diligently to increase internationally compliant bonds and are urging locals to partake in green investment through heavy subsidies. China is expected to continue to play a leading role in green bond issuance, and it's expected that the rest of the world will follow suit.

Other useful reports on green bonds in China

1. https://www.caixinglobal.com/2018-07-04/for-bond-investors-in-china-its-not-easy-buying-green-101292614.html
2. https://www.trucost.com/publication/environmental-performance-based-assessment-framework-support-china-green-bond-market/
3. https://www.climatebonds.net/files/files/China%202018%20H1%20Report_EN%20final%281%29.pdf

References

Bank of America. 2017. How Green Bonds Work. Retrieved August 20, 2019, from https://www.washingtonpost.com/sf/brand-connect/bank-of-america/green-bonds/?noredirect=on

Climate Bonds Initiative. 2019a. Explaining Green Bonds. Retrieved August 20, 2019, from https://www.climatebonds.net/market/explaining-green-bonds

———. 2019b. Green Issuance Surpasses $100 Billion Mark for 2019: First Time Milestone Is Reached in First Half: TEG to Open New Pathways Towards First $1 Trillion Says Climate Bonds. Retrieved August 20, 2019, from https://www.climatebonds.net/resources/press-releases/2019/06/green-issuance-surpasses-100-billion-mark-2019-first-time-milestone

———. 2019c. Labelled Green Bonds Data: Latest 3 Months. Retrieved January 1, 2020, from https://www.climatebonds.net/cbi/pub/data/bonds?items_per_page=All&order=field_bond_amt_issued&sort=desc

Climate Change News. 2018. Ex-UN Climate Chief Calls for Green Bonds to Hit $1 Trillion by 2020. Retrieved January 3, 2020, from https://climatechangenews.com/2018/03/21/ex-un-climate-chief-calls-green-bonds-hit-1-trillion-2020/

FTSE Russell. 2019. FTSE Russell Launches Chinese Green Bond Index Series. Retrieved August 20, 2019, from https://www.ftserussell.com/press/ftse-russell-launches-chinese-green-bond-index-series

Invesco. 2017. Bond Connect: Linking China's Onshore and Offshore Bond Markets. Retrieved August 20, 2019, from https://apinstitutional.invesco.com/dam/jcr:5368a863-2cf9-4f3f-81b3-a8ec9a3a68ee/FI_20171117_BondConnect LinkingChinaonshore-Nov2017.pdf

Ken, Hu. 2018. China Is Shifting Green Bond Market with Green Financing. Retrieved August 20, 2019, from https://www.scmp.com/business/banking-finance/article/2117507/china-shifting-green-bond-market-green-financing

Kenny, Thomas. 2019. How Green Bonds Allow You to Invest in Eco-Friendly Projects. Retrieved August 20, 2019, from https://www.thebalance.com/what-are-green-bonds-417154

Morris, Harvey. 2019. China Emerges as Key Player in Green Bonds Market. Retrieved August 20, 2019, from http://www.chinadaily.com.cn/a/201903/11/WS5c855866a3106c65c34edc7f.html

Moskowitz, Dan. 2019. Opportunities and Risks of Green Bond Investing. Retrieved August 20, 2019, from https://www.investopedia.com/articles/investing/081115/green-bonds-benefits-and-risks.asp

Municipal Securities Rulemaking Board. 2018. About Green Bonds. Retrieved August 20, 2019, from http://www.msrb.org/~/media/Files/Resources/About-Green-Bonds.ashx?

Oguh, Chibuike, and Alexandre Tanzi. 2019. Global Debt of $244 Trillion Nears Record Despite Faster Growth. Retrieved August 20, 2019, from https://www.bloomberg.com/news/articles/2019-01-15/global-debt-of-244-trillion-nears-record-despite-faster-growth

Yao, Wang, and Mathias Larsen. 2018. International Investors Eye China's Green Bonds. Retrieved August 20, 2019, from https://www.chinadialogue.net/article/show/single/en/10387-International-investors-eye-China-s-green-bonds

Zengkun, Feng. 2019. How China Grew Its US$30 Billion Green Bond Market. Retrieved August 20, 2019, from https://www.eco-business.com/news/how-china-grew-its-us30-billion-green-bond-market/

银行_财经_中国网. http://finance.china.com.cn/money/bank/. Accessed 31 Aug 2019.

20

Key Recommendations

Cary Krosinsky

A Ten-Step Investment Framework for Navigating China

With all of the above in mind, from China's long and more recent history, to its ongoing environmental and social conditions and governance challenges, the fact remains that China is one of the world's largest economies, expected to become the largest shortly, and so how can an investor best navigate the country's varying risks and opportunities?

A ten-step framework for investor consideration begins to emerge and will almost certainly evolve over time, but here's a useful, current-day perspective.

1. When looking on a global scale when it comes to what's necessary regarding climate change, as well as local conditions on the ground (and in the air), coal keeps coming up as a most critical issue that can be attacked head on. Investors should expect increased pressure on coal production and use in China (including utilities), both internally from its own citizens seeking better living conditions for their families and as alternative energy sources continue to become cheaper and more readily available. Investors around the world continue to commit to not financing coal-related enterprises, with Chinese banks increasingly seen as lenders of last resort. Investors would be wise to ensure that their investments across asset class, both active and passive, avoid companies that have significant involvement in coal-related industries, and to establish minimum standards in all sectors that help avoid the significant price crash that can come from "observation of the moment" recognition of companies and sectors that become no longer necessary or "excess to global requirements."

© The Author(s) 2020
C. Krosinsky, *Modern China*, https://doi.org/10.1007/978-3-030-39204-8_20

2. In addition to coal, the other perhaps most easily transformed sector of the Chinese economy is transportation, specifically cars and trucks, as the country has largely built its high-speed train infrastructure already. More subways are also fully expected in its increasingly important secondary cities. China has been putting as much effort as any country into battery storage research and the development and encouragement of electric vehicles. China's recent economic slowdown has lowered, at least for now, the local demand for automobiles, but Chinese policy continues to favor its citizens buying cars that qualify for "green" license plates especially in cities such as Beijing where air conditions will make these policies stick. Watch for China to become a global leader in electric vehicles and related technology, and to benefit from eventual global exporting. Warren Buffett became a large shareholder in BYD on this premise long ago, for example. More research and caution on a per company basis is always critically important, more on this in the Key Recommendations 2 section to follow.

3. China's ongoing race to be a leader in global technology more generally, as seen in the successful rise of its now largest companies from a market value perspective such as Tencent and Alibaba, is likely to continue. This is manifesting in many ways, from innovative venture capital opportunities across sectors such as healthcare and alternative energy technology to opportunities that help alleviate poverty such as providing credit access to more economically challenged regions, investment opportunities figure to manifest pretty much in every direction, including the largest companies and smaller startups that can quickly catch fire. The development of technology creates good jobs, even if it also at times eliminates less efficient segments of economies, arguably exacerbating inequality; it does encourage efficiencies which China more generally would likely benefit from, so expect the rise of technology to continue to generate a wide variety of opportunities.

4. Corporate strategy and culture is a critical component to the understanding of the potential success of any company as it competes within its sector for market share on a global basis. Watch for this to become the key lens for evaluating Chinese companies, more on this in the Key Recommendations 2 section that immediately follows. Strategy and culture are critical components to help understand whether companies have what it takes to thrive from a growth, productivity and risk management perspective, which is a lens any fund manager or analyst needs to know. Is the company I'm investing in growing at the rate I expect, and how is it likely to do regarding future market share, and are its products, services and operations more efficient? How is the company doing at understand-

ing and managing its risks, so it can avoid that sort of 50% price collapses seen in the recent past by a number of European companies? These are global dynamics such as the Value Driver Model describes in more detail (UN Global Compact 2013).

5. China is opening to foreign capital and increasingly allowing foreign investors to operate in the country. This is a recent phenomenon, but China has as a result opportunities to both (a) develop its own financial sector largely from scratch taking on modern techniques and strategies, and (b) allow for the setting up of publicly traded subsidiaries of foreign investors as well. Perhaps this latter possibility would be especially intriguing to watch out for and encourage. Modern Chinese financial institutions could, once successful in China, expand across Asia especially in ASEAN countries where economies will grow and opportunities will continue to emerge, and sustainability and impact-minded finance figures to play an ever increasing role at trying to solve societal challenges on the ground.

6. Trust and integrity are always important in business, but especially in countries such as China (see Chap. 21), and investible organizations that best develop trust will continue to emerge as winners. This is the essence of private equity, where companies have few owners, who have large if not majority stakes, making it a mandate to manage environmental and social issues, but most of all to ensure that there is trust and integrity in place and that it is maintained over time. During the recent trade war period, private equity and venture capital didn't slow down at all; in fact, renewable venture capital was larger in China than in any other country often enabled by Western investment (Bloomberg New Energy Finance 2019). Interestingly, the Chinese government of course is often a significant owner of every Chinese company, making the government in effect just another large strategic owner, much like private equity has become on a global basis. The difference between the two is increasingly down to who is best managing risks and opportunity, and who best develops trust and can maintain integrity, so the opportunity is the same. Both private equity managers and the Chinese government will benefit when well-run private organizations, including state-owned enterprises, can be turned into public companies at levels of high valuation, and managing for sustainability risk and opportunity (Krosinsky et al. 2008) is beneficial to such valuations.

7. The imperative for collaboration is clear, the focus of this book of course and the view of many leading investment experts such as Ray Dalio. Investment leaders such as Blackstone's Steve Schwartzman also have a

long-standing interest and many close connections to China and its government. The largest investment institutions such as Fidelity, Vanguard and BlackRock are all actively pursuing business, deals and market share in the country, mindful of the sizable opportunities. Investment opportunities are likely to arise directly from the cooperation imperative and across asset class, making this another category ripe for further examination and exploration. As climate change figures worsen, so does the urgency for collaboration and overcoming arguably more petty differences. The trade war is arguably a technology race and one that would and perhaps will occur between companies, as it would be expected to, and if we can successfully put that in the past, collaborative opportunities are likely to emerge, especially those underestimated and undervalued at present might prove to be the most lucrative of all to pursue.

8. Transparency is on the rise in China, with mandated disclosure already coming, and while most companies are being caught unawares (South China Morning Post 2020), companies who get this right figure to thrive in the new environment and will almost certainly be rewarded as more trustworthy. Expect improvements in transparency to increasingly be seen as driving financial opportunity.

9. The development of minimum standards across sector, the Seventh Tribe of Sustainable Investing (Krosinsky et al. 2017), figures to be a growing mechanism for positive change, especially given the growth of passive investing. Indexes will be strongest when avoiding the biggest financial losers and this dynamic also helps bring sustainability considerations into any necessary transition enabled by investment in public companies. Watch for more on this in the years to come, but ESG often has already been something of a red flag indicator, typically one of the more frequent applications of investment strategy within ESG integration. Data on Chinese companies is coming due to mandatory disclosure, making minimum standards potentially even more effective in a country such as China.

10. China's investments overseas continue to be an important dynamic; as per Chap. 18, the country has until recent times been one of the largest foreign investors in the world. In the 2020s, as China continues to learn and adapt, watch for opportunities to emerge in China as regards their ability to invest successfully and drive positive change elsewhere as underestimated investment opportunities of their own.

Measuring Chinese Companies on ESG+

We would like to suggest that in some ways the ESG conversation has been somewhat backwards.

Instead of building databases filled with static environmental and social data items and then trying to figure out what to do with this information, we should instead:

1. figure out what outcomes we seek,
2. pinpoint the strategies we need to deploy and that can be scaled for purpose,
3. determine what data we need to see how we are doing,
4. understand industry-specific policy frameworks within which companies are operating and
5. consider the government's political structure and stability where companies have major business exposure.

This way, ESG data can be both specifically helpful and useful.

The outcomes we seek would be best summarized by the sustainable development goals, making clear what we need to solve for by 2030. It's a great resource, but it doesn't come with a roadmap for investors.

Hence, step two is critical, what should investors do, and, most importantly, what are they doing already that works to satisfy both sustainability and financial goals.

Once we figure out the right case studies, then we can focus on deploying such strategies to necessary levels of scale and that's the main reason for the investor profiles we have provided earlier in the book, to start building case studies of success that we can build from.

It's also important to understand the context within which investments are made, and we increasingly feel that the qualitative aspects of investment analysis are the most important, especially when it comes to establishing financially successful ways to invest with sustainability fully embedded.

In particular, when you look at fund managers that are the most financially successful at sustainable investing, who manage to beat benchmarks after fees over time, it tends to be the more sophisticated, thoughtful managers such as Generation Investment Management of London who often do their own research at best using existing data from providers such as MSCI but more often do their own due diligence and arrive at their own conclusions.

Few funds can boast the performance numbers of Generation Investment Management of London, which has deployed a unique, financially outperforming, active approach to sustainable investing since its founding in 2004.

Their core equity fund regularly posts five-year returns around 18%, justifying their relatively high fee structure.

This is all the more impressive in an era where active managers struggle to meet benchmarks. Other firms that take similar approaches, such as Stewart Investors, also post similar performance strength and mostly do their own research to better understand the companies they intend to invest in, and this becomes something of a trend that any active investor should be considering given this financial success, especially as environmental and other societal issues are only expected to accelerate.

Enhanced green fundamentals add considerations of financial performance, corporate culture and strategy, government policy and political dynamics to existing fundamentals research, and this can and should apply not only to public companies, put also to privately run organizations as well including state-owned enterprises.

In our book *Evolutions in Sustainable Investing*, we offered a wider ESGFQ model, where F is the business or financial case, without which no sustainability strategy can be sustained, and Q is the quality of management, its culture and business plans as distinct and separate from traditional corporate governance measures such as board diversity or executive incentive packages.

On strategy, Generation, for example, first takes a thematic assessment of large global challenges whether climate change, access to clean water, healthcare and similar issues; they regularly liaise with a panel of experts to update priority issues seasonally then look for big picture solutions that can meet those challenges. This big picture approach leads to a short list of global companies for further attention where corporate strategies align. For example, low-carbon urbanization? Look for sustainable construction materials companies.

After finding focal points, they focus deeply on culture, performing interviews with company management, employees and customers, and examine reviews from supplier, consider compensation incentives and governance structures. Companies are people, and the best companies are where people put forth their best work. This requires adept management, trust and a purposeful vision that inspires its people. Each company receives a score, considered side by side with traditional financial fundamentals, and this usually takes hard work to ascertain.

Assessing corporate culture is difficult and comes with a cost, but this cost could be shared more broadly across more investors and minimized as a result. Both macro and micro perspectives can be equally important, and maintaining buy/sell disciplines that act on such research is important, and, as a reward for hard work, managers can uncover market inefficiencies to gain alpha as the likes of Generation and Stewart have experienced to the benefit of their end investors.

And as Generation and Stewart see things, we also see this as the best approach to understanding Chinese companies.

As presented later in the concluding Guanxi chapter, countries like China and ASEAN countries have their distinct historical and cultural backgrounds. In a society that was predominantly rural and built around families and closed communities, "relationships" or "networking" sometimes takes an important role over rules, regulations and even laws.

Political environments and industry policies that a company has to operate within can be very diverse, particularly to those multinationals that seek to regionally diversify such as General Electric, Microsoft, Facebook and General Motors.

For example, during the recent trade war between China and the US in 2019, Tesla was still able to construct and operate its first overseas Gigafactory in Shanghai, rolling out its first China-made Tesla car within 357 days of the launch announcement; while GM China's sales decreased 12.2% for the second quarter of 2019, slumping 17.5%.

What we call ESG+, as a result, involves integrating additional factors, not only F and Q, but also P1 and P2, alongside existing ESG considerations to provide investors a broader and more accurate picture of a company's business case in both micro and macro perspectives. Closely watching and constantly evaluating SDG-related industry policies (or what we call P1), such as electric vehicle developmental guidelines, and the political dynamics on future sustainable development (or P2) of the country, such have long been exhibited in President Xi's "2 Mountains Theory," can help investors better understand the environment within which a company is operating and which will have significant impacts on its long-term business survivability and sustainability.

Asian markets such as China are where this approach works particularly well, especially given a lack of reliable ESG data and where these expanded ESG+ factors are essential components to be considered.

See Appendix 3 for an example of a report assessing the strategy and culture of a prominent Chinese company attempting to assist the low-carbon transition through the manufacturing of electric vehicles, Great Wall Auto.

This profile does not emphasize non-decision useful metrics or rehashed news items. Rather, the focus is on company management, corporate culture and whether their strategy is positioned for success in the light of sustainability and financial trends.

Critical for success after all is whether a company can achieve its desired impact which requires that the company not fail financially but rather thrive and deliver its better impact through increased sales of its better products and so on.

At the end of the day, we need to know on a forward-looking basis which companies have (1) the right business strategy, (2) the best culture (including governance and stakeholder interaction) and (3) a business case with room to grow.

Companies and investors can achieve these three factors, creating the sort of positive dynamic that can tip financial markets in general in a better direction. When enough investors influence corporate strategy directly, companies improve, as does financial performance.

We believe ESG+ can and should be the future of all investing.

Reframing Modern Economies

Does anyone really believe China is still an emerging market?

Everyone I ask says no, and often of course not. The country is still coming up in many ways, especially on the basis of per capita GDP compared with a country such as the US, but we would like to suggest that the older frames no longer work work particularly well.

Here is a suggestion for what we think is a better way forward.

Whether it was the old first world, second world or third world categorizations or the more recent developed/developing/frontier market ways of defining country status, and such as are still largely in place, these seem to be falling behind in a world with a rapidly rising Asia including ASEAN countries becoming more significant, modern players.

What we would like to suggest instead is a sliding scale of

1. **mature** or
2. **evolving** or
3. **challenged** markets, countries and economies.

China is of course still evolving, but heading toward a stronger case for becoming recognized as increasingly mature. Much of Asia would be in the evolving category in fact. Countries at the bottom of the curve on various categories of economic, social and environmental performance remain challenged, including much of Africa, though some African nations too are evolving. A country such as Syria clearly is now fully challenged, while the more economically vibrant North American and European countries fall into a mature category fairly easily. A sliding scale could be developed across the world's 200-plus countries, with a dotted line dividing mature from evolving to challenged, giving investors more clarity on what is really going on.

In addition, what is arguably most important to know and understand is the directionality of countries moving across these dimensions, who is rising and falling over time and who has the necessary strategy and culture or is best developing such to most move up in the rankings in subsequent years.

The more countries we get over a minimum standard line on economic, social and environmental outcomes, the more we can say that we have sustainability fully embedded in the global economy, allowing the system to function properly going forward.

References

Bloomberg New Energy Finance. 2019. New Energy Outlook. https://about.bnef.com/new-energy-outlook/

Krosinsky, Cary, Robins, Nick, et al. 2008. *Sustainable Investing: The Art of Long Term Performance*. London: Earthscan

Krosinsky, Cary, Sophie Purdom, et al. 2017. *Sustainable Investing: Revolutions in Theory and Practice*. London: Routledge.

South China Morning Post. 2020. Hong Kong Listed Firms Get 'F' on ESG Report Card, Put on Notice as Rules Become Mandatory in 2021, January. https://www.scmp.com/business/article/3044106/hong-kong-listed-firms-get-f-esg-report-card-put-notice-rules-become

UN Global Compact. 2013. Value Driver Model. https://www.unglobalcompact.org/take-action/action/value-driver-model. Accessed 6 Jan 2020.

21

Conclusion

Huang Zhong and Cary Krosinsky

Guanxi

By now, anyone who did or is doing business with or in China will tell you how important it is to have the right *Guanxi* (pronounced "gwan-shee"). The famous Chinese saying sums this up nicely: "It's not what you know, it's who you know."

Fundamentally, Guanxi is about building a network of mutually beneficial relationships which can be used for personal, business or political purposes. In this sense, Guanxi is not all that different from typical Western networking. However, Guanxi is far more important in the Chinese context. In fact, *Guanxi* has arguably been the most important factor for getting things successfully accomplished in China for thousands of years.

For better or worse, Guanxi is the oil that keeps the wheels of community, business and politics running in China, more specifically, where there is a significant Chinese community where Confucianism and/or Taoism run through their social fabrics.

This book is in fact a living, breathing example of how *Guanxi* can work specifically, it being the result of trust built over time through such relationships off of other cases of success all coming together to then create a cohesive single, hopefully successful product.

Guanxi has great potential as a method to bring people together from different parts of the world with varying perspectives and priorities to tackle severe problems across environmental and societal categories.

We hope our book, a combination of experienced leaders from academia and Chinese business in Cary Krosinsky and Johnny Huang (Huang Zhong), partnered with leading students from one of the great teaching institutions in the world, Brown University can stand as a useful example.

© The Author(s) 2020
C. Krosinsky, *Modern China*, https://doi.org/10.1007/978-3-030-39204-8_21

Fig. 21.1 Huang Zhong and Cary Krosinsky. (Reproduced with permission from the Sustainable Finance Institute)

What Is "Guanxi"?

Guanxi is made up by two Chinese characters: 关系. The first *Guan* (in Chinese:关) means *gate*; the second *Xi* (in Chinese: 系) means *ties* or *connections*. So *Guanxi* literally means "Those inside the secured gate are closely tied and related to each other. Those outside won't be allowed in, unless they are endorsed by someone from inside."

Guanxi is often interpreted as "connections," "relationships" or "social networks". However, none of these terms do justice to the fundamental and complex concept of Guanxi and its central role in Chinese culture.

The sociology of many Chinese citizens involves the building of circles of trust in this regard, with this mentality having agrarian roots where people were largely on their own and built relationships as needed to get various things done, and kept out others who were unfamiliar as a form of protection. As a result, it can be argued that Chinese citizens over time have been more individualistic in some ways than Westerners. For more on Chinese sociology, we would recommend the excellent *From the Soil* (Appendix 4).

In a general sense, Guanxi is a network of contacts, which an individual can turn to when something needs to be done, and through which they can exert influence. These networks can have a direct impact on conducting business in China, such as involves market expansion or taking bureaucratic shortcuts.

Guanxi carries an element of trust. A lot of business in China revolves around circles of personal and mutual trust. For any outsider to do business in China they must take the time to form relationships and develop Guanxi. This has been a big obstacle for many Western businesses trying to enter the Chinese market. Business connections made through Guanxi must be maintained to ensure proper positioning for future business.

Guanxi, in essence, is an individual's ability to connect or network for productive business purposes. It takes time to build and even more effort to maintain. Abusing Guanxi through aggressive or dishonest business practices can jeopardize one's reputation or present opportunities for corruption. Aided by social media, behavior that damages Guanxi will have instant, detrimental and lasting consequences to one's business success.

Good Guanxi can minimize natural or man-made obstacles in doing business in China. Over time it may take some effort to maintain and nurture the needed amount of Guanxi to do business at different levels.

"Guanxi" and Its Historical and Cultural Roots in China

China's history has been marked by intense political upheaval—from the country's long and violent history including being attacked from the outside to internal civil wars amongst different factions and the coming and going of empires and dynasties. It's also a vast country subject to frequent natural disasters such as severe flooding, economic hardships and a long history as well of decentralized rule. Traditional Chinese society was predominantly rural and built around the family and closed communities.

Confucianism, the dominant cultural belief, emphasized the interdependence of social connections. Confucius maintained that a society organized under a benevolent moral code would be prosperous and politically stable and therefore safe from attack.

He also taught reverence for kinship. Confucius defined five cardinal relationships: ruler-ruled, husband-wife, parents-children, older-younger brothers and friend-friend. Except for the last, all the relationships were strictly hierarchical. Rigorous adherence to these hierarchical relationships can yield social harmony, peace and prosperity.

Community-based relationships bear four distinct features: loyalty, long term, selflessness and mutual trust.

1. Loyalty—the hierarchical nature of Guanxi always puts loyalty first more than anything else.
2. Long term—since communities are normally "boundary" spaces, everyone knows everyone. A transactional mentality is not going to survive to the next deal.
3. Selflessness—coming from Confucianism, communal experiences require one to be selfless in making contributions before seeking reciprocity from others.
4. Mutual trust—any harmonious society is based on the foundation of mutual trust.

Chinese businesses and societal relationships have deep historical and cultural roots. They rely more heavily on networks of trust and mutual obligations than on the rule of law and rules in general. It can be said that Chinese trust in only two things: their families (communities) and the money under their pillows.

Chinese "Guanxi" Versus Western "Networking"

According to John L. Graham and Mark Lam (Harvard Business Review 2003), one can easily make comparisons of Western versus Chinese ways of thinking and ways of action.
Ways of thinking:

- The Western way: information-oriented, egalitarian, reductionist, sequential, seeks truth and often establishing something of an argument culture.
- The Chinese way: relationship-oriented, collectivist, hierarchical, holistic, circular and often involves a haggling culture.

Way of action:

- The Western way: quick meetings, informal, making cold calls, proposals first, aggressive and impatient, attempting to "forge a good deal."
- The Chinese way: a long courting process, formalities, the use of intermediaries, explanations first, questioning and enduring and forging long-term relationships.

The cultural and historical backgrounds of Western and Chinese business perspectives project sometimes subtle, sometimes very distinct differences between the Western "networking" experiences and Chinese "Guanxi."

Many Western educated businessmen think that business relationships in China are only based on direct cash exchanges. Although this can be correct on some levels, it is not the norm today. Often "Guanxi" transactions are "hidden" and not made obvious to the casual observer. Although the direct giving of "gifts" is a common form of building "Guanxi," it isn't the only way.

For millennia, China has lacked a strong rule of law. Because laws have not often been able to provide legal protections as they do in the West, Chinese people needed to develop another means of ensuring trust amongst themselves in personal and business matters. Maintaining face or reputation among people within one's own network is also an important characteristic of Chinese business culture. Because of the importance of maintaining face, Chinese people will usually not take advantage of a person with whom they have Guanxi. This is true because if they develop Guanxi with them and they were to take advantage of them, all of the people in their network would know what they had done and they would quickly lose face within this network. By losing face they would also lose the respect of others in the group and potentially lose their connections with their network. Therefore, Guanxi has become a means of building trust that the law cannot always provide for Chinese people in both personal and business matters.

For these reasons, a Chinese company will feel far more comfortable doing business with a company where they have strong Guanxi because they believe it will make it far easier for them to trust their business counterpart. (This is seen in other ways in other parts of the world, such as when large US-based pension funds tend to work mostly with external fund managers and consulting firms that they already have long-standing relationships and successful track records with.)

To use a Western analogy, imagine Guanxi is like a bank account. You deposit something into your account, so that when you need money you can withdraw from it. The more you deposit into your account the more you can withdraw in the future. If you always maintain a good balance on your account, the bank may even give you credit that allows infrequent deficits, so long as you pay it back.

Building Guanxi takes a longer time to establish than does Western networking but the rewards can be useful and long lasting.

How to Build "Guanxi"?

Now that we have a general idea what Guanxi is, how can good Guanxi be created and maintained?

Not all Guanxi is equal. In fact, not two Guanxi situations are the same. The subjective nature of Guanxi makes situations intrinsically different each time (Fig. 21.2).

The strength of Guanxi generally relates to how long the Guanxi was established and has been in place. Guanxi can be created in many ways but it always takes time to develop. Good Guanxi should appear to be voluntary. The best Guanxi usually doesn't come with any direct exchange of financial interest. Think of the stronger forms of Guanxi: close friends and schoolmates. They don't involve an immediate exchange of favors and people involved in such Guanxi are initially forced to stick with each other for years (served in the same military units for three years, or shared the same classrooms for six years, etc.). As for family relations, they are bonded by blood and are therefore often the strongest versions of Guanxi of all.

Guanxi can be aided and built by having some general knowledge of China and its culture. This can assist to establish immediate connections to new Chinese contacts.

Because Chinese people prefer to do business with people they have a personal connection with, it can help if you are introduced to a prospective business associate through an intermediary. The higher the social status that your connection has, the more successful you are likely to be at being introduced to the right people and key decision-makers.

Guanxi in China is often more trust-oriented and personal than relationships elsewhere; therefore, a conscious and continued effort is required to

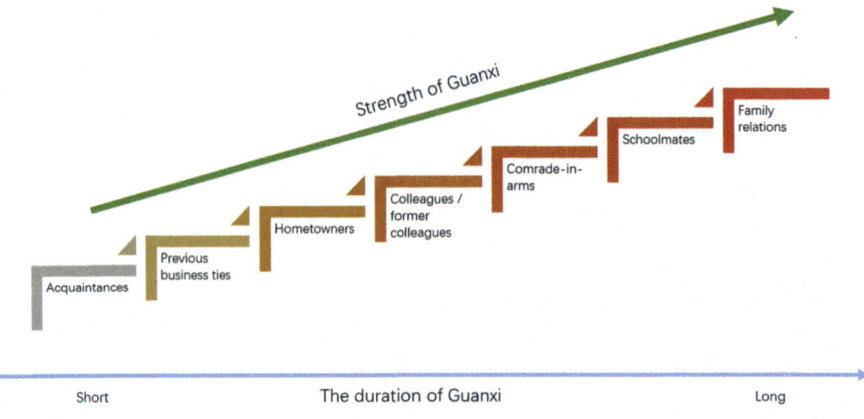

Fig. 21.2 Strength and duration of Guanxi. (Source: Huang Zhong)

develop and maintain these. It will require frequent visits, almost daily communication (preferably CEO/company director to CEO) and plenty of socializing.

Once you have established relationships in China, you are likely to be invited to dinners and other forms of entertainment including golf or massage. If you are invited for dinner at a business contact's house (which is generally a reserved honor) it is important to attend. Dining is commonly used to gently probe positions without having any formal commitment. Inviting or hosting dinners for prospective clients or business partners can create an environment for Guanxi.

Also, the exchange of favors or "inside information" may amount to good Guanxi. Those taking part in the acceptance of Guanxi are required to return Guanxi to the degree of previous Guanxi accepted. The key is to remain diligent and be aware that the reciprocal nature of Guanxi also dictates an informal obligation to "return a favor."

While developing Guanxi is important for doing business in China it is not necessarily easy to develop, especially for a foreign company. Having a full-time, long-term presence in China is essential for developing and maintaining Guanxi, and it will be helpful to have a native-born Chinese person responsible for developing these relationships. A native Chinese person will be familiar and comfortable with the cultural nuances involved. Your local Chinese staff or representative should meet regularly, in both formal and informal settings, with potential and current customers and any relevant government agencies to develop strong relationships on behalf of your company. Always set aside a comfortable budget for your local office to cultivate and maintain good Guanxi.

Doing business with something of a "zero-sum game" mindset in China is a strategy that is destined to fail. One might be able to get something by playing hardball and exerting full leverage of the unique strengths that China desperately needs. In the end, however, a zero-sum game will never create any meaningful payback from China. On the other hand, if one carefully crafts the proper Guanxi at various levels of social and political hierarchies, your business can flourish.

Good Guanxi takes time, don't rush for it.

Evolving "Guanxi"

Although numerous research papers and personal testaments show how Guanxi plays a key role in doing business in China, it is also important to point out that Guanxi is not the only thing that you need to know about doing business in and with China (Management and Organizational Review 2012). After all, Guanxi, like any country, is evolving in modern times.

Guanxi varies by region. At the beginning of China's drive to a market-oriented economy and related reform campaigns, Guanxi played a central role in almost all regions of the country. Almost all industries were centrally planned, highly regulated and subject to non-market forces. Good Guanxi with authorities and state-owned companies were critical to successfully doing business. After 40 years of development, many economists would claim that China is more capitalist than many Western countries. China is a very diverse country. (See Appendix 4 for books we like about China for those less familiar with the rich variety of cities and regions across China, a country as large in size as the US or the European Union.)

Some regions such as Beijing, Shanghai or Shenzhen may share more market-oriented business practices with the West. However, regions such as the Northeast, Inner Mongolia and the west of China tend to be subject to more traditional business practices where Guanxi still plays a key role.

Guanxi varies by age and education groups. Younger and well-educated millennials are more liberal and rule-conscious. They expect a more level playing field, respect rules of law, seek fairness and are often idealistic. They believe that Guanxi helps one to take "shortcuts" which could someday put themselves in an unfair and disadvantageous position. "Do unto others, do not impose on others." Young entrepreneurs do not want to get themselves into complex, time-consuming Guanxi building. They would rather spend more time doing concrete data analysis much like Western counterparts.

Guanxi can also affected by political agendas. In a recent speech published in the January 1, 2020, issue of the CPC's *Qiushi* magazine, President Xi is now pushing for the country's fifth modernization—the modernization of its national governance system—on top of the four modernizations first proposed by Deng Xiaoping 40 years ago, those being related to industrial, agricultural, defense and science & technology. It's quite possible that President Xi regards transforming China to a rule-based country is an outcome he is seeking to be part of his legacy. The results are yet to be seen, but it's already having impact on Guanxi.

In a system that is not based on explicit rules but on inexplicable and vague "Guanxi," there is always a fine line between Guanxi and bribery. In the age of the internet—despite government censorship—justice sometimes prevails in China, even for those with large amounts of Guanxi, especially as has occurred under President Xi's recent anti-corruption campaign and now the fifth modernization campaign.

Relationships built on Guanxi can fade or disappear if part of the "relationship chain" is put into question for any reason. The path to good Guanxi isn't an easy path to follow. Tipping to one side can put relationships made in this way a case for legal action, or in the worst case, a total disaster to a business. Creating Guanxi is in Deng Xiaoping's term "Crossing the river by feeling the stones" where you constantly have to feel your way through.

While Guanxi is an important part of doing business in China it is not the be-all and end-all. Having strong relationships alone will not ensure that you will be able to achieve your business goals in China. Your company will still need to have a strong overall business operation in order to be successful. You should also treat with skepticism those who claim that Guanxi alone can enable your company to succeed in China. While these connections can help you open doors and find new opportunities, your company will still need all of the other components of your business to be strong if you want to grow in China.

Guanxi in a closed networking environment is a double-edged sword. The Chinese respect real relationships more than artificial rules. These relationships are considered lifelong. You could lose touch with someone for years—even decades—after giving your initial favor and you can still call that person for a reciprocal favor out of the blue. However, those who gain a bad reputation are quickly removed from the circle. They will find that whatever Guanxi they had built up rapidly evaporated.

Do you have good *Guanxi* in China?

Final Thoughts

Inevitably, there are matters that remain unresolved or a work in progress on a subject such as the West's relationship to China, but we are convinced that cooperation is the only way to solve the serious issues of the day such as climate change, and we see clear scope for more research on how such collaborative environments can best be created.

A city such as Montreal, for example, rich in culture and enjoyable to visit has a history of being a successful venue for reaching global agreements, as does Kyoto. Building coalitions of the willing that meet regularly in the same safe, comfortable, neutral space is one way to achieve this, but we need to move beyond partial solutions such as the Paris Agreement.

Climate change is an existential threat, and a Manhattan Project of sorts is likely going to be necessary and until we recognize this and come together to solve such challenges together, we will continue to struggle and not come to agreement on necessary answers and pathways. Such answers will require cooperation.

We also have to find a way to avoid resource wars, especially in a future that may become increasingly resource constrained. This will hardly be easy; the South China Sea in particular figures to be volatile given the large degree of hydrocarbons thought to be in the ground there.

The answer on climate change will almost certainly have to come from shifts in demand, including in consumer demand from Asia including China. Products and services that use fossil fuel, as opposed to the production of fossil fuel, which is only 10% of the global footprint, is where the majority of carbon emissions occur. Lowering that demand is the only way to change the value of the world's supply. If profit cannot be realized, then resource wars on fossil fuel are less likely.

There's a lot more we could say about other resources as well, but China needs to join the world in being a mature player in the market, respecting the rights of communities. China learns quickly and will learn quickest of all the faster it is welcomed into the global financial system, treated as an equal, with investors able to demand minimum standards and ESG covenants in exchange for an ongoing flow of capital.

A number of major foundations and NGOs have recently been disappointed with the current situation in China; such relationships are always tenuous but most successful when governments and non-profit organizations come together and recognize that they have something positive to offer each other. Positive approaches create better answers, but there is work remaining to be done on this and we hope the government finds an increasing will to build such partnerships.

This could also include the future of Hong Kong.

We have to first of all be cognizant that China and the UK cut a deal which gives Hong Kong back to China in 2047, which is not all that long from now, certainly in the context of China's long history.

It is in some ways puzzling therefore as to why Hong Kong is protesting as much as it is as this inevitability has long been the case ever since the handover in 1997 well over 20 years prior to this writing though tensions had been increasing under the surface.

When we were over in Shenzhen in January 2019 for our most recent Sustainable Finance Institute event, there was a pervasive sense as we traveled the country from Shenzhen to Xi'An to Beijing and on down to Shanghai via the high-speed train that China was both focused and excited about its own future. Hong Kong was completely an afterthought.

China was and arguably remains primarily concerned about the economic strength and future of its own cities. Given the global need for China's economic vibrancy as outlined in this book's first chapter, this is a good thing that can aid China's own transition, but it could mean for Hong Kong a slow burn for the next 20 years while China ramps up innovation and focuses on its own future.

What then for Hong Kong itself?

Assuming the party maintains control of China, and it's hard to see that not happening (if anything China's necessary economic success due to climate change concerns will strengthen the party's hand), eventually Hong Kong will have to change and adjust to the new reality.

Singapore is already reaping the economic benefits of an immediate and ongoing flight of business away from Hong Kong. Real estate values in Hong Kong, always very high, have come down and its tourism economy has suffered.

But what many miss is that China was already trying to pull Hong Kong into China, not the other way around.

Right after our event in Shenzhen, in February 2019, the announcement of the Greater Bay Area plan made clear the extensive longer-term plans for Hong Kong, Shenzhen, Guangzhou and the region more generally. The recent bridge to Macao is also part of that equation.

By 2047, Hong Kong will almost certainly be fully part of China and the Greater Bay Area and one will be the same as the other. This becomes an opportunity for Hong Kong and the region could thrive as it adjusts.

For now, the protests of 2019 can be seen as a delayed but arguably to be expected reaction to the 1997 takeover, part of a psychological shift for Hong Kong having until 2019 more of a Western ethos. We must assume that Hong Kong and the Greater Bay will eventually be a sort of southern Shanghai, more Western than most of the rest of China but very much China as well.

Also, for now, announced plans for Hong Kong to become the Green Finance capital of China may slow down with such efforts shifting more to Beijing at least for the medium term, with satellite focuses placed where finance opportunities manifest across the country.

It is an opportunity also for cities like Shanghai and Shenzhen to take on, but perhaps most of all for Singapore, challenged by many of the same issues China faces, such as on water, but has yet to really sink its teeth into these sustainability-related opportunities which are only going to grow in relevance across Asia, so watch Singapore to become Asia's capital of Green Finance and the new bridge of comfort for the West more generally, if it doesn't cede this opportunity to China.

China has more to learn from Europe, the US and other parts of the world that are seeing increased benefit from bringing environmental and social considerations more into processes and strategies. The more China realizes that ESG+ considerations are competitiveness issues it can gain its rightful place in global markets, competing for market share fairly and on an equal footing to the benefit of the Chinese economy and its citizens. It is time for China to join the ESG conversation seriously for its own sake.

Ancient Chinese philosophy defines Yin and Yang as a concept of dualism, where seemingly opposite or contrary forces may actually be complementary, interconnected and interdependent, and how they may give rise to each other as they interrelate to one another. ESG+ issues are likewise interconnected and systems approaches are what make best sense in this situation.

Imagine what the US and China could do together, interconnected.

Then imagine what we won't do if we continue to grow apart.

References

Graham, John L., and N. Mark Lam. 2003. The Chinese Negotiation. *Harvard Business Review,* October.

Luo Y., Y. Huang, and S. Lu Wang. 2012. Guanxi and Organizational Performance: A Meta-Analysis. *Management and Organizational Review* 8 (1): 139–172. https://onlinelibrary.wiley.com/doi/full/10.1111/j.1740-8784.2011.00273.x

Appendix 1: Terminology

Terminology used by those who seek to resolve environmental and other societal challenges though investment varies in practice, causing understandable and unnecessary confusion. Commonly used terms include sustainable investing or investment, impact investing, responsible investing, ethical investing, socially responsible investing, divestment, engagement, gender lens investing, green bonds or green finance as well as conservation finance.

Suffice it to say, sustainable finance isn't one thing; our fourth book, *Sustainable Investing: Revolutions in Theory and Practice*, argued that it is in fact seven distinct strategies, featuring what has become known as "The 7 Tribes of Sustainable Investing" (Krosinsky et al. 2017), which includes:

1. *Negative Screening*—such practices typically focus on public companies whereby asset owners at times seek to avoid owning shares in specific companies or sectors, historically, such as tobacco, alcohol involvement in the Sudan or South Africa during the Age of Apartheid. Such practices might be known as "values first," and have their roots in religious mandates. However, negative screening at best meets benchmark financial performance, making this a less desirable primary approach for many thoughtful or fiduciary duty-minded investors. *Divestment* requests on fossil fuel production are a form of negative screening. *Ethical investing* practices in the UK have their roots in negative screening as does the now antiquated, less frequently used term *socially responsible investing* in so far as how portfolios were constructed.

2. *Positive Screening* (sometimes also called Best in Class)—in effect, the opposite of negative screening, positive approaches such as those deployed by successful investors such as Generation Investment Management and

the Brown Advisory Sustainable Growth Fund manage to outperform benchmarks after fees through successful identification of companies best positioned to financially succeed while also being sustainable in their own practices as well as regards the products they sell. In our first book, *Sustainable Investing: The Art of Long Term Performance* (Krosinsky et al. 2008), such positive approaches, or what might be called value first strategies, were what we suggested to be the best way to encourage more uptake by asset owners of *sustainable investing* across all seven of these approaches. Asset owners must legally consider their fiduciary duty, and so attempting to outperform through positive forms of sustainable investing that don't attempt to sacrifice on financial return offers the best opportunity to achieve the necessary scale from a supply-demand perspective. The East Capital case study in this book would be an example of an investor seeking to invest in this manner.

3. *Impact Investing*—typically involves investing to provide services for those less well off as pertains access to housing, healthcare, financial services and education. Some use the phrase impact investing to describe the entirety of these seven tribes, causing understandable confusion. Annual reports produced by the Global Impact Investing Network (GIIN) are useful to monitor progress in this targeted, at times niche, field, though one which is perhaps increasingly positioned to gradually encompass a growing percentage of philanthropy, and is thus very much an area to watch. The Ehong Capital case study in the book is an example of a long-standing impact investor.

4. *Thematic Investing*—would include tranches of investment across all asset classes in specific categories such as water infrastructure, sustainable agriculture as well as renewable energy and related enabling technologies such as innovation in battery storage. Often private in nature, such tranches of investing also encompass most green bonds and renewable energy project finance, and while the average investor can gain access to ETFs that invest in some related public companies, there arguably should be more ways for the average investor to participate in what would seem to be an essential area that needs to achieve scale as a requirement from a climate science perspective. *Green finance* is a term used often in China, and might often be correlated mostly with green bonds and other forms of thematic investing, but it is increasingly also a proxy term for all forms of sustainable investing.

5. *ESG Integration*—often the approach of the very largest fund managers, ESG Integration typically involves utilizing one or more ESG databases on public companies from providers such as MSCI, while developing formulas, processes and algorithms to help make decisions and gain understandings. China is moving to mandatory ESG disclosure in 2020, which should

increase the use and effectiveness of this technique in that region over time. For example, a company with a particularly poor score on ESG might be a trigger for further research to be performed prior to an investment commitment or decision.

6. *Shareholder engagement and advocacy*—often a key facet of *responsible investing* as well as the now less frequently used term *socially responsible investing*, shareholder engagement is the recognition that as a partial owner in a company, there is in effect a responsibility to ensure that owned companies perform to the expectation of their owner investors. Engagement is often, especially in Europe, performed in quiet, behind closed doors. In the US, when private engagements fail, shareholder resolutions are filed, and shareholders can vote on their proxy statements where results get announced typically at annual meetings. Topics of particular and increasing focus include diversity, compensation and climate change strategy. Groups such as the Climate Action 100+ are having an increasing influence on companies, and the case study on ChinaAMC in the book outlines how this is starting to occur in practice in China.

7. *Minimum Standards*—if you visit a restaurant in New York City, there will be a letter on the door telling you whether the restaurant achieved an A (clean bill of health, you can trust the food), B (there was one violation during the previous inspection) or Grade Pending, which is often construed as a restaurant to possibly avoid due to multiple violations. Yet minimum standards are often not applied to investing. Goldman Sachs's recent declaration that it wouldn't bring a company to market without at least one woman on its board is an example of a minimum standard. New York State Common Retirement Fund recently agreed to establish minimum standards on all of its investments, which is a way to bring divestment and engagement advocates together as part of a thoughtful investment process, such as Norges Bank Investment Management has long had in place; visit their website to see their fully transparent process in this regard. Minimum Standards have great potential to become a meaningful lever for positive change within investment.

Reference

Krosinsky, Cary, Robins, Nick, et al. 2008. *Sustainable Investing: The Art of Long Term Performance*. London: Earthscan

Krosinsky, Cary, and Sophie Purdom, et al. 2017. *Sustainable Investing: Revolutions in Theory and Practice*. Routledge.

Appendix 2: Understanding Climate Change

We believe all readers of this book have a common understanding of climate science; here are a few references and links to consider for those less familiar.

1. BBC on Climate Science https://www.bbc.com/news/science-environment-24021772
2. Black Bear Assets, "Warming up to the facts," http://nebula.wsimg.com/edf5b696c3bde9a8952279d5ef53f2a1?AccessKeyId=D9D974DEC5F930B854CF&disposition=0&alloworigin=1
3. Bloomberg, "What's Really Warming the World," https://www.bloomberg.com/graphics/2015-whats-warming-the-world/
4. Bloomberg Data Dash, "A Live Climate Scorecard for the World," https://www.bloomberg.com/graphics/climate-change-data-green/
5. Climate Scientists Virtually Unanimous, Anthropogenic Climate Change is True, Powell, 2016, https://journals.sagepub.com/doi/10.1177/0270467616634958
6. IPCC 2018 report on climate change https://www.ipcc.ch/sr15/
7. US Department of Commerce, NOAA, Climate Change impacts https://www.noaa.gov/education/resource-collections/climate-education-resources/climate-change-impacts

© The Author(s) 2020
C. Krosinsky, *Modern China*, https://doi.org/10.1007/978-3-030-39204-8

Appendix 3: Great Wall Auto

Great Wall Motors

 **Real Insights**

Real Impact Assessment
Neutral

Key Sustainability Trends

🚗 New Energy Vehicles	🟡 OKAY	
🔵 Artificial Intelligence	🔴 POOR	
🏭 Environmental Pollution	🟢 GOOD	

Real Impact

Positive Impact

Neutral

Negative Impact

Active Harm

Symbol: SHK: 2333; CH:601633
HQ: : Baoding, China
CEO: Wang Fengying
Chairman: Wei Jianjun
Founded: 1984
Industry: Consumer Discretionary -
Autombiles & Components

Great Wall Auto released their first New Energy Vehicle in 2017, though their growth in the sector lags behind rivals such as BYD.

In-house development of AI technologies such as self-driving cars is not a focus.

Great Wall are proud of their control of their environmental footprint within their manufacturing facilities, though their core product lines of trucks and SUV's inherently create air pollution.

Great Wall's independent culture prioritizes profitability over debt, but cedes the ability to lead investment into new technologies. A military-like discipline prevents corruption among employees, but creates a stressful working environment.

Strategy

As a fiercely independent, private company in a market dominated by state-backed companies, Great Wall differentiates through ruthless efficiency, manufacturing quality, and a specialization in profitable light truck segments. As a consequence of independence, Great Wall raises capital with little assistance from state-backed banks.

Great Wall's leadership has demonstrated strong capacity to adapt strategy to shifting market landscapes. At age 26, chairman Wei JianJun acquired what was then a struggling parts modifier. He resourcefully mustered the production of their first car, a sedan, in 1993. The following year, the Chinese government restricted sedan production to state-backed automakers, which excluded Wei's efforts. Instead of returning to parts modification, they rapidly built a pickup truck instead, launching their first model in 1996. By 1998, Great Wall had dominated the Chinese pickup truck market. Fortunately, this positioned Great Wall to capitalize on newfound affluent Chinese consumer appetite during the early 2000's.

Great Wall now seems to be positioning itself for three major changes.

1) While historically Wei insisted on in-house designs and forswore foreign joint ventures, Great Wall of late has frequently engaged foreign design consultants, and in 2018 Great Wall announced a large joint-venture with BMW to produce electric components for the MINI.

2) After decades of exclusive focus on gas and diesel trucks, Great Wall is expanding into New Energy Vehicles and sedans. Part of this move is in reaction to recent Chinese legislation restricting sale of gas guzzlers and mandating Zero Emission Vehicle production by 2020.

3) While Great Wall's competitiveness historically came from their vertical control of manufacturing, the company recently restructured divisions as wholly-owned subsidiaries. This will enable Great Wall to more rapidly switch suppliers as they diversify into new auto segments and energy technologies, and divest from underperforming segments. For example, in 2018 they sold off their Honeycomb Energy subsidiary, which had been manufacturing electric batteries.

Overall, Great wall's approach to NEVs has been conservative, which our financial strategy analysis suggests should continue. They produced the minimum amount required by the 2017/18 PRC NEV mandate, and lag far behind rivals BYD in CAPEX. Despite claims from CEO Wang Fengying that they will prioritize EVs, our financial strategy analysis (page 2) suggests that path is not an optimal strategy. Great Wall will maintain higher profitability by specializing in SUVs.

Management & Culture

Great Wall's founder and chairman, Wei Jianjun, remains the 'mastermind' behind strategic decisions, while longtime CEO Wang Fengying handles day-to-day operations.

Founder and Chairman Wei JianJun maintains their fierce independence through consolidating ownership — he currently controls 56% of shares. This stands in stark contrast to state-owned competitors.

Employees report adverse working conditions, with intense pressure to perform over long hours. High turnover is common. FT reports that chairman Wei Jianjun "does not allow mistakes... [which] can lead to staff dissatisfaction." Reports suggest that employees are allowed only one day off per week, and new hires undergo 'military-style' training.

On the other hand, this discipline inculcates against corruption. Two large engraved pillars stand at the company's headquarters, one listing the company's failures, and the other listing names of employees who gave in to corruption.

Core values are attention to quality, constant iteration, and quick reaction to changing regulatory and market conditions.

C. Krosinsky, *Modern China*, https://doi.org/10.1007/978-3-030-39204-8

Financial Analysis

Reporting Quality

The financial report, audited by Deloitte, is robust. Note that the Hong Kong exchange's adoption of IFRS 15 went into effect in 2018, which specified major change in revenue recognition practices. Great Wall reclassified the bulk of their receivables (notes receivable) as other current assets — their business model is to sell notes receivable as financial contracts. The reporting for 2018 achieves a strong Merton M-Score of -3.9, corresponding to a 0.01% chance of manipulation. Somewhat unusually, Great Wall opts for the 'direct' method for its cash flow statement. Great Wall carries little risk of exposure to misreporting fraud.

Earnings Quality

Our view is that Great Wall's earnings quality is average to above average. While the first half of 2019 saw a significant decline in share price, we believe the market to underrate the ability of Great Wall to bounce back.

The high current ratio exemplifies Great Wall's disciplined focus on profitability and independence from creditors. Great Wall behaves like a traditional manufacturer, not a tech company.

While SUV sales have slowed in China recently, Great Wall has demonstrated commitment expanding to foreign markets. Additionally, moves to restructure parts and manufacturing into wholly-owned subsidiaries will enable Great Wall to more flexibly change production in response to demand.

While the PRC pursues aggressive NEV policies, Great Wall has carefully made investments to keep pace with the changing technologies and comply with minimum regulatory standards while rivals assume debts to do the heavy lifting.

Scenario Analysis

The following scenario analysis explores two axes: whether the market demand shifts dramatically to NEVs within the next 5 years, and whether Great Wall invests heavily in NEV R&D + production.

MARKET CONDITIONS

The NEV-driven market assumes that 20% of new cars sold in China be electric within the next 5 years. In 2017, the PRC implemented a NEV mandate which required large automakers to produce EV's as a proportion of total units sold, between 4% and 12%. This scenario assumes additional aggressive policies are enacted.

The baseline assumes that the current segment mix, and segment growth rates, continue. SUV and luxury segments grow most.

GREAT WALL'S RESPONSES

As the stark difference between P/E, ROE, and Current ratios suggest, Great Wall behaves as a mature manufacturer whereas rival BYD behaves as a technology company. Now, Great Wall faces the choice of maintaining its profitability focus or transitioning back into a growth stage.

'Business as Usual' means continuing to specialize in SUVs. Dividends and debt remain stable, while sales growth slows for SUVs. EV sales growth maintains its current pace.

'NEV Investment' requires substantial operating and financial changes. Great Wall takes on debt for CAPEX into production facilities. EV sales rise to 20% of total sales.

Scenario Analysis Avg: Mean over T + 5 yr RMB	Market Stays Constant		(N)EV-Driven Market	
	NEV Investment	Business as Usual	NEV Investment	Business as Usual
Avg Current Ratio	1.0	1.21	0.9	1.7
Avg Sales Growth	0%	8.75%	7.37%	2.16%
Terminal Sales Growth	-3.2%	9.5%	14.9%	-0.34%
Avg RoCE	9.7%	13.3%	10.5%	11.5%
PV	6.6	9.0	8.0	7.2
PV Dividends	0.5	2	0.6	2
Fair Value	6.8	12.6	10.0	8.9

Multiples

07/2019	GWA	BYD	GM
P/E	11.6	36.4	6.34
Current	1.07	1.02	0.94
ROE	14.8%	6.1%	22.8%
Payout	40.3%	12.6%	24.2%

2018	GWA	BYD	GM
P/E	5.84	47.2	35.6
Current	1.21	0.99	0.92
ROE	10.3%	5.0%	21.4%
Payout	25.9%	15.6%	161.7%

NOTES

Data underlying financial models derived from Great Wall's FY 2018 Annual Report, released in Q2 2019, and additional research. Trade tensions from 2019 are outside the purview of this anaylsis.

Sustainable Insights

Primary Trend: New Energy Vehicles
Continued from Scenario Analysis

As you can see from the scenario analysis, the 'business as usual' strategy strictly dominates the NEV Investment strategy.

Going forward, the baseline 'Business as Usual' model assumes 40% growth in EVs and ~8% growth in SUVs, which is in line with analyst estimates of the growth of the SUV market. While trade and macroeconomic factors from Q1 & Q2 2019 may dampen market analysts, these figures represent the best available analyst estimates at the time of writing.

The following graphs demonstrate the current mix of auto sales by segment for Great Wall. Growth rates from 2017 to 2018 are labelled for each bar. While Great Wall's NEV segment grew 570% from 2017 to 2018, that year was an anomalous scramble to comply with regulations which mandated all automakers to sell a minimum % of NEVs by 2018. For perspective, the policy provides credits to automakers to produce up to 12% of autos as NEVs by volume, while Great Wall's 2018 NEV sales amounted to ~1% of sales. From 2017 to 2018, overall research and development from ~3.3b to ~1.7b RMB.

The "NEV Investment" scenario assumes that Great Wall increases their debt obligations to 150% of 2018 levels in the short term, reduces SUV production via a declining growth rate, and maintains a 80% growth rate among EVs year over year for the next half decade. In addition, Great Wall decreases dividend payout to 10% as they reinvest into development.

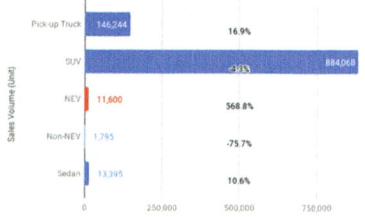

2018 Sales by Segment

Segment	Sales Volume (Unit)	Growth
Pick-up Truck	146,244	16.9%
SUV	884,068	
NEV	11,600	568.8%
Non-NEV	1,795	-75.7%
Sedan	13,395	10.6%

Secondary Sustainability Trends

Artificial Intelligence

Great Wall's investment into new smart car technologies seeks to keep pace with the newest trends, but not to lead the field.

This approach makes sense in context of the Chinese regulatory environment for self-driving cars. PRC regulators are drafting a top-down roadmap which would establish standards for communication among cars and standardize which technologies are implemented among manufacturers. Government-backed automakers are heavily investing in fundamental technologies.

In light of expectations that self-driving technology will not be a differentiator, it makes sense for Great Wall to wait for standards before implementation.

Environmental Pollution

Great Wall's core differentiator has historically been its efficiency and manufacturing, achieved through tight control. Due to this vertical control, Great Wall has been better able to implement responsible environmental practices compared to peers who struggle to maintain accountability among myriad suppliers.

For Chinese companies, the state takes a large role in environmental governance by setting detailed targets. Great Wall has a track record of meeting targets without scandal.

Balanced Scorecard

Reporting Quality
4/5
Earnings Quality
3/5
Management
4/5
Governance
3/5
Impact
1/5

Overall, Great Wall earns a "Neutral" assessment for Real Impact.

The company focuses on strong fundamentals and smooth operation. While Wei Jianjun's immense control may alarm some investors, and the military-like culture may stress many employees, these factors enable the company to operate "a tight ship" that minimizes traditional ESG risks from corruption and pollution. That said, this profitability focused manufacturer behaves like a stable manufacturer more than an innovator, and is positioned to follow the pack towards NEVs rather than lead it.

Appendix 4: Other Recommended Books on the Subject

While there are obviously many one might consider, we prefer books without a seeming political bias, much as we have tried to achieve with this text.

Here are three books you might want to consider within the realms of further understanding China and its diverse regions, unique sociology and fascinating, essential history.

1. Jonathan Spence's *The Search for Modern China* is very good, in fact arguably seminal, especially in its treatment of the more significant Chinese dynasties and emperors during China's evolution from 1600, when it was still the largest economy in the world, up through the 1900s and the start of the People's Republic of China some 70 years ago, but it has less to say on China's more recent economic period.
2. An excellent book on the thinking of the average Chinese citizen and how it was informed by China's agrarian, rural past is perhaps best captured by *From the Soil, The Foundations of Chinese Society*, a translation of Fei Xiaotong's *Xiangtu Zhongguo*. A fascinating read.
3. There are also many books describing China's diverse regions, useful if and when traveling to the country, something we strongly recommend to those interested in China. None perhaps are more beautiful and informative on all of the regions of China than the excellent *Eyewitness Travel: China* by Dorling Kindersley, which has been a companion for my own visits.

© The Author(s) 2020
C. Krosinsky, *Modern China*, https://doi.org/10.1007/978-3-030-39204-8

Index[1]

---

[1] Note: Page numbers followed by 'n' refer to notes.

Printed by Printforce, the Netherlands